No Right-of-Way

NO
RIGHT-OF-WAY

How
Democracy
Came to the
Oil Patch

PETER LEWINGTON

IOWA STATE UNIVERSITY PRESS / AMES

PETER LEWINGTON farms in Ontario, Canada. Also a farm writer, he has published extensively on agricultural and environmental issues. His books include *The Armbro Story* (1974) and *Canada's Holsteins* (1983).

© 1991 Iowa State University Press, Ames, Iowa 50010
All rights reserved
Manufactured in the United States of America
♾ This book is printed on acid-free paper.

First edition, 1991

Library of Congress Cataloging-in-Publication Data

Lewington, Peter.
     No right-of-way : how democracy came to the oil patch / Peter Lewington. − 1st ed.
          p.   cm.
     Includes bibliographical references and index.
     ISBN 0-8138-1677-7 (alk. paper)
     1. Land use, Rural−Government policy−Canada. 2. Soil conservation−Government policy−Canada. 3. Petroleum−Pipe lines−Government policy−Canada. 4. Land use, Rural−Government policy−Ontario−Case studies. 5. Soil conservation−Government policy−Ontario−Case studies. 6. Petroleum−Pipe lines−Government policy−Ontario−Case studies. I. Title.
HD316.L48   1991
333.76′13′0971−dc20   90-20444

No Right-of-Way is dedicated to people everywhere who care enough to make democracy work—and especially to all those wonderful people whose commitment contributed to bringing environmental, legal, and legislative reforms to the oil patch.

CONTENTS

I was very pleased when Peter asked me to contribute a foreword to his book *No Right-of-Way.*

No Right-of-Way is more than a book about a pipeline; it is an account of one man's concern for the environment and struggle for justice. Just as importantly, *No Right-of-Way* is a microcosm of the problem — the challenge — that faces us today: the need to educate everyone to be more responsive to the demands of agricultural land use and soil conservation.

Soil is our most basic natural resource. Civilization depends first and foremost on a steady supply of food. That ability to produce food depends on the quality of our soil. If we lose our soil, we threaten our society.

Only 11 percent of Canada's land base is capable of sustaining agriculture of any kind. Of more concern is the fact that 37 percent of our Class I and 25 percent of our Class II agricultural soils can be seen from the top of the CN Tower in Toronto. This land is very susceptible to urban encroachment.

Canada has been losing productive soils to urbanization, erosion, and soil degradation at an alarming rate. And it has been costing farmers dearly.

The cost of soil degradation in Ontario has been estimated at $68 million per year for water erosion alone. On the Prairies, topsoil depletion through erosion, salinization, and acidification is estimated to cost farmers $600 million per year in lost yields. The result has been higher production costs, a substantial reduction in net farm incomes, and a reduction in our ability to be competitive at home and abroad.

Several government and private reports have helped publicize the seriousness of the situation. These reports have made the point that we cannot rely upon science to increase food production while we allow our land production base to slip away. All levels of government must work with farmers to develop new conservation and farming technologies.

Peter Lewington, through his many publications, has contributed immeasurably to the education of farmers and governments on the need for soil conservation. *No Right-of-Way* is another step in this education process.

His dedication to conservation has not gone unnoticed. In June 1987, Peter received an honorary Doctor of Laws degree from The University of Western Ontario in recognition of his contributions to the fields of agriculture and conservation.

We must learn from the examples of Peter and other concerned Canadians: The soil is only borrowed by this generation from the next. It is up to all Canadians to learn to husband this critical resource for the future.

—THE HONORABLE JOHN WISE
former Canadian Minister of Agriculture

With plant scientist Paul Cavers poised with the symbolic hood, University of Western Ontario Chancellor David Weldon awards Peter Lewington an Honorary Doctor of Laws degree at the 1987 convocation. The citation read in part, "Peter Lewington, an environmental protagonist with elegant self-taught legal and communication skills, demonstrates that one man can indeed modify the laws of this country." (Photo courtesy of John Tamblyn, Inc.)

PREFACE

The saga began in June 1949 when I broke the knife of a tractor mower on a surveyor's stake concealed in a hayfield on a farm we were renting—my first warning that pipeline construction was imminent. The saga reached a climax some thirty years later when a judge of the Supreme Court of Ontario wagged his finger at a pipeline lawyer and said, "If you come into my home and break my leg, you'll pay for that privilege. And in future if you damage farmland, you'll pay for that privilege." That was September 1981, and it culminated our long struggle to minimize pipeline damage to farmland and assist in the reform of the law and some archaic federal legislation.

No Right-of-Way is only incidentally a pipeline book; it is about a lot of things that have a daily impact on the lives of millions around the world. It is about the need to conserve the precious resource of good farmland; a public-hearing system that doesn't function fairly or effectively; the National Energy Board (NEB), its willingness to be alternately a puppet of government and of the oil lobby, and its slowness to plug the environment into the energy equation. It is about all the expertise and involvement that must be orchestrated to accomplish change in the face of entrenched resistance by governments and industry.

It is fitting that a conflict between agriculture and energy is focused on Middlesex County in Ontario, north of London. Beginning in the 1860s London was the oil refinery capital of Canada. Two decades later, sixteen refineries merged to form Imperial Oil Limited. Imperial is the owner of that 1949 pipeline and a major shareholder in Interprovincial Pipe Line Limited, the owner of three additional pipelines through Larigmoor Farm, which is seven miles north of London. The controlling interest is now held by the Reichmann family of Toronto, which has said that it may sell Interprovincial to generate cash for the vast Canary Wharf project in London, England.

A common ploy of government officials and agents for corporations wishing to acquire rights to farmland implies that a dissenter is a lone voice and out of step with society. Following our challenge to the legal system, we began to get visitors from many parts of Ontario and telephone calls from the Maritime provinces to British Columbia. The case histories cited were infinitely variable; yet another hydrotransmission line; a proposed highway that would slice through a farm; a dam that would lead to the flooding of a valley; expropriation for an airport; a fire on the railroad right-of-way that was allowed to spread into and consume organic soil; and pipeline oil spills that polluted land and streams, and poisoned cattle. The common threads were that agriculture was under attack and that landowners found there was no one to turn to. In isolated but highly publicized cases, farmers driven beyond endurance brandished firearms. One of my elderly neighbours was so intimidated that he said, "What can you do . . . they've got the government at their back," and hid in the haymow of his barn.

In my travels I found that such problems were not unique to Canada. They can be found in the United States, Europe, Australia, and New Zealand.

Doubly disturbing was the weighting of the scales of justice against us. There was the continuing Tweedledum-Tweedledee syndrome of government and a major corporation. There was no redress from the courts, which were unsympathetic to agriculture and bound by legislation drafted in the heyday of the railroad barons in the nineteenth century. Arrayed against us was Interprovincial Pipe Line Limited, the largest pipeline system in the Western Hemisphere, a major factor in the pipelines in both Canada and the United States and a corporation tracing its ultimate ownership to Exxon, which vies with General Motors as the largest corporation in the world. The engineering and other consultants for Interprovincial worked for Bechtel, the largest corporation of its type in the world. And then there was musical chairs, played out by former dominant figures in the federal cabinet who would metamorphose, like monarch butterflies and emerge as directors of oil companies or Bechtel. It was small wonder that politicians from the municipal to the provincial and federal level, with some notable exceptions, didn't want to get involved. Worse yet, the expertise in universities and government, which might have been used on behalf of agriculture, was often siphoned off by corporations that appeared willing to spend any amount of money to avoid precedents that could mitigate damage to agriculture and the environment.

In spite of these odds, the National Energy Board Act has been amended to protect the rights of landowners. There have been changes in access to expropriation, which had been granted with wanton profligacy. The sections of the Railway Act that undermined landowners for a century were successfully challenged. No longer can a pipeline lawyer tell a judge, "You shall grant us a warrant; we can go in and make a wasteland if we wish to."

Who cares? A letter from Sarnia lawyer Douglas Beatty, who has no connection with our struggles, states in part, "In this age of increasing conflict with big industry and big government your book will find readership among lawyers involved in the areas of real property, administrative, municipal, environmental and corporate law. Your book will be widely read by geographers and other academic disciplines concerned about the impact of man on the environment." Later chapters are devoted to the changing attitudes of the NEB and pipeline companies, the creation of their own environmental or agricultural departments and more enlightened policies on land use. Beneficial change was ultimately accomplished.

As a farmer and farm writer, I had some advantages. As a farmer, I could record and monitor the impact of pipelines on agriculture. As a farm writer, I had the experience and the exposure that gradually formulated a philosophy that a better way was not only desirable but economically feasible. I found that in the neighbouring state of Ohio, land strip-mined for coal could be restored to levels of greater productivity. Even more important was the existence of a practical formula for paying for the costs of energy and protection of the environment. By law, the strip miner had to pay one way or another for land restoration. This was simply budgeted as part of the cost of coal extraction. The costs were then recoverable on sale of the coal to a thermal electricity-generating utility. In turn, the utility was awarded rates to compensate for the cost of environmental protection. And so the final user paid not just for the energy but for the protection of the environment. A residual benefit for consumers was access to newly created parklands, which contrast with the eyesores of much of the strip-mined areas of Ohio, Pennsylvania, and Virginia. A contractor (who was acknowledged by Dr. Roy Kottman, then the influential dean of agriculture at Ohio State University, as the best in the business) told me that he had never made so much money in his life; using the good practices of restoration for drastically disturbed lands, he could move, on completion, to a neighbouring property, as farmers had grasped that their farms could yield coal and subsequently better crops when sensible policies were implemented.

My wife Jean and I were privileged to visit the International Institute for Land Reclamation and Improvement at Wageningen in Holland. We later saw every phase of land being reclaimed from the sea. We were shown the technique of pipeline construction that could preclude soil damage, even through an aquifer. In Brazil, where agriculture is the engine of economic growth, we witnessed giant strides in land and water use.

Contrast this with the Canadian situation. When Interprovincial celebrated its twenty-fifth year of business, it had still done no environmental-impact research. In 1974, when the president of the company was asked when he would halt pipeline construction through Class I farmland in the event of adverse weather, he replied under oath, "When we can't find enough riprap to hold up the machines." When the National Energy Board authorized the third Interprovincial pipeline in 1975, there was still no oil-spill policy in place. And perhaps the most damning indictment of all was that my wife and I, with our puny resources, had funded more research to mitigate the impact of pipelines on farming than the provincial and federal governments and the entire oil industry combined, in the entire history of pipelining.

There is a price to be paid for almost everything in this imperfect world; I am the first to concede that in tackling apparently insuperable odds, some of that price was paid by my wife and partner, Jean. She typed letters by the hundreds and briefs by the score, and yet maintained both good humour and the ability to criticise constructively. But for her, I would not have become involved with law reform. She urged my involvement with the advice that "You'll regret it later in life if you don't get it out of your system now." Without her steadfast and stalwart support, there would have been scant progress to report and no book.

Our children, Ann, Jennifer, and Roger, all lost and gained while growing up amid the tension of the perennial pipeline. Our daughters witnessed the tyranny of a judge who gave no indication that he was qualified to sit in judgment. Our son witnessed the partisan bias of the Ontario Municipal Board, which heard my appeal from the ruling of that judge.

They also gained an awareness that if democracy doesn't work, with a little bit of luck, it just might be made to work. Now that they are pursuing their own careers, they have some residual benefits. As a planner, Ann values the wise counsel of Norman Pearson, a valued friend of long standing and a planner whose Ph.D. had its roots at Larigmoor Farm. Jennifer, a journalist, was the first female to receive a *Globe and Mail* foreign-bureau posting and reported for the *Globe and Mail* from Washington, D.C. She is now a Nieman Fellow at Harvard University. Earlier, she was her paper's energy reporter in Ottawa and in the course of her work interviewed many people I had done battle with in earlier years. Some had been quite junior in government when I first encountered them and have subsequently risen to deputy minister level while Roland Priddle is now NEB chairman. I was pleased to find that our efforts had opened doors rather than closed them for her.

Roger's work involved erosion control and pollution abatement. The foundations of most of his complex projects are the structure and characteristics of soils; Dr. R. M. (Bob) Quigley, whose applied research and precise testimony were pivotal to our success in the courts, is now also Roger's friend as much as ours.

A heartwarming aspect of our protracted battles through the courts was the camaraderie that developed among our consultants. Some of them formed the prestigious panel that criticized this manuscript. They were joined by others who were not involved but who have demonstrated interest or expertise in the environment. Mere words cannot express my appreciation for their prompt, perceptive, and detailed critiques. Responsibility for any errors of commission or omission that escaped their vigilance remains my own. I thank the Canada Council for a welcome grant to defray some of the costs of researching *No Right-of-Way.* That grant came about as a result of the combined recommendations of Dr. Norman Pearson; Mr. Gordon Hill, a successful Huron County farmer, a former president of the Ontario Farmers Union and the Ontario Federation of Agriculture and chairman of the Ontario Bean Producers Marketing Board; and Dr. Gordon MacEachern, who was then president of the Agricultural Research Council of Canada and is now the deputy minister of agriculture in Prince Edward Island.

My sincere thanks go to all these fine people as well as our neighbouring farmers Stuart and Jocelyn O'Neil, Roberta Tilden, John Walker Elliott, and John Martens, whose faith never wavered.

I am indebted to Richard R. Kinney, director of Iowa State University Press and his associates for appreciating that *No Right-of-Way* involves a complex of farming, democracy, government and corporate responsibilities, and both the needs and means of achieving legal, environmental, and legislative reforms; it is a plea for policies and planning, for conservation and common sense.

I have been most fortunate in my editor, Sandra McJimsey, and her colleagues and recognize their interest and expertise. I have yet to meet anyone from Iowa State University Press, although I am familiar with the university and have traveled widely in Iowa. However, I already count them among the legion of friends — the unforeseen bonus of bringing democracy to the oil patch.

No Right-of-Way

CHAPTER 1

Gossamer Threads

All the silvery gossamers
That twinkle into green and gold.
—ALFRED, LORD TENNYSON

C all it chance, luck, or good fortune—a reality of life is that there are improbable and delicate gossamer threads that link the events of our lives. Together, those threads make a cobweb as complex as any encountered at dawn in a fall pasture. Sometimes the gossamer threads fulfill Tennyson's flight of poetic fancy.

In 1947 Jean and I were among the first postwar emigrants from England to settle in Canada. We allocated a couple of weeks to gather an overview of agriculture in Ontario before going to work on a farm. On making inquiries at the Ontario Department of Agriculture in Toronto, we were promptly ushered into the office of Cliff Graham, the deputy minister. With him was Dr. William Reek, president of the Ontario Agricultural College (OAC). The gregarious Dr. Reek invited us to visit OAC, where we were astonished to be treated to a faculty dinner. So began a rewarding association, which continues to flourish.

It was natural to turn to OAC for professional consultants when we faced the first Interprovincial pipeline. By 1956, Reek had been followed by Dr. J. D. MacLachlan, who was to guide the first three colleges at the Guelph campus into the University of Guelph. I was disappointed to be denied my request on the ground that he did not want OAC to become involved. However, he assured me that no member of the faculty would appear for either farmers or the pipeline company. (Interprovincial Pipe Line Limited is now part of Interhome Energy, Inc.) It was with some astonishment that the very next week a visitor appeared at Larigmoor Farm and introduced himself as "A professor of the soils department at

3

OAC." Maintaining my faith in Dr. MacLachlan and OAC, I questioned the visitor for some ten minutes until he threw up his hands and declared, "I have no association with OAC. I am an appraiser hired by Interprovincial."

Why would an official of a federal government agency, moonlighting as an appraiser, stoop to such misrepresentation? It certainly contravenes everything the Appraisal Institute of Canada stands for. Its Code of Ethics and Standards of Professional Conduct specifically state, "It is unethical for a member to claim professional qualifications which may be subject to erroneous interpretation or to state professional qualifications which he/she does not possess." Why would a company of the standing of Interprovincial fail to disassociate itself from such deception when it was made known to company counsel? The bottom line was that the deception effectively undermined the position that Arthur Pattillo, Q.C., of the law firm of Blake, Cassels & Graydon sought to establish on behalf of Interprovincial.

What were the odds against the moonlighting appraiser misrepresenting himself to the one farmer in the entire Dominion of Canada who would question his credentials and credibility?

For twenty years at Larigmoor Farm we studied all the intricacies of growing bird's-foot trefoil as forage for our beef cattle and as a certified seed crop. When I detected an error in a published report on the use of herbicides on bird's-foot trefoil, I telephoned Dr. Paul Cavers of the plant sciences department at The University of Western Ontario (UWO). He advised that Rudy Brown, of the Ridgetown College of Agricultural Technology, had already alerted him to the error. Dr. Cavers then asked if we would make some of our farm available to Roy Turkington, a native of Ireland, who was doing postdoctoral research at UWO; that gossamer thread lead to the involvement of Roy as our plant ecologist.

I happened to meet Jim Lind, our Liberal member of Parliament, at Toronto airport and persuaded him to appear on behalf of farmers when the National Energy Board (NEB) convened hearings in London later in May 1967. What Interprovincial did not know was that Lind planned to make a cursory appearance and then proceed to Ottawa. For some reason, Bob Burgess, Interprovincial's counsel, asked in public, "Mr. Lind, are you deaf as well as stupid?" Three days later, Jim was still doing battle with Interprovincial. As a member of Parliament, he was able to commandeer every photocopying machine in the federal building where the NEB was holding court, so that the nineteen farm-oriented intervenors could produce the three copies of each brief demanded by Burgess. In subsequent years, Jim pursued the interests of farmers in the

House of Commons. Why did Interprovincial, by such a gratuitous insult, turn a bystander into an implacable enemy?

In 1975, in preparation for a major court case, Bechtel Canada Limited, on behalf of Interprovincial, and ourselves and our consultants were all assiduously gathering evidence. I advised Bechtel that a certain day was inappropriate for their visit since both Jean and I would be away. When we returned home, our friend Tina DeBoer, who had been keeping house for us, advised that an unidentified person representing himself as a "long-standing business associate" had entered the farm to gather soil samples. I promptly telephoned the Ontario Provincial Police to report the theft of some soil. The sympathetic officer responded with "We'll nail the bastard!" And they did. As I suspected, I had never met the clandestine soil sampler, and I continue to be amazed at such tactics.

In Canada's centennial year of 1967 I was seconded by the Dairy Farmers of Canada to research and write the Documentation on Milk Recording. This was eventually presented to a conference in Ottawa and to the World Conference on Animal Production at the University of Maryland. My research inevitably took me to the state of Wisconsin, which has more dairy cows than all of Canada. As I began dinner at a Madison, Wisconsin, hotel, I was paged for the telephone. When I responded, the line promptly went dead. Moments after I returned nonplussed to my table, an apologetic Roger Clute, chief engineer with Interprovincial, introduced himself with the comment, "I thought it was you! But I had to check as I could see no logical reason why you would be in Madison." So began a very fruitful exchange of ideas, and I was pleased to learn that Clute was sympathetic to the concerns of farmers. It was certainly to his credit that when he later testified at NEB hearings, his ideas coincided exactly with those expressed informally to me in Wisconsin. Yet another improbable gossamer thread which helped shape events.

When I appeared before the NEB in Ottawa in 1974, I was singled out by NEB counsel, whom I had yet to meet, for treatment that differed radically from that accorded to all other intervenors. Lawyer J. H. Hendry, on behalf of the NEB, demanded that "Mr. Lewington will have to be kept within strong confines." I can only conjecture who might have poisoned Hendry's mind. However, by the evening of the second day, having apparently been reassured by my conduct in the pipeline hearing, he became my legal coach. Acting on his advice, I was able to initiate procedures for acceptance of our consultants' reports, which years later were to be vital for our success at several levels of the courts.

And what were the odds against establishing that Interprovincial's chief witness against us was concurrently and covertly doing research on pipeline damage to farmland under contract to Agriculture Canada? This was established only through the involvement of such concerned scientists as Dr. A. D. (Al) Tomlin of the London Research Centre of Agriculture Canada and questions in the House of Commons by a backbencher, John Wise, who later became Canada's minister of agriculture in two Progressive Conservative administrations.

There are literally thousands of landowners directly affected by pipelines in North America. The O'Neil family of Denfield was the only farm family prepared and committed to go the distance with us in the courts, regardless of the costs and hazards. The odds against finding such commitment in a neighbour who shared our local telephone exchange must be astronomical. To telephone even across our easterly line fence involves long-distance charges! The evening before we and the O'Neils were to face Interprovincial in our first joint legal venture, Stu, relaxing on the golf course, struck up a conversation with a fellow member whom he knew to be a lawyer. Recalls Stu, "I asked Geoff Bladon how we should proceed the next morning, and he said, 'Get a good lawyer!' " We not only got a good lawyer; we got a most unusual one. With no opportunity for adequate briefing, Geoff appeared on Stu's behalf in a series of court sessions. An unusual feature was that while the O'Neils and Lewingtons jointly shared the legal costs, I continued to represent ourselves in the courts. That gave us two cracks at the whip on every issue. Once we reached the stage of calling witnesses, Geoff took over with impressive zeal and authority.

Just prior to a three-week trial before Judge Gordon Killeen in 1975, I realised that we had a gap in our battery of witnesses. We needed a professional agronomist to link the soils work of Dr. Quigley and the plant ecology of Dr. Turkington. The ideal expert was Jim O'Toole, head of the agronomy department at the Centralia College of Agricultural Technology and a national authority on crops and herbicides. I telephoned Jim, and he readily agreed to appear as one of our expert witnesses. A short while later, I received an animated telephone call from Geoff Bladon, who said, "In my nine years of practising law, I've never had such an experience. A guy comes in off the street and says, 'I don't know quite what it is, but would you serve me with a subpoena?' " It was Jim O'Toole who had been advised by the deputy minister of the Ontario Ministry of Agriculture & Food (the former Ontario Department of Agriculture) that he could appear only if he was subpoenaed; Jim had rightly surmised that I would never have risked compromising his position by seeking a subpoena.

It was this commitment of professionals that led to a camaraderie, a feeling of a team effort, and finally a synergism; the combined efforts of our expert witnesses were far more effective than their individual efforts would have been.

Without in any way detracting from the awesome contributions on our behalf by Geoff Bladon and subsequently John Robinette, it was indeed fortunate for us that Interprovincial stuck with John Brownlie as their top legal gun. Like Pattillo before him, Brownlie is from the large Blake, Cassels & Graydon stable, but cut from a different cloth. If Arthur Pattillo had not chosen to become the leading barrister of his day, he might have achieved comparable fame on the stage. In addition to having a keen legal mind, he was infinitely flexible and resourceful. He employed lightning changes of mood and a rapier wit. In contrast, Brownlie reminded me of the sort of World War I general who, faced with failure, promptly repeated the same strategy.

Of all the flimsy gossamer threads, the flimsiest was spun while Jean and I sailed our diminutive Flying Junior on a lake in Ontario's beautiful Muskoka country. In a light wind, the Flying Junior sails best with a couple of people. When the wind is brisk, we make the greatest speed with some additional ballast. With a crucial NEB hearing imminent, what were the chances of finding that our "ballast" was a judge with a rare insight into the NEB?

In my first brush with the NEB, I had assumed that they were honourable men who had not been made aware of the threats pipelines posed for Class I farmland or farmers' water resources. As the dreary years passed, I became increasingly disillusioned and cynical over the workings of the NEB. I finally concluded that they were not only operating against the interests of agriculture but were contemplating hearings that were illegal. As a lay person with no legal training, it was a great relief to sail the Muskoka Lakes — and learn from a unique legal authority that my concerns were indeed valid.

CHAPTER 2

A
Flawed
System

"The rule is, jam to-morrow, and jam yesterday – but never jam today."
"It must come sometimes to 'jam to-day,' " Alice objected.
"No, it can't," said the Queen. "It's jam every other day: to-day isn't any other day, you know."

— LEWIS CARROLL

The pipeline debate of 1956 turned the Canadian Parliament into bedlam and led to the rise of John Diefenbaker and a then unprecedented Progressive Conservative majority. The following year Liberal Walter Gordon's royal commission on Canada's economic prospects reported, and in 1958 came the Borden Commission Report. These were the major steps that led to the passage of the National Energy Board Act in July 1959.

The act gave the NEB sweeping powers that have relevance and impact for all Canadians and many U.S. citizens. The NEB became the energy czar of Canada. An NEB Certificate of Public Convenience and Necessity is an essential prelude to the construction of any interprovincial or international pipeline in Canada. Anyone who wants to export oil, natural gas, or electrical power, or import oil or natural gas, must obtain a licence from the board.

When the Law Reform Commission of Canada investigated the NEB in 1977, it noted that "the Board consists of nine members appointed by the Cabinet for seven years . . . the current Board members all have extensive professional training in relevant fields as well as considerable industry or related experience. . . . Board staff during our research was organized into seven separate branches. These were: administration, economics, electrical, engineering, financial, law and oil policy." While this may sound innocuous, it contains the seeds of all the discontent that stem from the realities of the NEB.

First, take that expertise that is stated as "extensive professional training in relevant fields." Such relevance proved to be too narrow a definition for the Canada of the 1980s. Board members were largely recycled civil servants, retreaded oil and gas executives, or holdovers from earlier political patronage appointments. The board members came in assorted shapes and sizes, but they exhibited disturbing uniformity in my experience regarding the way they thought or acted. The NEB would be more effective and would be perceived to be objective if members, from time to time, were drawn from other professional disciplines, such as the environment and agriculture. The shortcomings in these areas are evident in the board's staff; the omission of any branch with relevance to the environment exacerbated the bias farmers perceived in the NEB.

NEB board members lacked the discretion of Caesar's wife. The *Globe and Mail,* in September 1976, reported that "the chairman of the National Energy Board, two federal cabinet ministers and their aides went on a High Arctic fishing trip in August as guests of Panarctic Oils Ltd., which is soon to ask the government to approve a $5-billion pipeline from the Arctic Islands. Marshall Crowe, the NEB chief, was in the north five days, four of which were spent fishing for Arctic char in the waters around an Inuit-run camp on Baffin Island. . . . Energy, Mines and Resources Minister Allistair Gillespie and C. M. Drury, Public Works Minister at the time, joined the group for two nights, flying in a government plane. . . . Members of the party included Mr. Gillespie's wife and son."

A subsequent chairman, Jack Stabback, later conceded that Bob Blair, head of the giant Nova Corporation, had met privately with NEB panel members while a public hearing of the NEB was delayed.

Canadian Business, of May 1980, reported that the then NEB chairman had continued such practices. "Edge had specifically told me that no private meetings on substantive matters ever took place after a hearing date was set. He now had admitted, in public, that he had been involved in just such meetings."

These are the sort of indiscretions that inevitably detracted from the credibility and integrity of the NEB in the eyes of intervenors, who are never privy to such discussions. The seriousness is underscored by this perspective of *Canadian Business:* "The NEB's enabling statute, the National Energy Board Act of 1959, gives it the attributes and powers of a superior court. Cabinet may only accept or reject its decision on exports and pipelines — it cannot amend them. The Federal Court of Appeal may reverse the Board only on matters of law or jurisdiction, not on substance. The Board is a court of record. Evidence in hearings is given under oath. It has the power to compel testimony, to cite for contempt, to have its orders registered with the Federal Court and treated as a court order."

The credibility of the NEB was further impaired by some highly publicized flip-flops on Canada's energy resources. For instance, in June 1971, the board estimated that Canada had nine hundred years' reserves of natural gas and four hundred years' reserves of oil. Later that year, this was amended to a shortfall by 1991!

The NEB Rules of Practice and Procedure confirm that the NEB does not have to exhibit the knee-jerk reaction to government and the oil lobby that has become painfully apparent to farmers who intervene before the board. For instance: "At any time after the filing of an application and before the disposition thereof by the Board, the Board may require any applicant, respondent or intervenor to furnish the Board with such further information, particulars or documents as the Board deems necessary to enable it to obtain a full and satisfactory understanding of the application, reply or submission." And further: "The Board may at any time allow the whole or any part of an application, reply or submission filed with the Secretary to be amended."

In September 1975, with some of our friends and neighbours, we decided to test the efficacy of the NEB public-hearing system. As always, Jean had done considerable typing of briefs and so on to ensure that we qualified as an intervenor. There were veterans of NEB skirmishes — Roberta Tilden, John Walker Elliott, and John Martens. Also involved was Morley Salmon, an undergraduate at The University of Western Ontario and the son of a farmer who had suffered pipeline problems under Union Gas. Morley had telephoned to say, "Whenever you go back into court, I want to carry your briefcase!" Morley did much more than that; his help in promptly finding relevant documents in that hearing, which began at 9:30 A.M. and concluded at 12:15 A.M. the next morning, was most welcome. We were joined by Stu O'Neil, about to have his first brush with the NEB.

We arrived at Sarnia well in advance of the scheduled start of the hearing, convened to decide on expropriation for Interprovincial's third pipeline through our farms. It was no surprise to find that comfortable padded chairs, tables, carafes of water, and glasses had been provided for the NEB panel, the NEB staff and officers, and expert witnesses on the staff of Interprovincial (IPL). It also occasioned no surprise that the clerk of the court ushered us to metal folding chairs at the back of the court. I advised the clerk that this was not the accommodation we required; we intended to be treated like the board staff and the pipeline company. This request was summarily dismissed. Next, Ian Blue, NEB legal counsel, made a further rejection. Surprisingly, we were then harassed by some of the media people, who criticised us for delaying the hearing. Our response was that the appointed hour had not yet arrived and that in any event, we were not going to indulge in a controversy with them.

We continued to remain standing until Jack Stabback, as chairman, and his panel of W. A. Scotland and J. Farmer sought to convene the hearing. We asked to "have the same sort of facilities as the board enjoys, which the Energy Board staff enjoys, and which the applicant enjoys."

Eventually, our request was met. This was crucial to our subsequent effectiveness. Instead of juggling papers while perched on metal chairs, we won the opportunity to compete on equal terms. The boost to the morale of our troops sustained them throughout the protracted hearings, at the end of which Ian Blue feared we might all turn into pumpkins.

As the morning hours slipped by, Stabback tried to get his show on the road, only to find that he had to deal with motions to cancel the hearings, to postpone them, to disqualify the NEB panel, and to take action on my concerns, which included

•The research said to justify this pipeline was still kept secret.

•IPL had failed to negotiate rights prior to seeking expropriation.

•The research that could mitigate damage to Class I land had not been done by the NEB or IPL.

•Retroactive remedial action to alleviate or compensate for my problems tracing to earlier pipeline construction had not been initiated, as requested, by the NEB or IPL.

•No policy had been enunciated regarding oil leaks and the propensity of IPL for igniting oil spills in our drainage basin.

•The NEB had enunciated no policy on pipeline abandonment.

•IPL had failed to produce the requested procedures of good pipeline practices.

•Yet again, the NEB had failed to notify affected farmers by registered mail of a hearing pertaining to their farms.

The expertise of my legal coach, which had been shared while we sailed Muskoka, was proving valuable. But it was not enough.

In seeking further use of expropriation from the NEB, Interprovincial had predicated its submission to the NEB on the claim that the requested land could not be obtained by negotiation.

Having taken the precaution of routinely using registered and acknowledgment-and-receipt mail for all letters to the NEB and IPL, I was able to prove to the satisfaction of both organizations that I had expressed concern that expropriation initiatives had preceded negotiations and further that I had expressed a willingness to negotiate. Such documentation counted for little in the *Alice-in-Wonderland* world inhabited by the NEB. Declared Ian Blue, "My submission is . . . and I do not say this triumphantly, but it is just the way that the act is written . . . that there is no obligation on any person to negotiate prior to coming before the board for leave to take additional land."

I further questioned the autonomy left to the NEB when the federal minister of Energy, Mines and Resources had already declared that the line would be built no matter what. Responded Blue:

> I think the issue which Mr. Lewington raises is a question of whether there is such a thing as institutional bias; that is, if the minister of energy makes a statement, because he is minister of energy which affects something which the board must do because it is the National Energy Board, is that a question of bias or is it a question of law? That question has recently been decided by the Ontario Court of Appeal which held that there could be no such thing as institutional bias, and that was not a basis for either stopping or quashing any proceedings of an administrative board.

Was the proposed pipeline necessary and in the public interest? Stabback quoted from the NEB Report to the Governor-in-Council, dated May 1975, which states: "The Board is satisfied that the pipeline is and will be required by the present and future convenience and necessity and has taken into account all such matters as appear to be relevant."

To this I responded, "Does that include the Sylvain Cloutier Report?" Blue promptly squelched that with "It is quite improper to cross-examine the panel on what reasons went into a decision."

Sylvain Cloutier was one of those civil servants who wore many hats; he was then chairman and president of the Export Development Corporation. In the early 1970s, as deputy minister of National Defence, he had chaired an interdepartmental task force that selected the pipeline route through southern Ontario. Or more precisely, it was said to make such recommendations; notwithstanding sustained and documented requests for that report, it continues to remain a secret of government.

That southern route, incidentally, was vigorously deplored by Gordon Hill, as president of the Ontario Federation of Agriculture, and William A. Stewart, as minister of Agriculture & Food in Ontario.

So we were all involved in the ritual dance of a public hearing while the basic documentation remained unavailable. Small wonder that *Maclean's* magazine had earlier noted, "The Board is a Keystone Cop, even if its antics contain more potential for tragedy than comedy."

When Stu O'Neil made his debut before the NEB, he learned, as others had before him, that he was addressing his concerns to the "wrong court."

Finding the "right court" is what reduces the NEB public-hearing system to a sham. When pressed to identify what the right court was, Ian Blue, in a subsequent search of the files of the Board of Transport Commissioners for Canada (the forerunner of the NEB), concluded that no evidence could be found that the right court had ever been advertised so that concerned farmers could participate or endeavour to protect their interests and their land.

Throughout the long day and into the night in Sarnia, farmers continued to document their concerns; some of these will be explored in a subsequent chapter, "A Micro View," on what it is like to be in the path of a pipeline.

Gordon Sheasby, who had taken over from Bob Burgess as IPL counsel, struggled valiantly on behalf of Interprovincial. Not infrequently, he was handicapped by the absence of company expert witnesses and by the inability of those present to give satisfactory answers.

Ian Blue began to voice his changing attitude when he said, "I feel we are faced with the difficult task of reconciling some very valid concerns expressed by the people present. . . . [The board is governed by] a convention that has been in effect since the time of William the Conqueror. No one can explain it or give a reason for it; it is just the way things are done; it is a convention." Blue then cited a 1927 precedent that concluded that "power should be exercised only in plain cases. There is always some danger of a pruner cutting off a fruitful bow, mistaking it for an unfruitful one." Noted Blue:

> This case establishes that if there is any doubt in your minds as to whether one of the paragraphs of these replies or submissions should be cut out, the doubt should be resolved in favour of the person submitting the reply, that is, in favour of these gentlemen not in favour of Mr. Sheasby. . . . The same principles that I have just enunciated have been decided by the Exchequer Court of Canada, the predecessor of the Federal Court of Canada, the

Court to which any appeals from decisions of this Court go . . . the matters he (Lewington) raises are matters which the Board could take into consideration in determining whether to attach conditions to granting Interprovincial temporary working rights in those lands, and therefore Mr. Sheasby's application with respect to them should be dismissed.

By early October 1975, the NEB had rendered its Reasons for Decision. The board chose to ignore our pleas and even the advice of its own legal counsel. I promptly wrote to Stabback that "the marathon Sarnia hearing was a searing indictment of the NEB and the current and long-term practices of IPL. The detailed and documented charges of farmers have not, and cannot, be refuted. The decision of the NEB to grant expropriation, without attaching many of the conditions that it was asked to attach, must be deplored in the strongest possible terms."

In a similar vein, I had written to the then agriculture minister for Canada, Eugene Whelan: "R.I.P Agriculture Canada. When the crunch came yesterday in NEB expropriation proceedings involving some of the best farmland in Canada it was the farmers who alone had to carry the fight. Your department could have, and should have had dedicated personnel there with expertise in soils and in crops."

CHAPTER 3

Farmland, the Limited Resource

From the top of Toronto's CN Tower on a clear day, you can see 37 percent of Canada's Class I prime land.
—DR. E. W. (TED) MANNING,
Environment Canada

In that Sarnia NEB hearing, Jack Stabback and his panel might claim indifference but they could not claim ignorance of the importance farmers attached to their good farmland. Stu O'Neil, a graduate of the University of Guelph who farms land first cropped by his family in 1819, had given the panel what amounted to a short course in the use and abuse of soils.

An NEB panel is reminiscent of the three brass monkeys: They hear no evil, see no evil, and speak no evil. They appear preordained to reach programmed conclusions and decisions, regardless of the evidence placed before them. Member of Parliament and NDP energy critic Max Saltsman in fact referred to the NEB as "Canada's National Monkey Board" in a speech in the House of Commons.

A debilitating aspect of NEB hearings for farmers who intervene is the pretence indulged in by both the board and applicants that issues have been "dealt with." It is a serious flaw in the public-hearing system. In a typical response, Gordon Sheasby declared in Sarnia: "Mr. Chairman, it may be of concern, but it was dealt with specifically at the hearing in Ottawa."

To this I responded: "Several times Mr. Sheasby has made reference to 'deal with,' and this, I think, is a fundamental area of disagreement. We have spelled out our concerns to the board, to its predecessor, and to

Interprovincial over two decades, and we do not consider that 'dealing' with problems. We have detailed them ad nauseam, ad infinitum. We want some honest action. . . . The question is, what will be the [construction] procedure. . . . I would like to know what progress has been made since 1957 to avoid and mitigate unnecessary damage to Class I land."

Unfortunately, the answers became available only during the winter and early spring of 1975–1976 when Interprovincial, aided by Bechtel, installed the third pipeline through Larigmoor Farm.

Two vivid images are etched in my mind forever. As the construction went remorselessly through a field that had earlier won first prize for us in an Ontario Soil & Crop Improvement Association contest, the ditching equipment inevitably breached our aquifer (see Glossary). The predictable flooding was the same as it had been in 1957 and 1967 when the earlier lines were installed. The equally predictable response of Interprovincial and Bechtel was "So it really rained here!"

The second indelible memory involves the start of Interprovincial's vaunted "restoration program." It began with a truck driven as close to the construction-created quagmire as it was safe to, without getting stuck. For the remaining few hundred feet, workers carried on their backs bags of Sakrete, a mix of aggregate and cement that turns to concrete on contact with water. They dumped the Sakrete in the heart of what had been our award-winning field in an attempt to stabilize soil prior to replacing the Lewington Drain (see Chapter 11).

How could this happen in an era of supposed environmental enlightenment? How could this happen after all the documented concerns, reports of select committees, and all of the organizations and departments at the provincial and federal levels that have some concern and responsibility for the land? Such questions can be answered only by the brass monkeys, for they alone had the authority to make good pipeline practice mandatory.

Even as Interprovincial was doing its best (or its worst, depending on one's viewpoint), the Science Council of Canada published *Food Production in the Canadian Environment*. It states in part: "There is a universal tendency among affluent people to take food for granted. Canadians enjoy a food production system which demands no more than $\frac{1}{5}$th of their income, in contrast to the $\frac{4}{5}$th's required in most developing countries. . . . We tend to take our agricultural environment and resources for granted."

For years, the warning bells have been ringing for those who cared to listen. Norman Pearson, writing in the *Agrologist,* the journal of the

Agricultural Institute of Canada, observed in 1973 that "the preservation of our best farmland is now a national imperative; whatever else may be said, the limiting resource is good farmland. Our society has not yet evolved machinery for preserving the prime soils in climatically-favoured areas and it is vital we do so quickly and effectively. Land planners and agrologists must unite and concentrate their efforts to protect such land. The stage is set for danger in Canada. Agriculture is in retreat to poorer soils. . . . It needs to concentrate on the best soils in the climatically-favoured areas. . . . To lose the best land is to lose the capacity to feed the nation and to build diversified industries on the agricultural base. It implies diverting extra resources for remedying the inadequacies of soil or climate, and it means that the more urbanized Canada becomes, the more dependent it becomes on poorer soils."

The following year, the Ontario Federation of Agriculture, in its annual brief to the Ontario Cabinet, noted that "our land is the basis of our livelihood. . . . If urban development is allowed to sprawl over fine farmland at today's ravenous rate, within 50 years our best farmland will all be under concrete and pavement. . . . Every hour you delay, 26 acres of Ontario's improved farmland go out of production. We repeat, the need is urgent." In subsequent years, Norman Pearson continued to express his concerns in every available forum. Among his multitude of interests he managed to find time to write and edit *The Land Economist,* the journal of the Association of Ontario Land Economists.

Perhaps the most ironic concern was that expressed by the Agricultural Institute of Canada in 1983 when it told the Macdonald Commission on Canada's Future that "unless a strong agriculture and food system is ensured, a bright future for Canada will be impossible." The chairman of the commission, Donald Macdonald, has been privileged with more opportunities to encourage beneficial change in Canada than most of his 26 million fellow citizens. Macdonald has been variously federal minister of finance, federal minister of Energy, Mines and Resources, and a director of Gulf Canada, a shareholder in Interprovincial.

Under the Canada Land Inventory, the mineral soils (this does not include the high-organic muck soils) are grouped into seven classes on the basis of soil survey information:

• Class I: Soils that have no significant limitations for crop production.
• Class II: Soils that have moderate limitations that restrict the range of crops or require special conservation practices.
• Class III: Soils that have moderately severe limitations that re-

strict the range of crops or require special conservation practices.

•Class IV: Soils that have severe limitations that restrict the range of crops or require special conservation practices, or both.

•Class V: Soils that have very severe limitations that restrict their capability to produce perennial forage crops.

•Class VI: Soils that are capable only of producing perennial forage crops, where improvement practices are not feasible.

•Class VII: Soils that have no capability for arable agriculture or permanent pasture.

If all the rhetoric had been followed by reality, Canada's precious Class I farmland would not have become such an endangered species.

When the Ontario minister of agriculture and food, Bill Newman, spoke to the Middlesex Federation of Agriculture on January 19, 1976, he was clearly aware that he was in the county that had been in the forefront in the preservation of farmland. Said Newman: "It is vitally important that we preserve the productivity of Ontario's valuable agricultural land, as Middlesex has some of the most valuable — about 75% Class I. The government is determined to minimize any adverse effects of pipelines and highways and Ontario Hydro rights-of-way. Our Food Land Development Branch was involved, with other concerned ministries, in filing a formal intervention with the National Energy Board. It helped draw up guidelines accepted by the board last year, and Interprovincial Pipe Line Limited agreed to them." This of course was too little too late. Even as the devastation of pipeline construction took place at Larigmoor Farm, George Jackson, the associate director of the Food Lands Branch, gazed at the havoc and declared, "We don't want to get involved." He did not explain such detachment.

People, pipelines, and "progress" have a common denominator; they like easy digging. Land costs are a relatively low budget item in pipeline construction; it is cheaper to install a pipeline through Class I farmland than to blast through bedrock. Similarly, people like to live in the most favoured areas. This puts the greatest competitive pressure on the fertile farmlands of such places as the Lower Fraser Valley in British Columbia.

Southern Manitoba has some of the richest, deepest soils in Canada. It is impressive to stand in a field of 640 acres with grain-corn rows stretching to the horizon. It is significant that Manitoba Agriculture has issued a publication, *Land — The Threatened Resource*.

Saskatchewan has even more limitless horizons. It is all the more significant that Saskatchewan Agriculture published *Land Use Conflicts in Saskatchewan.* "As population and industrial development increase, so does the demand for land for utilities. . . . Power lines, telephone lines, microwave towers and power stations use relatively small amounts of land, yet they are a source of conflict. They create inefficiencies in field tillage operations and represent a hazard to machine operation. Hydro reservoirs occupy a significant amount of farmland and often sizable tracts of fertile alluvial soils are flooded. . . . Urban sewage disposal ponds are farmland consumers. Cities such as Regina and Moose Jaw have sewage lagoons which occupy hundreds of acres of prime farmlands. . . . The future demand for land by railroads is likely to be in and around urban centres. Rail relocation will result in farmland adjacent to the City of Regina being withdrawn from agriculture."

The threats to farmland in Canada have to be seen in the perspective of both soil and climate. Early in the summer of 1985, farmers were combining their grain in Alberta's Peace River District and in Saskatchewan; the rub was that it was the 1984 crop. As the costs of crop production continue to increase, it becomes increasingly difficult to grow profitable crops in the face of any constraints of soil, water, or climate.

While the United States has rather more than 1 billion acres of farmland, there are accelerating concerns over land use and abuse. In 1923, the year I was born, the United States had 10 acres of farmland per person. By 1943 this had dwindled to 8, and by 1958, to 6.5 acres. Now it is around 4 acres, and less than half of that is suitable for the production of food or fibre. The Council for Agricultural Science and Technology in its publication *Preserving Agricultural Land,* puts those dwindling acres in perspective. "There are relatively few acres in the United States with proper combinations of soil, climate, water, topography, and clean air which are essential for growth of crops such as oranges, grapefruit, lemons, avocados, cranberries and artichokes."

The Soil and Water Conservation Society of America, concerned with an annual loss of 1.8 million acres of farmland each year, has zeroed in on the protection of prime farmland, which is defined by the United States Department of Agriculture as "that land having the best combination of physical and chemical characteristics for producing food, feed, forage, fibre and oilseed crops."

The state of Iowa has one of the world's most abundant land resources. It is significant that Iowa is a leader in changing attitudes about the use of prime farmland. Soil loss due to erosion is an indictable offence in Iowa. Although corn is grown fence-to-fence in parts of Iowa, this is the state that is a leader in developing Corn Suitability Ratings as a tool in county zoning.

The buck stops with Dr. Ted Manning in matters relating to land use at Environment Canada. When he spoke at the 1985 conference at the University of Waterloo on "Canadian Agriculture in the Global Context; Opportunities and Obligations," he put Canada's prime farmlands in clear perspective:

> The world view of Canada is a huge storehouse of resources. But, Canada's high capability forest lands comprise only 4% of Canada's area. Only 11% of Canada has any capability for agriculture and only 5% of Canada's area is capable of crop production. Because of climate and topography, agricultural land with no serious limitations to production constitutes only one-half of one percent and is located along the southern borders in small nodes of favourable climate. Ours is a history of failure to consider the long-term maintenance of the land resource. Old attitudes die hard. A country of frontier mentality, Canada still carries with it the myth of plenty. We continue to build on the very best land (nearly all major Canadian cities are surrounded by Class I agricultural land — Montreal, Toronto, London, Winnipeg, and Edmonton) and to manage the land as if it was easily replaceable. But the resilience is no longer there. We ignore the limits at our own peril, and already some of the consequences are becoming apparent in higher costs of production and in serious degradation of farm and forest land. Canada's farm production depends upon continuing intensification of use of its best land. Forty percent of Canada's Gross National Product and 25% of its jobs are directly related to the land resource.

This chapter began with a quotation from Environment Canada. It concludes with another very appropriate quotation: "The nation's farmland is important to Canadians not only for food but for much of our export wealth. What happens to that farmland should therefore be of considerable concern to all Canadians."

CHAPTER 4

A
Micro
View

No race can prosper till it learns that there is as much dignity in tilling a field as in writing a poem.
— BOOKER T. WASHINGTON

F arming is sometimes a way of life and sometimes a business; at the best of times it is both. Farming can also be a blend of the senses — sight, sound, smell, and taste. It is rewarding to watch a thick stand of legume hay in the early-bud stage fall before the mower. There are the colourful sights and sounds of bobolinks and meadowlarks, and nimble swallows that scoop hapless insects jarred from their habitat.

Like most pieces of farm equipment, the hay mower generates its own monotonous and soporific sounds — when all is well. But imagine my surprise when suddenly the rhythm, the mower blade, and Pitman shaft all shattered at once. Climbing down from the tractor, I discovered that where there should have been alfalfa there was also, inexplicably, a surveyor's stake, jammed between the mower guards. It was the summer of 1949, and my education into the perils of pipelines had begun. It was my first indication that a pipeline was imminent.

We then held a five-year lease on a highly productive, self-draining, fertile farm lying in a bend of the Thames River, north of London. We grew hay, silage corn, and spring grain for our registered herd of Holstein dairy cattle. A thriving secondary enterprise was supplying London's four A&P stores with our Grade-A1 eggs. To help the cash flow, we raised and retailed Broadbreasted Bronze turkeys for the Thanksgiving and Christmas markets. No one from Canada Trust, which administered the lease, or anyone from Imperial Oil Limited, the owners of the

21

projected pipeline, had offered the slightest shred of information about pipeline plans or construction.

In 1947, when Imperial's first gusher blew in at Leduc, Alberta, it was just an interesting item in the news to us. But by the summer of 1949, a pipeline had snaked its way from Redwater, Alberta, to Sarnia, Ontario, and was under construction through the farmlands of southwestern Ontario to supply some of the cities enjoying the explosive growth of the post–World War II period.

The priorities of pipelining soon became apparent. Pipelines tend to follow the most direct route and the one where the digging is easy. And so it was with our first pipeline. The trench was excavated diagonally through the farm. Logistics, the scheduling of men, equipment, and supplies, are essential parts of pipeline profit. Among the elite in the hierarchy of construction workers are the welders. They are kept supplied with innumerable welding rods needed to connect the lengths of steel pipe. Every one of those rods is flicked to the ground when it is reduced to about two and a half inches — and that is the ideal length of a piece of metal that can kill a cow. Cows have a legendary capacity for ingesting feed, and along with it, any stray pieces of hardware. The metal gravitates to the rumen, one of a cow's four stomachs, and if it lodges strategically in the rumen wall, it can work its way to the heart and cause a painful and lingering death. I have watched that happen.

For unexplained reasons, pipeline construction was tediously slow and greatly inconvenienced our farm work throughout the growing and harvesting season. By Christmas, the line was finally in the ground and a "pig" was projected through the pipe as part of a routine testing procedure before introducing petroleum products. The pig, instead of sailing serenely down the line, got stuck. The heavy equipment that had so recently departed returned, and the pipe was dug up, leaving an open trench across our farm lane. At quitting time, the pipeline workers left us marooned. This might not have been too serious had they made the repairs in time for the arrival of the milk truck the next morning. But on that day it was almost a fatal blunder.

Jean and our newborn son, Roger, had just come home from St. Joseph's Hospital in London where, like all of our children, he had been delivered by our beloved family doctor, Vince Callaghan. Roger, just two weeks old, suddenly had difficulty breathing and began turning a frightening blue colour. The problem was later diagnosed as an overactive thymus gland, which required immediate hospitalization. We are never likely to forget the difficulties of crossing that gaping pipeline trench, made all the more hazardous by snow and ice.

By the following summer, there had still been no offer of compensation. I fired off a telegram to the president of Imperial Oil, advising him that unless steps were taken to achieve a prompt and fair settlement for our crop losses, I would sue. This brought a quick response. In came a covey of Imperial officials. I was to learn over the years that oil-industry people never travel alone and seldom in pairs. Too often, if a farmer does make any progress in negotiation, he will never see the same company representatives again.

About a mile away we rented other land from a different landlord. It was now July 1950, and the wheat planted the previous September was ripening for harvest. I went to have a look and to my surprise found that the city of London had drilled two wells in the wheatfield and cut a swath through the crop to install a water pipeline to the city. By now, the pipeline pattern was not entirely unexpected. No one representing the city of London ever sought my permission or offered any compensation.

Finally, I called on the assistant general manager of the Public Utilities Commission (PUC) and gave him my bill. Wheat was then selling for $2.25 a bushel, and the bill totalled $34.90. To my astonishment, Vern McKillop declined to pay on the grounds that "you farmers always double your charges. I'll pay you half what you ask." We haggled for much of the afternoon until I eventually had to go home to milk our cows. I left with some $20.00 in my pocket and a sour taste in my mouth for pipeline practices.

At that time, the city of London, like many cities, relied on well water. With the subsequent doubling of the city's population, farmer after farmer found that his well was going dry as the city remorselessly lowered the water table. In frustration, the Middlesex Federation of Agriculture convened a protest meeting that attracted some four hundred farmers. McKillop was spokesman for the PUC. McKillop was a distinguished-looking man with an autocratic demeanour. He told the meeting that he would not receive a delegation of farmers but that he would see farmers individually, by appointment. I took my turn at the microphone and recounted my pipeline experiences with McKillop. I said, "If you listen to this man, he will pick you off one by one." McKillop moved rapidly across the stage, put his arm around my shoulder like a friendly uncle, and advised the meeting that perhaps something might be worked out. It was.

The solution (a mixed blessing) was a pipeline to bring the water of Lake Huron to London. While the scars of that pipeline are still evident from the air nearly three decades later, there was some improvement in pipeline practices, primarily due to the involvement of Ontario Agriculture Minister Bill Stewart, who represented our riding, the one most affected by pipeline construction.

In 1952 we purchased our present farm and said good-bye to landlords and to pipelines. Larigmoor Farm had some of the best Class I farmland and was free of stones. Our friend R. W. (Bob) Packer, a geography professor at The University of Western Ontario, established by soil profile that the farm was once a glacial lake. In later years, when Roger researched his thesis at the University of Waterloo, he found the surveying notes of Mahlone Burwell, who had staked and surveyed our farm before he left to serve in the War of 1812.

Another attribute that prompted us to buy Larigmoor Farm was the shallow well, legendary for both purity and dependability. With a favourable climate, excellent soil, and adequate water, we had the ideal environment for an expanding dairy herd. We were fortunate in our choice of sires available through artificial insemination from Western Ontario Breeders, Inc., of Woodstock, Ontario. The cows did well on official Type Classification, and their milk and butterfat production, recorded by the federal Record of Performance, rated them third among herds in the very competitive county of Middlesex. The growing of grain and forage seeds became a secondary enterprise. We took an interest in crop competitions, and our hay samples won first prizes in the farm shows in both Middlesex and Oxford counties.

Then, after a six-year hiatus, we found ourselves again embroiled with pipelines. In 1956 the reeve of London Township came to the door with the news of the first of Interprovincial's (IPL) pipelines. The reeve was moonlighting as a right-of-way agent and was paid a fee per signature. This was an inspired choice by Interprovincial. By using a local and respected farmer, most easements were swiftly obtained, despite the fact that the agent was given no details of where and how the pipeline would be constructed. There is a world of difference between a pipeline installed along a line fence and one that severs a farm in two. Similarly, there is a world of difference between a pipeline that usurps the level needed for a gravity-tile drain and one buried deeper.

The latter reality was borne home to Roberta Tilden and her late husband, Ken, when they reluctantly paid for the added cost of a siphon and two catch basins when their own main drainage system surrendered pride of place to the pipeline. It was to take a quarter of a century to establish the principle that a farmer's drainage system could be effective only if it took priority over a pressure pipeline.

The level of township or municipal government is the one closest to the people. The rapport between farmers and their elected representatives breaks down when a man primarily associated with municipal government dons a pipeliner's hat. The gulf between farmers affected by pipelines and their municipal council grew wider and wider as the municipality found that pipelines were a licence to print money. By the 1970s we had ten pipelines in our tiny Medway Valley, and the corporation of the township of London was taking in more tax dollars from pipelines than from any other source.

The prospect of our third pipeline in 1957 was far from pleasing. We now farmed fine-textured soils that require systematic drainage if they are to achieve optimum production and profit. I tried, unsuccessfully, to find out from Interprovincial exactly where the proposed line would go and at what depth it would be installed. Such facts were needed since the installation of the Lewington Municipal Drain was imminent, following two years of debate in the community and innumerable meetings with London Township Council, which had routinely been delegated drainage responsibilities by the Ontario government.

Pipelines that cross provincial boundaries then came under the jurisdiction of the now defunct federal Board of Transport Commissioners. I wrote to them, explaining the nature of the problem. I expected that the secretary of the board would check the extensive and documented trail of the planned municipal drain by contacting the Ontario Department of Agriculture and London Township Council.

Instead, the board limited its enquiries to a letter to Bob Burgess, then Interprovincial's legal counsel. Burgess arbitrarily and incorrectly advised the board that "the Lewington Municipal Drain is the figment of his [Lewington's] imagination." And that ended any involvement or intervention by the Board of Transport Commissioners. The actual expropriation involved the county courts. IPL used the provisions of the Railway Act in 1957 to seek expropriation of a 60-foot easement for the installation of pipelines – plural and unlimited, both in number and time. County Court Judge Ian McRae briskly brought down his gavel in granting expropriation, with the terse comment that "drainage is no concern of this court." The court gave no protection to farmland or the environment.

The inevitable result was that Interprovincial installed its pipeline where and when it wished. It chose to go right through the middle of Larigmoor Farm. Exacerbating the impact was the route that went through the lowest part of the farm and usurped the depth essential for the Lewington Municipal Drain. The drainage criteria had been established long before any of us in the community had even heard of Interprovincial.

Farmers generally accept the not inconsiderable biological and environmental hazards inherent in crop and livestock production. Experience had taught us that hail, icing rain, and tornadoes could all be endured. But nothing had prepared us for the pure hell of trying to farm amid pipeline construction that owed nothing to common sense or good practice.

When Interprovincial excavated the trench, our aquifer was breached. This water-bearing stratum, located some fifty-two inches below the surface, served two important functions. It was the groundwater supply for our shallow well, which had been infallible since the land had been cleared of virgin bush to build our huge barn. And the aquifer contributed to land underdrainage, in effect an underground stream.

If the pipeline contractors had used the techniques mandatory in Holland, or merely used a little common sense, this would not have become such a serious problem. However, as land is the lowest priority in a pipeliner's plans, the trench was dug far ahead of the installation crews, just to make sure that there would be no construction delays. Perish the thought that a welder, then paid an astronomical $1,500 weekly, should experience any downtime at the pipeline company's expense.

Standing beside the gaping trench, which bore no relationship to the pictorial pleasantries beloved of pipeline companies, one could hear the plop of soil by the ton as it fell into the soupy mess created when the flowing aquifer inevitably caused the trench sides to cave in.

When I reproached pipeline representatives for this avoidable destruction, they inevitably responded, "Well, you must have had a heavy rain." Their myopia precluded any need to check with the London weather office where they would have learned that there had been no rain. Drainage tiles exposed and severed by the excavation became silted with the slurry in the trench. As the pipeline crews used the right-of-way for access to other farms, vehicles of all kinds could be expected at any time of the day, and many of the drivers routinely neglected to shut gates. Down into the pipeline trench fell one of our best brood cows, and by the time we had winched her out, she was crippled with dislocated stifle joints.

As hay and grain harvest approached, the pipeline presented new problems. The obstacles to crossing the farm were not restricted to the open trench. On the far side, for a full six weeks, the welded pipeline sat mounted on eight-inch-square wooden blocks. When I asked for a bridge to gain access for the tractor and pickup baler and the self-propelled combine harvester, the pipeliners obligingly built a bridge. The "bridge" over the elevated pipeline consisted of some of those wooden blocks and a few scoops of soil—it was such a narrow and precarious structure that even an agile mountain goat would have hesitated to use it. Half of our farm remained inaccessible.

Many people have a home and a separate place of business. For farmers, everything is wrapped up in the land they farm. When pipeline construction occurs, especially in the absence of good pipeline procedures, the peaceful enjoyment of their land is shattered, and the ability to manage crops and livestock is drastically impaired.

As the protracted construction drew to an end, the topsoil, the subsoil, the glacial till, and the gravel from the aquifer were shoved higgledy-piggledy into the trench, together with construction debris of wood and steel. Left on the surface was a gray plastic clay, devoid of nutrients, organic matter, or biological activity. Our elder daughter, Ann, then aged 10, found it the perfect material for modelling clay figures. The material could be shaped as desired, and when it set naturally, it was as solid as concrete. Her models are still intact today.

For the next decade we continued to farm, though hampered in the aftermath of that first Interprovincial pipeline. Then, in Canada's centennial year of 1967, back they came again. Our opposition and pleas for better procedures fell on deaf ears. We were even more hampered this time as the company continued to enjoy the fruits of expropriation, granted without preconditions by Judge McRae.

Those first two 20-inch pipelines of 1957 and 1967 were followed eight years later by a 30-inch line that was to stretch to Montreal and beyond. Interprovincial quickly served notice that it had learned nothing about agriculture. Garnet Bloomfield, our reeve and later our member of Parliament, was sufficiently concerned that he hired an aircraft and flew over the right-of-way. To his horror, he found that despite the arrival of winter, IPL had as much as seventeen miles of open and unprotected trench through prime farmland. But this time it was all going to be different! IPL had promised that it would be better, and the NEB had chosen to accept these assurances. Reality was something else. When IPL president David Waldon appeared under oath as the pipeline's chief expert witness, he had asked me rhetorically, "What more damage can we do to your property?" Now we had the answer as the pipeliners worked over the easement and the additional land granted as working rights. They succeeded in making a wasteland.

Waldon is a big man, at least physically. Prior to construction I had challenged him with the prospect that "Interprovincial can be a hero in the Province of Ontario. Why don't you fund projects for the Ontario

Soil & Crop Improvement Association, which could lead to policies and procedures to mitigate damage to farmland?" This suggestion was summarily dismissed. It was just one of several rebuffs. As far back as 1958, we had entertained Arthur Pattillo and J. F. Howard (IPL lawyers) for luncheon and afternoon tea at Larigmoor Farm. We had shown them how we had constructed a farm pond with no adverse impact on the environment. For starters, we had stripped the entire area of topsoil. The dragline, in excavating the pond, deposited the good soil on subsoil, not on topsoil. When the dragline had completed its work, we spread the topsoil, which had been carefully saved, over the "spoil" and the steep banks of the pond. We were then fortunate in getting a good "catch," or growth, of legumes and grasses, which prevented erosion and provided feed for our dairy herd. The pond was securely fenced, and the cattle had access to pond water only through a pasture pump, which they operated themselves. Such pumps are popular in Holland but less well known in Canada. In principle, they are rather like a hand-operated pump of yesteryear; the difference is that a cow pushes with her nose on a steel plate, which has the same effect as a person operating a pump handle.

While Pattillo might be ruthless in the courts on behalf of his client, he never lacked courtesy. Typically, Jean received a delightful thank-you letter from him.

In retrospect it was tragic for agriculture and for Canada that Interprovincial chose to ignore the simple procedure we used to construct a pond. It could have been used most effectively in pipeline construction. The company continued to fight such a practice until John Robinette, Q.C., eloquently convinced the Supreme Court of Ontario that pipeline companies must mitigate damage or pay the consequences. Topsoil did not have to be sacrificed. I have long contended that Interprovincial might have finally understood the place of agriculture in the economy if a senior officer or member of the board of directors had found time to visit with us during construction. They never did. If people at the top don't care, why should the foot soldiers? It was all the more to the credit of those construction workers who did exhibit concern. Earlier I singled out Interprovincial engineer Roger Clute for his courtesy, common sense, and integrity. IPL's Gordon Frew was another who consistently endeavoured to make the construction as painless to farmers as possible. Not infrequently, he went out on a limb to overcome the drainage problems that resulted from pipeline construction. He authorized additional and remedial drainage tile for John Martens and us.

In his Ph.D. dissertation, "Impact of Pipelines in South-Western

Ontario," Norman Pearson listed the following as characteristic problems during pipeline construction:

1. Pipelines running contrary to the grain of the farm field system.
2. Disruption of field drainage and irrigation systems.
3. Operations not confined to the actual right-of-way or ownership.
4. Soil disturbance, mixing of topsoil and subsoil, or inadequate restoration measures.
5. Fencing problems.
6. Damage to trees and woodlots.
7. Failure to remove stones or to clean up adequately after construction.
8. Contouring inadequate, creating wet areas difficult to work because of contrary slopes.
9. Blasting effects in rock areas, particularly on farm wells.
10. Operational trenching problems (erosion, collapses, subsidence, access disruption).
11. Stock losses or damage.
12. Permanent fertility losses due to effects of construction on soil.
13. Compaction of soils by heavy machinery.

The experience of farmers invests that catalogue with even deeper meaning. Reported Peter Hennaert while president of the Lambton Federation of Agriculture: "Pipelines have caused my neighbours all kinds of crop loss problems." The same could be said of Middlesex. Roberta Tilden looked out of her kitchen window to see a terrifying wall of flame and dense smoke. Interprovincial had ignited an oil spill and had not bothered to alert affected farmers. Destroyed in the fire was John Walker Elliott's good grove of white ash trees. Our corner of Middlesex County suffered a variant of the scorched-earth policy of Vietnam.

IPL and the NEB have been given case histories by the score. Lawrence Markusse, of Wyoming, Ontario, told them, "We have 150 horsepower tractors, but when we come to that pipeline we have to stop and shift into the lowest gear. When we get through the pipeline again we shift into a higher gear and there is a cloud of smoke; every time there is a half-gallon or a gallon of fuel gone. . . . The natural drainage can't go across the pipeline any more. . . . They crushed all my tile. . . . For 20 years I have grown nothing there."

Some problems are more subtle and obscure. When Stu O'Neil checked the deed to some of his land, he found that there was a cloud on the title. This was a lingering footprint of Interprovincial from the time when it thought it would expropriate additional land — and then decided not to do so. However, they had not bothered to correct the record of the County Court.

On the national scene, the Canadian Federation of Agriculture urged, "There must be a coherent, combined federal and provincial approach to measures for the preservation of our agricultural land base." Agricultural historian Dr. Hiram Drache adds a global context.

> If America wants to avoid economic catastrophe it will have to make faster progress in agriculture than we have made in the last half-century. If we cannot maintain our supremacy in food production we will suffer economic catastrophe. At the time of Christ there were only 250,000,000 people in the world; by 1650 half a billion; by 1830 there were one billion; in 1927 the total was 2 billion, in 1957 4 billion; in 1984 there were 5 billion; 6 billion are predicted by 1993 and by the year 2000 7 billion people will be on this earth's surface. Does this help you to understand the challenges of agriculture?

As Interprovincial became the longest pipeline system in the world, it could be considered to have leadership responsibilities in resolving energy/environmental conflicts and issues.

CHAPTER 5

A
Macro
View

If oil is the lifeblood of Canadian industry,
pipelines are its arteries.
                                    – DON HICKS,
                                    Bechtel Canada Limited

Interprovincial is just one of many pipeline systems. But its pipelines alone pass through the land of over nine thousand owners in Alberta, Saskatchewan, Manitoba, Ontario, and Quebec in Canada, and North Dakota, Minnesota, Wisconsin, Illinois, Indiana, Michigan, and New York in Interprovincial's Lakehead division in the United States.

It is appropriate for a pipeliner's pipeliner to provide the perspective between the micro and the macro view. Declared Nova's Bob Blair: "Pipelines do great things for the places they go to ultimately as markets, and something for the places they come from, but they are of strictly limited benefit to the places they go through."

Today, Calgary and Houston are the energy capitals of North America. Just as Canada's oil and gas industry was born in such Ontario places as Petrolia and Oil Springs near Sarnia, so the United States has its Oil Springs in Pennsylvania.

It was in Pennsylvania that John D. Rockefeller put together the monopolistic Standard Oil Company. Standard was to turn out to be a many-headed hydra and lives on in such giants as Exxon. It was also in Pennsylvania that some of the first gas pipelines were installed. However, it was in Canada that the first oil pipeline was built. That was in 1862, and it extended a few miles, from Petrolia to Sarnia. Petrolia is now a small town known for its oil museum, while Sarnia has become

Canada's petrochemical capital. By 1911, Calgary could boast the longest 16-inch-diameter pipeline in the world. A 180-mile pipeline brought natural gas to serve the city.

Canada's energy needs have been growing ever since. Canadians hold the dubious honour of having the highest per capita energy consumption in the world. We consume more energy per capita than the United States, twice that of West Germany, and nearly four times that of Italy. The reasons can be found in the cold winter climate of Canada and the vast distances that must be travelled by energy and all other consumer and industry requirements.

No politician in Canada has been more involved in getting energy to consumers than C. D. Howe. It was his intransigence that led to the defeat of the Liberals in the Pipeline Debate of 1956 and his personal defeat at the hands of an NDP neophyte, Douglas Fisher, in his northern Ontario riding. Howe exhibited scant patience for the democratic parliamentary system. Witness his comment: "I will see to it that the Board of Transport Commissioners settle on an application for export quickly. Time is of the essence." Howe's energy and integrity were never questioned. TransCanada's pipeline would probably not have been built — and certainly not when it was — had it not been for Howe's considerable influence. It was Howe's excesses that led to the creation of the National Energy Board. Another of Howe's links with the NEB was the appointment of his former executive assistant Douglas Fraser to the board; we will see more of Fraser later, but it is worth noting in passing that among his attributes was a welcome sense of humour.

By 1973, it was estimated that if laid end to end, Canada's major pipelines would circle the globe three and a half times. They have continued to proliferate ever since. A gasline from the Mackenzie alone could add 2,500 miles. The gas-distribution system of Nova now stretches to over 8,200 miles. Interprovincial is the oil and hydrocarbon heavyweight, with well over 6,000 miles of larger-diameter pipelines in Canada and the United States.

Pipelines not only keep getting longer; they get bigger. A doubling in the diameter means a quadrupling of pipe capacity. Larger-diameter pipes can mean greater efficiency in transportation costs. Interprovincial has been a consistently profitable company, and the oil that flows through Larigmoor Farm, sight unseen, is moved by IPL at a tariff of just $3.69 per cubic meter from Edmonton, Alberta, to Montreal, Quebec, through its Canadian pipeline.

Pipelines are a major phenomenon of the twentieth century. Pipelines have long laced the oil-rich nations of the Middle East and the Persian Gulf. When I researched an earlier book, *Canada's Holsteins,* I kept coming across pipelines and energy initiatives in countries as disparate as Mexico, Brazil, Scotland, Holland, and Italy. Groningen, in Holland, is close to the birthplace of the world's most popular dairy cow, the Holstein. Groningen is also the start of a pipeline that takes natural gas all the way to Italy. And as so often happens, one finds the same cast of multinational corporations. The Groningen gas field is rated as Europe's largest reserve of natural gas and is owned primarily by Exxon and Shell. Perhaps the pipeline of greatest political and economic significance is the Soviet natural-gas pipeline, which now operates over three thousand miles, from the gas fields of Siberia to West Germany.

Just a century ago, Africa was literally the Dark Continent, largely unknown to Europeans. Even the source of the Nile remained a mystery for much of the nineteenth century. Now, a U.S. $15-billion pipeline is proposed to snake all the way from the Red Sea to the Atlantic Ocean. On completion, it would pass for 3,520 kilometers through a number of countries, including Sudan, the Central African Republic, and Cameroon.

The ramifications of the ubiquitous pipelines are all around us. When the southern portion of the Alaska Highway gas pipeline was approved, the *Toronto Star* headlines were "The Pipeline Kept the Glow on Bay Street [Canada's Wall Street]," and "Pipeline Approval Spurs Bay Street." The *Globe and Mail*'s Report on Business headlined, "Clamour for Pipeline Participants Gives TSE [Toronto Stock Exchange] Strong Gains." In a similar vein, the stock of Caterpillar Tractor shot up on the New York Stock Exchange with news that the company had landed an order for two hundred pipe-laying tractors for that Russian gas project.

Pipeline construction usually sparks a significant demand for credit. Indicative that financial institutions value that business is the full-page, four-colour item in the 1984 Annual Report of Royal Trust alerting readers that "TransCanada Pipelines and other Canadian and foreign countries have benefitted from our corporate loans program."

Some of the beneficial spin-offs of pipeline expansion are direct and easily measured: for instance, the jobs that are created with a burgeoning need for pipe from such suppliers as Stelco in eastern Canada and Ipsco in western Canada. Less easily quantified are the multiplier effects that ripple through such diverse industries as fertilizer, herbicide, plastic, and many other segments of economic life that depend on the products conveyed by pipelines. Even the concern for pipeline breaks and leaks creates demand in the aviation and marine industries. The surveillance of pipelines through land is variously routinely monitored by light aircraft and helicopters. Where Interprovincial pipelines cross the Straits of Mackinac at the junction of Lakes Michigan and Huron, surveillance is done by a minisubmarine with a crew of two. The concerns for the environment following an oil leak have already been referred to. The hazards with high-pressure natural-gas lines can be of even greater concern. In Ontario over the last thirty years there have been twelve major failures of the TransCanada pipeline, and six involved explosions. In addition, on October 17, 1985, a farm drainage machine struck the company's line near Oshawa. The resulting explosion and fire killed one man and injured four others.

In the transmission of energy, pipelines are all-pervasive. Despite the access to numerous all-weather ports, pipelines are used to convey 80 percent of the crude oil to U.S. refineries. But pipelines are by no means restricted to crude oil and natural gas.

If the grandiose plans of Ontario Hydro are ever matched by consumer demand for electricity, steam, a by-product of generating electricity from nuclear power, could be conveyed by pipelines to create major greenhouse production in the vicinity of nuclear power stations. Some energy initiatives can be beneficial to agriculture. Farmers are big users of many forms of energy. They may also benefit in the future from pipelines used to move grain pneumatically. Pipelines are also used to convey wastes. One notorious pipeline abuse involved the waste "disposal" system installed by Amax of Canada, which discharged tailings fifty meters below sea level at Alice Arm, British Columbia. Only in recent years have the enormities of some waste pipeline projects come to light. A highly publicised one is the lingering aftermath of the Manhattan Project, which gave birth to the first atomic bomb. That aftermath includes revelations of the cyanide-type wastes that were discharged into the Niagara River by the U.S. Atomic Energy Commission, and a hazardous radioactive and potentially explosive pipeline that was used to convey atomic wastes before being abandoned.

And then there are sewage pipelines, such as those proposed by the Ontario Ministry of the Environment to dump the wastes of London and St. Thomas into Lake Erie. It is a revealing aspect of human nature that proponents of such schemes depend upon upstream water supplies. London draws its water from Lake Huron; Toronto, where the beaches are periodically closed to swimmers because of pollution, is now looking north to the relatively pure water of Georgian Bay for its future supply.

And then there is the relatively new technology of pipelining solids such as coal in slurry form.

Perhaps the most bizarre proposal was reported in the *Manchester Guardian Weekly* of September 2, 1984. "The Americans have suggested installing an underground pipeline filled with liquid explosive along the Oder-Neisse line in Central Europe as one of a variety of barriers to a Soviet land attack. The proposal was outlined to M.P.'s from NATO countries at a meeting here last week." The perestroika that led to the removal of the Berlin Wall in 1989 made such prospects obsolete.

Who owns the oil and gas pipelines? Well, many people, including Jean and I, have a stake in pipeline companies; this toehold was fruitful in obtaining information for Chapter 24, which records how some companies are reacting to a new era, one that includes environmental concerns.

Beyond the publicly traded and privately held shareholdings, the ownership is incredibly complex. Interprovincial began as a consortium of major Canadian oil companies, led by Imperial Oil. For most of its existence, Interprovincial has relied on the revenue from tariffs paid by anyone who chooses to use the system. The Canadian tariffs are set by the NEB. Interprovincial does rather better in the United States with its subsidiary Lakehead Pipe Line Co., Inc., which has been generating over 60 percent of Interprovincial's profit. Under then chairman R. K. (Bob) Heule, IPL ownership became much more complex.

In 1983 there was a share swap, giving Hiram Walker Resources a 34 percent share of Interprovincial and Interprovincial a 16 percent share of Walker. This was motivated by a provision of the National Energy Program that was intended to encourage Canadian ownership. The share exchange ended the long period of foreign ownership. The previous majority shareholder, Imperial Oil with 22 percent, continues to be 67 percent owned by Exxon Corporation of New York. In 1986 the Reichmann brothers expanded their resource holding company, Gulf Canada Corporation, by buying up the Walker conglomerate, including IPL. The merger with Home Oil created the current company Interhome Energy, Inc. Hiram Walker was a pioneer Canadian distiller with a history dating before the confederation of Canada in 1867. The modern company is a major distiller and distributor of distilled spirits in Canada and the United States. Its liquor cabinet includes such brands as Canadian Club, Ballantyne scotch, Kahlua liqueur, Courvoisier cognac, and most recently, a 100 percent ownership of Tia Maria Limited. But Hiram Walker Resources Limited was much more than a liquor company; those resources included Consumer's Gas Limited, Home Oil Company Limited, and a piece of the oil action in Western Canada, the Beaufort Sea, and the Scotia Shelf of Canada's Atlantic coast. Such energy projects generate 53 percent of Walker's earnings.

The role of the government of Canada can be best equated to a referee who has the opportunity to score the winning goal in the Stanley Cup. With the stroke of the pen, legislation can be introduced (like the late and unlamented National Energy Program), and the same Canadian government appoints members of the NEB. The Canadian government is also the biggest stakeholder in the oil patch. Petro-Canada, Canada's crown-owned oil company, was established with the buyout of Atlantic Richfield's Canadian assets and has continued with the purchase of Pacific Petroleum, Petrofina, BP's refinery and marketing assets, and most recently Gulf's refinery and marketing assets in Ontario and western Canada. Petro-Canada also includes a 45 percent share of Panarctic Oils Limited, about a quarter of the shares of Westcoast Transmission Co. Limited, and major holdings in the Tar Sands of Alberta and the now shelved Polar Gas project. A rather different creature of government is the Canada Development Corporation, which remains 49 percent owned by the government of Canada; its oil and gas interests include those previously held by French-owned Aquitaine Co. of Canada.

Canadian provinces have oil and gas interests. In British Columbia, BC Hydro is a natural gas distributor, and the government share of Westcoast Transmission was turned over to British Columbia Resources Investment Corporation. The BC Petroleum Corporation markets natural gas. The government of Alberta is the major stockholder in Alberta Energy Co. and also owns a piece of Nova and the right to appoint directors to that board. The government of Saskatchewan is involved in both exploration and oil and gas production. In 1981 the Ontario government spent $650 million to buy 25 percent of Suncor, Inc., of Toronto, which was then owned almost exclusively by Sun Oil of Pennsylvania. Quebec has two crown corporations involved with oil and gas. Yet another provincial crown agency is the Nova Scotia Resources Corporation. Newfoundland created the Newfoundland and Labrador Petroleum Corporation.

Through the labyrinth of these corporate structures, governments at the federal and provincial level hold financial interests in many of the pipeline companies. Petro-Canada, for instance, holds a 20 percent interest in Q&M Pipeline Limited, which was formed to distribute the natural gas of western Canada to the more easterly provinces.

TransCanada Pipe Lines owes its origin to the enthusiasm of C. D. Howe and U.S. entrepreneurs. The company's finances and fortunes have been unusually convoluted. Until 1990, control of TransCanada was vested in Bell Canada Enterprises. TransCanada has assets of over $5 billion in Canada, the United States, and other countries. TransCanada's pipeline interests include 50 percent in Great Lakes Transmission Company, which operates in the states of Minnesota, Wisconsin, and Michigan. TransCanada also owns 50 percent of Q&M (Trans Quebec & Maritimes Pipe Line, Inc.). It also has a 44 percent interest in Foothills Pipe Line and a 30 percent interest in Northern Border Pipeline Company. TransCanada has pipeline interests in California and Alaska. TransCanada is a truly multinational business, with involvement in Indonesia, Australia, Italy, the Dutch and U.K. sectors of the North Sea, and Egypt.

Westcoast Transmission Company Limited, not untypically, is partly owned by other interests and in turn has financial interests in other initiatives such as the Alaska Highway Natural Gas Pipeline Project. Westcoast also reflects a broad trend to diversification and is involved with LNG and the manufacture of fertilizers. It is another multinational.

The interlocking pipeline interests of Nova, an Alberta corporation, are too complex to detail. Through its ownership of Husky Oil Limited, Nova has an indirect interest in all of the major oil plays in Canada and in Colombia, Indonesia, the Philippines, and New Zealand. Nova also has major investments in the petrochemical industries, but it was a greater financial success when it was simply Alberta Gas Trunk Pipe Line Ltd.

For many years, Darcy McKeough was the most forceful figure in Ontario provincial politics. He held such major portfolios as Energy and Municipal Affairs and was also provincial treasurer. McKeough was foiled in his bid to become premier. One of his last major moves in provincial politics was to squelch the opposition of several of his fellow cabinet ministers to ensure that Interprovincial's third line went through southern rather than northern Ontario. McKeough went home to Chatham, Ontario, and the presidency of Union Gas Limited. With its natural-gas distribution system to half a million customers in western Ontario, the company affects more of Canada's fine farmland than any other energy company. McKeough now heads Redpath Sugar. This is an ironic change as Chatham still mourns the demise of its sugar-beet refinery.

Corporate quiet reigned at Union until McKeough spearheaded the creation of Union Enterprises Limited as a prelude to the acquisition trail. This took Union beyond the orbit of the Ontario Energy Board and its ownership provisions. In 1985, in one of Canada's bitterest corporate battles, Union was devoured by Unicorp, a much smaller company but one with powerful friends in the liquor, oil, and gas businesses. In a countermove designed to reduce the percentage of shares held by Unicorp, Union diversified into Palm Dairies Limited, Stafford Foods Limited, Burns Meats Limited, and Canbra Foods Limited. Canada's second largest gas utility had become a very different animal. By late 1989, there was another metamorphosis of Unicorp Canada Corp., the parent of Union Gas. With closer ties to Hees International Bankcorp, Inc., and Brascan Limited, it was scheduled to become an operating energy and utility company.

However, in 1989 Unicorp was thwarted in its attempt to buy Dunkin' Donuts, Inc., of Randolph, Massachusetts, with its 1,850 outlets in fifteen countries. Doughnuts are ubiquitous, and in this instance they involve two continents and three countries directly. Unicorp lost in this doughnut-bidding war to the British conglomerate Allied-Lyons PLC. Ironically, it was also Allied-Lyons which had earlier gained majority control of some of those Walker liquor interests only recently acquired by the Reichmann Brothers. Allied-Lyons is a modern conglomerate that had its roots in Joe Lyons's Cornerhouses; I well recall a splendid high tea in one of these popular restaurants after watching a test match at Lord's cricket ground in London, England. It was a simpler world then, in the 1930s; now it appears that the tentacles of pipeline bids, ownership, and the conglomerates that include pipelines in their portfolio have achieved new complexities.

Can anyone in the entire United States and Canada claim that his or her daily life is not influenced in some way by pipelines?

CHAPTER 6

Railroaded

Government is everywhere to a great extent controlled by powerful minorities, with an interest distinct from that of the mass of the people.

–D. L. DICKINSON

R ailroads were to the Canadian economy in the latter nineteenth century what pipelines have become in the latter part of this century. No examination of the impact of pipelines on the Canadian economy would be complete without reference to the railroads. This is partly because archaic railroad legislation was used effectively to force pipelines across Canada.

When Interprovincial sought to acquire a right-of-way across Larigmoor Farm for its first and subsequent pipelines, it did so under the expropriation provisions of the Railway Act. This century-old legislation has been incorporated by reference in the NEB Act to deal with pipeline expropriation; where there are references to *railways,* simply read the word *pipelines.* The Honourable Patrick Hartt, while chairman of the Law Reform Commission of Canada, described the Railway Act as "archaic." When Middlesex County Court judge J. F. McCart heard Interprovincial's subsequent request for additional working rights to install its third pipeline, he referred to the Railway Act as not only archaic but also unfair to landowners.

It first dawned on me what a superb weapon pipeline companies enjoyed in the Railway Act when I watched Arthur Pattillo orchestrate Themes on the Railway Act in court in 1957. I had not then met Pattillo, but I knew that I would shortly have to do so. As the Interprovincial initiatives in Oxford County happened to precede those in my own Middlesex County, I seized the opportunity to observe Pattillo, at what must have been the height of his power, in a Woodstock, Ontario, courtroom.

Pattillo appeared to be a lean and lovable figure with the disarming appeal of everybody's uncle. The court was hearing the damage claim of a dairy farmer whose 200-acre property had been traversed by IPL's pipeline. The dairyman's expert witness on property values was an experienced appraiser employed by the Canada Permanent Mortgage Corporation. The appraiser had prepared himself well for the court appearance. His knowledge of Oxford County property values was encyclopedic, and his recall was total. Pattillo was clearly impressed by the expertise and authority of the witness and generously complimented him. The witness visibly relaxed; it became evident that he did not relish court appearances and was glad that he had survived this one unscathed at the hands of such a renowned courtroom lawyer.

But Pattillo was far from finished with the witness. Continuing in his avuncular vein, he broached the matter of tile drainage, which was and is a major concern of farmers who work some of Canada's best farmland. The witness was encouraged to talk at length about the importance of tile drainage while the farmer's lawyer, involved in his first and possibly last such case, watched with benign satisfaction.

And then with startling suddenness the tranquil mood of the courtroom was shattered. If not exactly Dr. Jekyll and Mr. Hyde, Pattillo had the capacity for chameleonlike changes in demeanor. Now he had become the rapier-sharp interrogator. His questions related entirely to drainage and never touched on the topic of property values in which the witness had qualified as an expert. By the time Pattillo asked his final question, it had become the unequal contest of the stoat and the baby rabbit. "I put it to you," asked a dominating Pattillo, "that having severed 33 tile drains on this farm, that if we drive across the surface with a road grader we will have completed the restoration without any damage to the farm?"

"Yes, sir. That is exactly true," agreed the hapless witness. On the contrary, such grading would have no beneficial effect on the buried tile drainage system.

Pattillo had once again triumphed, but even he would have given credit to a provision of the Railway Act. In nearly a century of use, a maximum of three witnesses was allowed in each case. When you look at all the disciplines involved in documenting pipeline damage on a modern farm, it is evident that three witnesses are not enough. An understanding of the conflict may involve expert witnesses in such diverse fields as appraisal, planning, agronomy, farm management, soils, drainage, crop ecology, geology, agricultural economics, statistics, and geography. The rub for farmers was that restriction to three witnesses meant they faced difficult choices. It really narrowed down to Hobson's choice, no choice at all. If the farmer used three witnesses and they were kept to their specific areas of expertise, numerous issues could not be alluded to. The alternative was to allow a witness such as the appraiser to be lured into a quicksand of a different discipline such as drainage.

It was there, in an Oxford courtroom in 1957, that I decided that if we ever went the distance with Interprovincial, it would involve a challenge to the archaic Railway Act. Mercifully, I then had no idea of the complexities of law reform that would dominate our lives for the next two decades and more.

How did Canada get such laws, which could have been written by the railroad interests? The simple answer is that is precisely who dominated the scene during the drafting and enactment of the nineteenth-century legislation that later cut the ground from under twentieth-century farmers.

The way history is depicted in Canada and the United States is just one of the differences between two countries that have many similarities and common interests. U.S. history has all the drama of the shoot-out at the OK Corral. Canadian history has all the excitement of Mr. Milquetoast. Both extremes are of course ludicrously inappropriate and inaccurate.

When Doug Hamilton reviewed Professor Arthur Lower's book *Colony to Nation* in 1978, he made this appropriate comment:

> The professor tries valiantly to write crisply, without pedantry or cant. He falls short in many places because he ignores many of the colourful aspects of the personalities who helped mould Canada. Let's take Sir John A. Macdonald for example. He was often a cantankerous, manipulative man, who was impaired by alcohol on many occasions. Yet Lower mentions little of this. He, like many of our historians, opts for a homogenized account of history. He all but shuns many of the scandals that several of Canada's first governments were involved in. Historians have a duty to expose the charlatans and scoundrels in Ottawa that concocted deals with avaricious real estate and railway promoters that were against the public interest.

Gustavus Myers, author of *A History of Canadian Wealth,* could never be accused of pulling any punches when he explored the roles of politicians and railroad promoters. His book was published in the United States in 1914, but a Canadian edition had to wait until 1972. Every review I have found acknowledges the accuracy of Myers's research, although some challenge his interpretation of the facts. As Myers launches into an examination of the inception of the railroad power, he notes that the railways of Canada, owned, controlled and ruled privately by individual groups or corporations of capitalists, cover more than 26,000 miles. These are the privately-owned railway systems, but this is not to say that their proprietorship has come from the application of private cash. The funds that paid for their construction come largely, if not fundamentally in whole, from the ever-accessible public treasury which the railway promoters early began to plunder, extending and elaborating the process with time and opportunity.

Canada had been explored by enduring and intrepid men travelling by canoe and on foot. Clearly, if Canada was to become a nation from sea to sea, the railroads were a prime prerequisite. To encourage railway construction, the federal government granted rights to over 56 million acres to the builders of railroads. Other incentives included the infusion of cash and bond guarantees. Similarly, the ambitions of every town could be fulfilled only after it could boast a railroad station. I suppose that in modern parlance we'd call it a slush fund. But every community that aspired to be part of a railway system was able to generate incredible amounts of cash to encourage the railway promoters to bend in their direction. So far, so good. Much of Canada was then virgin territory, and the challenges facing the railroad builders called for herculean accomplishments.

It was the elected politicians who derailed the railway ideals. As Myers observed,

The prime and first consideration of railway ownership was the ability to get legislation giving certain definite rights and privileges. This legislation conferred what was called a charter of incorporation. Having the power, as the legislative politicians did, to grant to themselves these charters, it was not an astonishing outcome that the promoters should have so often been the politicians themselves. This was particularly so inasmuch as many of the politicians, then so-called, were not politicians in the sense that they exclusively followed politics. Not a few of them were landowners of considerable holdings, and it was not a far step for them to promote railways, the operation of which would increase the value of their timber and other lands. Other Members of Parliament were traders, merchants or shippers, as well as land speculators, and had a personal and immediate interest in bringing about modern methods of transportation. Still other Members of Parliament were lawyers, who were either connected with landed or trading families, or who were often themselves interested in capitalist undertakings or inspired to become so. At the same time, the parliamentary railroad promoters were compelled by the exigencies of politics to put on an appearance of great concern for the public welfare while engaged in the very act of seeking to enrich themselves; they assiduously presented themselves as law makers having at heart the development of the resources of Canada and the expansion of its wealth.

Nowhere in Myers's book did I find the term *conflict of interest*. But the following are just some of the examples given of the links politicians had with the early railroads of Canada:

• Allan N. MacNab was an M.P. (member of Parliament), speaker of the House, prime minister, a baronet, and promoter of the Gore Railroad Company, and president of the Great Western Railway. MacNab was also chairman of the Legislative Assembly Standing Committee on Railroads.

• The Canada, New Brunswick and Nova Scotia Railway involved a lengthy list of M.P.'s and the mayors of Montreal, Toronto, and Kingston.

• P. J. O. Chauveau was a prominent M.P., cabinet minister, and the first premier of Quebec after confederation; he also headed the promoters of the Quebec and Saguenay Railway Company.

• Involved in obtaining the charter for the Amherstburg and St. Thomas Railway Company was a quartet of M.P.'s. Another quartet from the House of Commons was among the incorporators of the Canada Western Railway Company.

• When the charter was granted to the Toronto and Owen Sound Railway Company, five M.P.'s were involved.

• The Quebec, Montreal, Ottawa and Occidental Railway involved members of Parliament, both as promoters and directors. This was a railroad that received a grant of 2.7 million acres from the Quebec legislature. Coincidentally, J. Cauchon, prominent in Quebec politics, was crown commissioner of lands, involved in federal politics, and the chief promoter of the railway.

• When the European and North American Railway received its charter, the incorporators included the speaker of the House of Assembly, the provincial secretary, the attorney general, and twenty-three members of the New Brunswick legislature.

Such a list could go on and on. Suffice it to quote Sir Allan N. MacNab, who summed it up with the comment "Railroads are my politics."

Of necessity, in the 1880s, a railway company had to be incorporated to exist; it had to be created by a special act of Parliament. It was routine procedure for a private bill to be introduced and backed by M.P.'s and senators. Myers provides this perspective:

It was during this brisk session that the Parliament of the Province of Canada passed an Act with a preamble asserting the principle that in a new and thinly-settled country, where capital was scarce, the assistance of Government could safely be afforded to railway lines, "and that such assistance is best given by extending to Companies constructing railways under charter the benefit of the guarantee of the Government for loans." One delectable point was omitted in this preamble, namely, that the members of the very Parliament that enacted this law were largely themselves railroad promoters, or planning to become so. . . . Often these legislative and other capitalists sold or leased charters to themselves as heads of other railways, profiting exceedingly thereby. . . . There was thus hardly a member of the Parliament of the Province of Canada or of the other legislative or executive bodies who was not in some way zealously pushing railway or other projects in which he or his associates were personally interested. . . . The whole power of the state could be infallibly depended upon to pass whatever additional laws were necessary, and to give gratuities in loans, bonuses and land grants.

Concluded David Mills, who was to become dominion minister of the interior: "Corruption taints the majority of railway enterprises from their inception to completion."

The most significant railroad in Canadian history is of course the Canadian Pacific Railway (CPR). The centennial of the departure of the first scheduled transcontinental passenger train from Montreal to the West Coast terminal of Vancouver was celebrated on June 28, 1986. The building of the Canadian Pacific is indivisible from Canadian history. On November 7, 1885, the celebrated last spike was pounded into place, bringing to a successful conclusion a venture that had survived all manner of financial, political, and scandalous incidents. Just nine days after Donald Smith pounded in that last spike, watched by such railroad giants as William Van Horne, Louis Riel unleashed his rebellion. The role of the fledgling railroad in effectively moving troops to put down that rebellion lifted from the CPR the spectre of bankruptcy and the last vestiges of criticism that the railroad was not in the national interest.

Not that that ended all criticism. "God damn the CPR!" cried the apocryphal prairie farmer as he saw the drought wither whatever grain the grasshoppers had overlooked. When the CPR encouraged colonization in the 25 million acres given to it by a grateful government, little was known about the management of fragile prairie soils or drought cycles. The frustrations of prairie farmers were compounded because the CPR got them coming and going: They paid a high price for freighting the inputs manufactured in eastern Canada, and they had to pay the going rate to get their grain to the markets back east.

I must confess to never damning the CPR. When Jean and I tried to emigrate to Canada in 1947, we were initially thwarted by the shipping shortage; air travel was still in the future. Our last hope of emigrating had died at Canada House in London, England. As we walked disconsolately across Trafalgar Square, Jean spied the CPR office. We went in, in some desperation, and pleaded that there must be some way of working one's passage to Canada. To this, the suave agent responded, "That, sir, will not be necessary. I am sure our emigration department can accommodate your every wish." They could, and they did. Two weeks later, we sailed to Canada aboard the aging *Aquitania*. Accommodation was allocated by the Ministry of War Transport, and some of the berths had been given to the CPR, which, like most other shipping companies, had suffered grievous wartime losses.

A more recent CPR link occurred when twenty numbered copies of the special edition of *Canada's Holsteins* were sold at public auction by Brubacher Brothers and Shore Holsteins. One of the successful bidders was CP Enterprises; their link with Holsteins went all the way back to the CPR Demonstration Farm at Strathmore, Alberta, which was awarded the third Master Breeder Shield by Holstein Canada in 1932.

CP Enterprises had been spun off by Canadian Pacific Limited in the early 1970s for CPR's nonrail interests. It is interesting to note that in the mid-1980s, 70 percent of CPR's profit comes from Canadian Pacific Enterprises; and CPE is doing well because of its oil and gas interests, which include PanCanadian Petroleum Limited of Calgary. In 1985 CPR made an about turn and absorbed CPE.

Most of those early railroads have long ceased to exist as independent entities. The major survivors are Canadian National and Canadian Pacific. The most enduring survivor of all was the Railway Act, and that made the railways germane to pipelines — until the 1978 judgment and the subsequent decisions of the Supreme Court of Ontario.

Pipeline ventures are not infrequently referred to in the same breath as transcontinental railroad construction and even the Panama Canal. Prime Minister Pierre Trudeau declared in 1972: "A transportation system (gas and oil pipelines, a communications' network and a highway through the Mackenzie Valley) is the key to national development in the North. This northern transportation is mind-boggling in size. But then so was the very concept of a continent-wide fur trade 100 years ago. It's expensive too, but so was the Canadian Pacific Railway a century ago." It now appears that the Mackenzie Valley pipeline could become a reality in the 1990s.

When Prime Minister Pierre Trudeau and President Jimmy Carter met in September 1977, it was to approve in principle the largest-ever pipeline project, the Alcan Highway Pipeline to carry Alaskan natural gas through Canada to the lower forty-eight states. Commented Trudeau: "We were successful in one other giant project, a generation ago on the St. Lawrence Seaway. This one is even bigger; in terms of energy, it is certainly more important." Responded Carter: "We have decided to embark together on this historic project which holds the promise of great benefits to both countries and which confirms anew the strength of the ties that link us."

Amid such brave hopes and eulogies there was no room for reference to the Railway Act, the act that got the railroads built in the last century and railroaded farmers in this one. Railroads and pipelines have been boon and bane to farmers.

In 1876, about the time that the Railway Act was created, the intrepid pioneer farmers on Canada's Prairies faced incredible difficulties in getting their produce to market. The first wheat shipment, a mere 857 bushels to go from Manitoba's Red River Valley to eastern markets, went via a convoluted route through Minnesota and involved both land and water transportation. In the latter part of the nineteenth century, the modes of transportation included the oxcart, covered and Conestoga waggons, mule teams, steam boats, and canalers. For the United States, the completion of the first transcontinental railroad was celebrated at Promontory, Utah, on May 10, 1869. The tracks of the Central Pacific and the Union Pacific were joined to create a link of three thousand miles and just seven days' duration for travellers. Nowhere between St. Louis and San Francisco was there then a town with more than 35,000 people. At that time, 60 percent of all U.S. steel production went into building railroads. It was also the heyday of circus promoter Phineas Barnum, and the suffragette movement was active. Chiefs Crazy Horse and Sitting Bull had overwhelmed Custer and his cavalry. The number of U.S. blacksmiths then outnumbered lawyers by three to one. Europeans and others were adapting to the telephone, the bicycle, and the typewriter.

It was such a different world that it was an incredible blunder of Canada's legislators to rule that a century later the Railway Act should apply holus-bolus and that anyone using the act should merely substitute the word *pipeline* for *railway*. If legislators and lawyers had been more perceptive, the many problems that afflicted agriculture and the environment could have been avoided.

The railroads have been overwhelmingly good for agriculture. The problems ranged from right-of-way access through farms to weed and fire problems and more recently to rail-line abandonment, which pulled the plug on the prosperity of some rural communities. The dichotomies relating to agriculture and pipelines are also marked, but they are very different. Farmers too benefit from pipelines. Agriculture is a big user of energy and energy by-products such as those created in the manufacturing of fertilizers and plastic drainage tubing; these products are key factors in increasing farm productivity and efficiency. The problems relate primarily to the individual farms, and as you will see, such problems trace to a misuse of bureaucratic powers, a myopic pipeline industry, and incredible ignorance of the significance of agriculture and the environment.

The root cause in Canada was the use of that archaic Railway Act and its application to pipelines and agriculture. When the Railway Act was drafted, it was a very different world. The creation of such Canadian provinces as Alberta and Saskatchewan were still a quarter of a century in the future. The use of the Railway Act in the nineteenth century was good for Canadian development. Its abuse in the twentieth century has been an unmitigated disaster for agriculture and the environment. It took a long time but the energy industry and its regulators have now accepted this reality.

CHAPTER 7

Without the Owner's Consent

Bad laws are the worst sort of tyranny.
— EDMUND BURKE

Expropriation is a legal taking, without the owner's consent. The full implication of this sinks in when it is your farm, your home, or your business. (The terms *expropriation* and *condemnation* are both used in the United States.)

"Expropriation is a very unpopular word for a very unpopular action. It happens when property is taken from its owner, without consent. Almost invariably, the owner is irritated, upset and shocked. And understandably so." So began Working Paper 9, issued by the Law Reform Commission of Canada on expropriation. The straightforward writing style and the absence of Latin or ten-dollar words were welcome to anyone facing that blunt instrument called expropriation. I expect it owed something to the commission's consultant in its expropriation law project, Gaylord Watkins. Getting to know Gaylord and having the privilege to contribute my ideas on law reform were beacons of hope and encouragement for us during some particularly bleak years of what often seemed futile struggle.

The commission chairman, Patrick Hartt, later wrote to me, "I understand that you have discussed with Gaylord Watkins the need for reform of certain federal statutes that give the power to expropriate to pipeline companies. . . . The reforms we will be recommending, if implemented, would help to prevent the kinds of situations and frustrations that some people have experienced. But it is, admittedly, these very experiences that point out the need for reform and activate the process of change." And then Hartt made a very interesting comment (a decade ago): "Recent discussions with Mr. Gary Homer, Chairman of the Land Right-of-Way Committee of the Canadian Petroleum Association indicate that most pipeline companies will support our initiatives in these areas."

I found that comment easy to accept. On three occasions I have accepted invitations to address the International or American Right-of-Way Associations. When the first Canadian seminar was held in Ottawa in 1972, I got an incredibly chilly welcome from the six hundred attending — and later a standing ovation. I learned that many of the members were concerned that the rotten apples in the barrel were giving the whole of their business a bad odour. I believe that the reform of archaic laws would have come much more rapidly but for the atrophied conscience of such influential bodies as the NEB. As recently as 1979, the Canadian Senate Special Committee overseeing the then proposed Alaska Highway Gas Pipeline concluded that the federal procedures used to acquire rights-of-way were "inadequate and placed the owner in an untenable position."

My own views have not changed since *Saturday Night* published my article "Expropriation and the Farmer" in 1959:

> Farmers realise the need for the installation of various utilities but the dice are loaded rather heavily against the farmer. The thoughtful landowner questions whether the virtually indiscriminate use of expropriation powers can be justified. That they are necessary to some extent is not questioned, but when they come to be used instead of reasonable, straightforward negotiations, they can only fall into disrepute. This is not a narrow argument against necessary powers of compulsion, but rather that they be used with far greater intelligence and understanding.

As my friend and neighbour John Walker Elliott once observed, "There are too many people, with too little knowledge and too much power!"

Expropriation was used in the Roman Empire and by the ancient Greeks. Despite the antiquity of taking something without the owner's consent, there is still some confusion about the precise meaning of the word *expropriation*.

The definition in the *Dictionary of English Law* describes *expropriation* as "compulsorily depriving a person of a right of property belonging to him in return for compensation."

The *Canadian Law Dictionary* definition is "the compulsory purchase of land or other property of a person by municipal or other governmental authority usually in return for fair compensation. The right to expropriate is vested in the state by reason of its eminent domain and only the amount of compensation payable is a justifiable issue." And that is where I part company with the legal system and most of its practitioners.

First, there should be a mandatory provision for negotiation. If it can be shown that there was no attempt at negotiation or that the negotiation was conducted under threat of expropriation, then expropriation should be denied. I made this point in briefs to the NEB, to cabinet ministers at the federal and provincial levels, and before the Ontario Law Reform Commission.

Another important issue in the laws governing expropriation is the omission of responsibility to mitigate damage and to consider environmental concerns. In our case, we had not only pleaded for negotiation and procedures to avoid damage; we had given Interprovincial and the NEB copies of our consultants' reports, which would have prevented most damage had they been implemented. Throughout the actual construction of Interprovincial's third pipeline in 1975–1976 and the subsequent court cases, there was considerable media coverage of the damage to farmland. Despite such publicity, the damage escalated and became more serious than any experienced in 1957 or 1967. From the vantage point of those experiences, there can only be grave misgivings for the fate of native people and the fragile environment when pipelines are installed in the sparsely populated northern areas of the continent.

Admittedly, there have been changes. From an earlier era when there was no environmental-impact research, we have moved to an era when whole forests were needed for the paper to publish reports like *Northern Frontier, Northern Homeland* by Mr. Justice Thomas R. Berger, the *Report of the Environmental Assessment Panel on the Alaska Highway Pipeline,* and *Forgotten Land, Forgotten People,* published by the Northern Pipeline Agency.

François Bregha, in his book *Bob Blair's Pipeline,* had sounded a warning note: "The government had allied itself to powerful business interests to advocate one concept of northern development, but paid little heed to the native people." The environmental issues will continue to surface until exploration, exploitation, and distribution are made compatible with stewardship of land.

The 1985 annual meeting of IPL heard a gung ho presentation from its president and a future chairman Bob Heule on vistas of a pipeline to the Beaufort Sea. Heule claimed that the recently constructed Norman Wells pipeline had "demonstrated that a pipeline can be built in the harsh, yet delicate, northern environment when properly engineered and managed." This provoked the response of Stephen Kakfwi, president of the Denendeh National Office in Yellowknife:

> Certainly the IPL pipeline has been built, but the Dene, who live in and use the surrounding land and water, are concerned that all is not well with the environment and the processes involved in environmental management. We have concerns with contaminated fish downstream of the oil-field development, inadequate water quality standards and insufficient and untested oil-spill contingency planning. . . . We live here. The full environmental impacts of this pipeline will not be known for a long time. Already the quality of our land and water is being eroded. . . . All is not well with the land, animals, fish and people of Denendeh.

Once again, the trail of responsibility leads back to the NEB, which has repeatedly chosen to permit expropriation in the absence of such sensible precautions as practical oil-spill procedures. In this instance, the NEB did reject the initial IPL environmental impact work as inadequate.

However, one wonders how much has really changed in North America since the response of Chief Seattle in 1854 to the request of the U.S. government for the sale of tribal land:

> We know that the white man does not understand our ways. One portion of the land is the same to him as the next, for he is a stranger who comes in the night and takes from the land whatever he needs. The earth is not his brother, but his enemy, and when he has conquered it, he moves on. . . . He treats his mother the earth, and his brother the sky, as things to be bought, plundered, sold like sheep or bright beads. His appetite will devour the earth and leave behind only a desert.

As a lay person, I have further concerns with the sort of legal niceties explored in *The Laws of Expropriation and Compensation in Canada*. For instance, "The market value of land expropriated is the amount that the land might be expected to realise if sold in the open market by a willing seller to a willing buyer." In 1957, Interprovincial, using expropriation, acquired the right to lay pipelines forever through Larigmoor Farm. The financial settlement was on the basis of what local land was selling for in 1957; companies that enjoy the fruits of expropriation are consequently immune from inflation. I recall that in 1947, the year we landed in Canada, an automobile cost around $1,500. In 1991, a comparable model costs over ten times as much. It would have been very nice for us to have been awarded the rights in 1947 to replace our cars forever as they wore out, at 1947 prices! Farmers have to live with inflation; those who take the land do not. Such inequality is also evident when cities expropriate land banks. Farmland is thus acquired at current prices and sold at industrial development prices.

And then there are disturbance damages, which "may be defined generally as personal economic loss suffered by an owner by reason of his having to vacate the expropriated property." Here, my objection is the use of the adjective *economic* to qualify loss. When we bought Larigmoor Farm in 1952 it had no esthetic attributes. That pond that was shown to Interprovincial representatives back in 1957 continues to be as clean and pure as the day it was constructed. It is spring-fed and on the highest point on the farm, so that there can be no surface drainage to the pond. Since Arthur Pattillo and his colleague looked at the pond, the trees around it have matured. Another pond beside the barn offers fire protection and is stocked with fish; the trees and hedgerows around it are now inhabited by many species of birds that have come in the years since 1952. We have planted thousands of trees, and the bush is managed under a long-term conservation agreement with the Ontario Ministry of Natural Resources. Through the bush we have a horse-riding trail that serves winter duty as a ski trail and provides access for woodlot management. A large part of our lives has gone into making these improvements. But would any court consider them "economic"? In Canadian law, where there is no legal redress, there is deemed to be no legal injury.

In the light of these experiences and concerns, I turn with sympathy to the section on *expropriation* in *The Synonym Finder.* A synonym is not a precise alternative to definition, but it does invest a word with additional flavour. For instance, "Seize, commandeer, confiscate, dispossess, strip, evict, eject, steal, et cetera." *Steal?* The *Business Quarterly,* a sober bastion of Canadian business, observed in a 1973 feature on expropriation, "There are no constitutional safeguards here. In one of his classic outbursts, The Honourable Mr. Justice Riddell once said that in this country government can do anything — even steal with impunity."

In the same forty years that I have had concerns about the ways farmland is expropriated, some of the same characters keep emerging with different hats. Arthur Pattillo, apart from his courtroom appearances for Interprovincial, was general counsel to the Borden Commission, which led to the creation of the NEB, and he was, among many other things, president of the Canadian Bar Association. The study paper that originated the Law Reform Commission of Canada's reform recommendations was authored by John W. Morden, who later became a judge of the Supreme Court of Ontario and its Court of Appeal. After he left the NEB, Ian Blue became legal counsel to the Dene, a major opponent to pipeline construction methods.

And then there is the enduring John Turner, who while federal minister of justice created the Law Reform Commission of Canada. Turner's subsequent reincarnations included a directorship of Bechtel, and he was leader of the opposition in the Canadian Parliament until his retirement in 1990.

I was to find over the years that there were many fruitless leads and dead ends in any examination of expropriation. I went to Toronto in 1957 and met with federal transport officials who then held the mantle subsequently given the NEB. They exhibited no awareness of or interest in the problems a right-of-way through a farm can create for a crop and livestock farmer. Finally I said to them, "You can see nothing wrong with the forceful taking of our land and rights. You have no concern for the disruption of our farm business. Will you accept my expropriation of four inches across the middle of your desk, so that you cannot reach the other side, and will you be content with the prorated payment, based on the appraised value of your desk?" Unfortunately, this ploy merely confirmed to them that I was stark raving mad.

Some twenty years later, I used the same gambit when I appeared before Judge J. F. McCart. With the aid of court officials, we measured the courtroom and gave Judge McCart a right-of-way through his court that equated to the right-of-way through Larigmoor Farm. Judge Mc-Cart began to understand the concern of the farmer who could not gain access to half his farm during the growing and harvesting seasons. He promptly acknowledged the inconvenience he would suffer if a right-of-way through his court precluded return to his chambers and washroom!

When I appeared before the Ontario Law Reform Commission, I pleaded for reform of expropriation and the appointment of judges on competence, not patronage. A sympathetic and understanding member of that commission was the former Ontario chief justice, the Honourable James C. McRuer. Among his other contributions to justice was his chairmanship of the Ontario Royal Commission Inquiry into Civil Rights. That inquiry concluded:

> The mere existence of the power to expropriate property is in itself an encroachment on the rights of an individual in the sense that the security of his rights to property has been diminished. There is general agreement that the existence and the exercise of this power in actual cases constitutes an invasion of civil rights in our current legal system. Notwithstanding this, the power conferred and exercised in proper cases and according to proper principles is in the public interest. The great weight of criticism was not

directed against the principle of expropriation as an instrument of government, but against the promiscuous manner in which the power is conferred and the methods by which it may be, and often is, exercised.

McRuer went on to detail no less than fifty-three basic changes his commission felt necessary in the reform of expropriation laws.

McRuer's counterpart on the federal scene was Judge Hartt, and the report of the latter's commission began:

> Our concern for expropriation began in 1972. . . . We soon learned there were solid grounds for continuing to improve federal expropriation law. The 1970 [Expropriation] Act left untouched more than 1,200 expropriation powers — including some that could be used without any obligation to provide compensation, let alone fair procedures. . . . Many powers are governed by the clearly inadequate provisions of The Railway Act that date from the last century and give no right of notice or hearing to the landowner. . . . We initially hoped that the Expropriation Act of 1970 could simply be extended to govern all federal expropriations. But, we soon discovered that many powers outside the Act, and particularly those available to strip-takers such as railway and pipeline companies, have procedural and regulatory needs that the Act does not meet.

The commission report explored what is called some of the essentials of good expropriation law. These included equality. This, we were able to show, had not been practised by Interprovincial, which had decided to negotiate with some farmers but not with others. It will be recalled that the NEB found these kinds of concerns of no substance.

And the report had this to say on openness: "Openness — by all expropriators acquiring land by purchase or expropriation, in providing information about plans, rights and procedures, appraisal methods, prices paid and settlements reached." In this regard, IPL displayed a cavalier disregard for openness in the county court that granted expropriation of part of Larigmoor Farm in 1957. The company declined any and all requests for information, and the court decided that such things as drainage "are no concern of this court."

The Hartt commission next addressed the crucial question "Who should be able to expropriate?" It noted that in the years since confederation, the Canadian Parliament had been very generous in conferring expropriation powers. Since many of the parliamentarians in the preconfederation and early postconfederation periods were also promoters and participants, such largesse was not surprising. This era ended in 1920 when the government of Canada took over many private railways and formed the Canadian National Railway, the CNR.

The report noted:

> It [Parliament] has given the power to virtually anyone that, in meeting a public need, might require land. As a result, expropriation powers are held by a wide variety of governmental and non-governmental entities. Some 29 governmental entities—the Cabinet, individual Ministers, Commissions, Crown Corporations, and other public authorities have been granted the power to expropriate. . . . The vast majority of private enterprises that may expropriate are railway and pipeline companies regulated by federal agencies, the Canadian Transport Commission and the National Energy Board, respectively. . . . Many companies—at least 1,234 at last counting—have been granted expropriation powers by general or specific legislative enactments.

Chapter 4 explored the aftermath of expropriation. The constraints on farming extended far beyond the area of the expropriated right-of-way. In this chapter, we have seen the narrow legal definitions of *injurious affection*. The conclusions of the Law Reform Commission of Canada in this regard were particularly welcome to farmers.

> The 1970 Expropriation Act allows owners to claim compensation for injurious affection for damages caused by the construction or use of any public work on the part of the land that was taken. Damages, however, could arise from a project situated on land other than the land taken. And in this event, the owner would have no recovery under the Act and questionable recovery under the common law. We find the Act's approach narrow and unfairly restrictive. A recent reform in the United Kingdom allows compensation for injurious affection of land retained to be assessed with reference to the whole of the work and not only the part situated on the land required. Federal expropriation legislation in Canada should adopt this reform.

Concerns over the use and abuse of expropriation are surfacing in many quarters. The ubiquitous Norman Pearson, writing in the *Appraisal Institute Magazine,* had this to say: "Because private property rights are intimately and inextricably intertwined with political freedom, the question 'private property rights—for how long?' is vital to the future of our kind of society. If we are to avoid a new Dark Age it is imperative."

The Canadian Federation of Agriculture convened an expropriation meeting and concluded that "in no place in Canada, under either federal or provincial authority do procedures and principles followed in connection with the expropriation of land and of rights to the use of land give farmers an entirely fair break and often their legitimate interests are very seriously neglected."

The Canadian Broadcasting Corporation TV Ombudsman explored expropriation nationally. Ontario farmers like Lorne Dodge recounted their problems of farming amid a complex of pipelines and Ontario Hydro transmission lines. Commented CBC reporter Jim Wray: "The biggest battles over the expropriation in the West have been in Alberta, where 90% of Canadian oil is produced. . . . Pipelines are considered by governments, and the Supreme Court of Canada, as being in the public good, since they are designed to bring resources to the people at large. However, since the contracts are drawn up by oil company lawyers, there is a natural bias in favour of the oil companies."

Among the farmers who drove hundreds of miles to visit with us and share their expropriation experiences was Thorold Dupré of Napanee, Ontario. Dupré's immediate concern was that a third pipeline of Interprovincial threatened his remaining productive, thriving sugar bush. Dupré is among those unfortunates who have experienced a multiplicity of utilities. His rights and ability to farm have been variously impaired by expropriation for the four-lane Highway 401 (the Macdonald-Cartier Freeway), by Richmond Township for a road intersection and by Ontario Hydro for a power line. Multiple expropriations can render a farm uneconomic.

The Senate of Canada has long been regarded by its many critics as a sleepy sinecure and home for defeated politicians and party faithful. But it was the Senate that grasped the nettle and contributed to reform of expropriation laws. The Special Committee on the Northern Pipeline was chaired by Bud Olson, whom I first met when he was minister of Agriculture Canada. The concerns of Olson and his committee surfaced in the Senate as Bill S-12, an act to amend the National Energy Board Act. It was passed by the Senate on March 14, 1979. The numerous amendments replaced the sections that had previously brought into play what the Senate called "the outmoded Railway Act." They would bring pipeline right-of-way acquisition into line with modern federal and provincial expropriation statutes and would institute procedures more suited to conditions that foresee a growing number of major pipelines crisscrossing the country in the next few years. The bill incorporated some of the recommendations of the Law Reform Commission of Canada.

Any rejoicing for reform in expropriation could only be tempered with the realisation that it took an unconscionably long time.

CHAPTER 8

Style,
Tile,
and Bile

Hope is a good breakfast,
but it is a bad supper.
— FRANCIS BACON

There was a time, long ago, when I held no views about the members of the NEB; I had yet to meet them. What more promising day to rectify that omission than St. Valentine's Day? My debut before the NEB, on February 14, 1967, in Ottawa, began with a feeling of pleasure at the relaxed style of the board as it listened to my pleas. Later in the day, there was a startling revelation about tile—drainage tile, that is. But the aftermath of that hearing was pure bile.

From the hindsight of over twenty years, I now realise that I was naive, but all the vibes had been good, and there are probably greater sins in this life than naivety. The vibes had been good from the start. Having read, by chance, a CP (Canadian Press) story that Interprovincial planned to loop its pipeline, I had written to I. N. McKinnon, then NEB chairman, to inquire if the proposed expansion would affect Larigmoor Farm. Indicative of how little I then knew of the NEB was the fact that the letter was simply addressed to The Chairman, The National Energy Board, Ottawa. It concluded with a request in the event that his reply was in the affirmative; "I trust that I may be favoured by your early reply and an invitation to attend and participate in the hearings."

The vibes continued to be good. On receipt of an affirmative response from the NEB, Jean typed my brief. That brief was discussed in detail with my neighbours and received their endorsement. Long before dawn on St. Valentine's Day, we made our routine checks in the barn;

none of our Simmental beef cows, which were heavy in calf, gave any sign that they would calve in the next twenty-four hours. Leaving the farm in Jean's capable hands, I set out for London Airport. There was a brief station stop in Toronto, and again the vibes were good. I was met by a courier from Ontario agriculture minister Bill Stewart with documentation on the topsoil-stripping options that had been made available by the province during the construction of the Lake Huron water pipeline to London. Later that month, Stewart was to endorse my brief in the Ontario legislature, one of the many positive moves he made to encourage good pipeline practice. He had an empathy and an understanding of agriculture unequalled among provincial ministers of agriculture. Some of this was acquired on his own crop and livestock farm in London Township; it is now a dairy farm operated by the Stewart's eldest daughter and her husband.

On arrival at the NEB, which was then on Bronson Avenue and convenient to the airport, I was greeted with friendly warmth by Fred Lamar, then senior counsel at the NEB. The helpful advice of Lamar and other members of the NEB staff on how to make my presentation was much appreciated.

It is not always understood by courts and tribunals that a lay intervenor is under considerable stress and can appear only by sacrificing business and family. Costs ruled out retaining legal counsel; in any event, I knew of no lawyer with any expertise who might appear effectively on behalf of farmers. Anyway, I still had a vivid recollection of that lawyer in a Woodstock court who might have saved the day if he had simply advised the court that his expert witness in real estate appraisal had not qualified as an expert witness on drainage.

It was nearly time for the NEB to convene, with all the authority of a federal court. I felt some empathy with the hapless slaves who entertained Roman emperors in their amphitheaters. The welcome from Interprovincial lawyers Bob Burgess and Gordon Sheasby was polite yet restrained. Burgess fielded his first team. Representing Interprovincial were President T. S. Johnston, Treasurer John Blight, Roger Clute, manager of engineering, and A. B. Jones, manager of planning and economics. This was just great. Finally I would have an opportunity to inform the decision makers of IPL directly about the problems that had festered for a decade.

It looked as though we were in for a fairly quiet hearing. The only other intervenor was Ross A. McKimmie, on behalf of his client, the Northern Pipe Line Company; he was there to ensure that the company was not disadvantaged by any decisions that might result from the hearing. McKimmie, incidentally, is now a Q.C.; his business interests included being a board member of Sulpetro Limited, which is involved in oil and gas in both the United States and Canada, and he has also served as chairman of the Board of Governors of the University of Calgary. NEB hearings usually involve a panel of three; this time the panel was headed by McKinnon, assisted by Douglas Fraser and Maurice Royer. As C. D. Howe's executive assistant, Fraser had enjoyed a unique vantage point. A biography of Howe observes: "Scorned by the press of the Fifties as a calculating manipulator who rammed approval of the Trans-Canada Pipeline through Parliament and sold out Canada's resources to the Americans, C. D. Howe was acknowledged by critics and admirers alike as Minister of Everything."

As I looked around the small assembly in the court, I had to conclude that the vibes were also good for Interprovincial. There were no representatives or observers from any environmental or agricultural department of the federal or provincial governments. Also conspicuous by their absence were representatives of any federal or provincial farmers' organizations. I realised that I was the only person there to oppose the IPL application and the only farmer involved. If I did not ask some of the questions of concern to farmers, those questions would never be asked.

Bob Burgess was never one to overlook an exposed Achilles' heel. "Where is the Federation?" he asked, implying that if the Ontario Federation of Agriculture was not there and the Canadian Federation of Agriculture, located down the street, did not bother to attend, then I was alone out there in left field. As with so many of Burgess's provocative outbursts, this was shortly to boomerang.

What neither Burgess nor myself knew at that stage was that my neighbours, led by Gib Sleight, had generously passed the hat to defray the costs of my appearance in Ottawa. Evidently, some people did care, even if they were not participating directly in the hearing. A heartwarming moment occurred when Lamar rose to say, "I have a telegram here, and I have shown a copy of it to Mr. Burgess. It is a telegram which arrived on my desk this morning, and it is signed by a number of gentlemen who, I believe, are your neighbours — are they not? — who support the ten-point program urged by Mr. Lewington. I would suggest that I might file this as an exhibit." That telegram, which was addressed to McKinnon and signed by Jack Legg of Birr, read:

At an open meeting held in London Township on February 13, 1967 the following resolution was passed unanimously by citizens who are affected by the Interprovincial pipeline. Stop. We urge in the strongest possible terms the adoption of the ten points of principle which have been drafted by Peter Lewington. Stop. All farmers affected by the proposed pipeline are convinced of the justice of these principles. Stop. We commend them to the immediate attention of the Board for implementation prior to granting the company authority to lay a further pipeline. Stop.

Much of the morning was devoted to the technicalities of pipelining, and figures in the millions of barrels of oil and millions of dollars of investment were freely bandied around. Then, after the luncheon recess, Johnston got into his policy statement:

Interprovincial is occupied exclusively in the transportation of hydrocarbons at published tariffs. We attempt to be in a position to provide new facilities whenever it is feasibly possible and economic. We also tend to accept oil of any other parties who desire to ship. We accomplish this by extending our facilities through expansion of the system by horsepower and/or by looping. . . . In view of the forecast demand we consider it extremely important that we be permitted to undertake this construction at this time and as promptly as possible.

As Burgess observed in his final argument, "It is a perfectly normal application for additional facilities." He was right in that most of the evidence presented was of a technical nature affecting pipeline construction, matters such as the grade of the steel pipe and all the minutiae of pipeline construction. Where he was wrong was that this, the second time around, there was some input from agriculture. It was the first such hearing that I had learned of in time to participate.

It transpired that Burgess, too, had an Achilles' heel. I asked the board to request from Interprovincial the costings which went into their offer to landowners. It involved the princely sum of $10 for the crossing of any farm, regardless of size, exclusive of damage! Conceded Burgess: "We are not proud of it, and perhaps there may be a change."

McKinnon subsequently pursued this point, to which I responded, "You asked, sir, whether farmers were competent to judge whether it [an agreement] was fair or not. I think the fact that 135 signed for a fee of $10, which Mr. Burgess now doesn't think is adequate, would indicate that if people come along with virtually any piece of paper, some people will sign it." Interprovincial subsequently made a new and much better offer to every affected landowner.

When in the latter part of the afternoon I had an opportunity to speak, I felt that the board was receptive.

It is high time that the NEB and the utilities which seek authority from it should become conversant with their impact upon farmers and agriculture in general. In order to illustrate my viewpoint, it will be necessary to make reference to some personal experience. However, in no sense is this a narrow or selfish presentation. I am here today to seek your support on some basic principles. It is my submission that the NEB should consider these principles and then enforce them upon such companies as the Interprovincial Pipe Line Company, which come under the board's jurisdiction.

Here, in summary, are those principles:

1. The NEB should consider the interests of individual farmers who would be affected by a utility, *prior* to granting authority to construct pipelines or additional facilities. "If you neglect to protect his legitimate interests, he loses the first and crucial round."

2. All farmers and landowners shall receive, by registered mail, notice of any board hearing that may affect them. The board should alter its procedures so that from the outset, the farmer can be acquainted with projected construction plans that affect his property. In Ontario the board has been content to require Interprovincial to insert notices of this hearing in the *Sarnia Observer* and the Toronto *Globe and Mail*. I pointed out that "in my own township, not a single farmer who is affected subscribes to the *Sarnia Observer*, and only one subscribes to the *Globe and Mail*. A legal notice in the *Afghanistan Times* would have served as well. In simple terms, gentlemen, the farmer is kept in ignorance. Having been kept in ignorance of the provisions of your orders, he is then technically excluded from participation in your deliberations."

3. The board should place itself beyond all suspicion of partisan action. I referred the NEB to its own secretary's letter received just prior to the hearing, which said, "I am forwarding one copy of your letter and this reply to the Interprovincial Pipe Line Company for reference." It seemed to me that the scales of justice, already weighted heavily in the company's favour, suffered further imbalance if my correspondence to the board was routinely shared with IPL. But the board did not feel a similar constraint to share the company's correspondence with me.

4. This principle called for the appointment of an independent inspector with authority to resolve problems during construction. I pointed out that it was unreasonable to expect Ontario farmers to have to resolve their differences, without any authority, with contractors from Texas, Oklahoma, or wherever, whose job it was to ram the pipeline through.

5. This principle called for mandatory identification of all company representatives. I cited the phoney "professor from the Soils Department of the Ontario Agricultural College." This brought Burgess angrily to his feet with the comment "We know nothing of this, and we deny it flatly." I countered by saying, "Mr. Burgess was informed of this in my own living room in the presence of Mr. Arthur Pattillo, Q.C., and my wife; this is not the first time Mr. Burgess has been acquainted with this." The chairman noted Burgess's objection and offered him the opportunity to explore the issue further, but he made no effort to do so. My concerns were not restricted to misrepresentation. I had found many instances in which farmers subsequently appeared at a grave disadvantage because they had neglected to find out the name and the affiliation of the person to whom they had been talking.

6. This amounted to a plea for pipeline practices that would mitigate damage to farmland. It was sparked by memories of miles of open ditches and pipeline practices that maximized damage and disturbance of farming operations.

7. This principle dealt with the importance of tile drainage, the need for remedial action stemming from the first construction, and the protection and repair of drainage systems in future construction. I said, "I have no power to force them [Interprovincial] to do those things which they are morally obligated to do. Only the NEB has such power, and I trust it will exercise its authority."

8. Having alluded to the very limited extent of Class I farmland, I urged mandatory stripping of topsoil and an endeavour to restore the soil strata in the original position.

9. My ninth principle called for a change in the wording of damage releases. I urged that they be effective only to the date of signing, so that they did not exclude subsequent documented and legitimate claims. Experience had shown that many problems were not apparent immediately after construction and that crop losses could be experienced for many years.

10. This principle called for the recognition of *nuisance* as a valid claim. As we saw in the preceding chapter on expropriation, injurious affection is a difficult loss to quantify and prove.

That was the substance of my ten points, points that I urged should be implemented before the NEB gave the green light for construction. Throughout my presentation, there were many parries and thrusts from Bob Burgess. It is a miracle to me that the official reporters, Nethercut & Young, who do the work under contract, can prepare such accurate transcripts and have them completed overnight.

To assist the board in understanding the problems faced by farmers, I had filed numerous pictures. When Burgess spied the breached aquifer and the consequences, he predictably launched into the figment of "heavy rain." And when I urged acceptance, as a matter of principle, that a gravity tile drainage system should take precedence over a pressure pipeline, Bob Burgess asked, "Would you carry that one step further and say that the Indians have precedence over you?"

But overall, it had been a successful day. Bob Burgess had agreed that there should be a new offer to all landowners, and he had offered to strip the topsoil in a narrow strip above the planned excavation. And he had wound up the day with a much appreciated comment when he said, "I think this is a problem which bothers Mr. Lewington, and no doubt it does bother him, and bona fidedly bothers him too. . . . In spite of some of my remarks, I have a great admiration for Mr. Lewington." The questioning of Douglas Fraser had underscored the importance of my ten principles and the requirement that they should be universally adopted to benefit all landowners.

The hearing had also been a forum for tile drainage. Tile drainage has long been accepted as a fundamental requirement for profitable crop production in the best lands in Canada and the United States. Tile drainage now benefits from such things as laser technology, but in principle it has not changed. The 1881 (*sic*) Report of the Ontario Agricultural Commission included these observations:

•The most economical depth for general draining is about three and a half feet.

•Nothing is more certain than that underdraining, in ninety-nine cases out of one hundred, would prove a most profitable investment.

•The healthiness and vigour of the plant promoted by well-drained soil would enable it to resist attacks that would be fatal to less-thriving crops.

•The wetland that has been drained is the finest land on the farm. [I have underdrained a good deal with tile, stone, and wood; I prefer tile.]

•The proper drainage of land cannot produce drought; it has the opposite effect. Well-drained land holds moisture longer than any other land and holds it evenly.

•When land is properly drained, we can get on it earlier in the spring, and this is a saving of time, labour, and seed.

Inasmuch as tile drainage and its benefits have been widely understood and appreciated for so long, it is pertinent to record, in its entirety, Fred Lamar's cross-examination:

> *Q.:* One small point, Mr. Lewington, on exhibit number eleven, your diagram. About the middle of the page you have this line which you label "actual open ditch," and then to the right you have painted in a double line which you have labeled "actual tile outlet"?
> *A.:* Yes.
> *Q.:* I did not quite understand how the tile outlet related to the ditch. Is there some physical connection between the two?
> *A.:* The tile empties into the open ditch.
> *Q.:* In other words, the tile collects the water from the ground.
> *A.:* Yes.
> *Q.:* Is it a surface tile or a subsurface tile?
> *A.:* This is below the surface. Our surface level is here, at the top line.
> *Q.:* So these sort of subterranean tile outlets feed into the open ditch which is open to the surface?
> *A.:* Yes.

It came as a stunning blow to find that the NEB, which had by then over a period of eight years authorized the construction of pipelines through thousands of miles of farms, had done so without the slightest understanding of what a tile drain was, let alone its significance.

It had been a great day for agriculture, and it was going to get better. Ross McKimmie, who had been an interested bystander for most of the hearing, invited me to share his cab back to the airport. We flew to Toronto together and ruminated on the day's proceedings. "I think you carried the day!" said McKimmie, chuckling, as we parted company in Toronto.

As on the outward flight, the Toronto stop was put to good use. I was interviewed by George Atkins, senior farm commentator for CBC Radio. I told him (and listeners across Canada) that the NEB hearing had been a splendid success and that farmers could confidently anticipate a new deal involving pipelines and agriculture.

That euphoria didn't last long. The roof began to cave in when Bob Fraleigh who was then a geologist with Dome Petroleum in Edmonton sent along the only published report I ever saw of that hearing. *Oilweek* headlined its report: "No opposition to IPL expansion application." There was no by-line for the story, which went on to say, "Interprovincial Pipe Line Company met with no opposition last week when it asked the National Energy Board for authority to construct additional pipeline capacity and associated facilities. . . . The only jarring note at the hearing came from a disgruntled Ontario farmer who asked the board to adopt a 10-point program for protecting the rights of farmers against pipeline companies. The 90-minute intervention by Peter Lewington of Ilderton, Ont., was at times heated, controversial and amusing."

I promptly wrote to the editor, Earle Gray, that "this is an extraordinary conclusion for your reporter to make; I specifically asked the board to implement ten points of principle before authorizing any further construction. I trust that, upon investigation, you will take steps to publish a correction." There was no response, retraction, or reaction forthcoming from *Oilweek*. However, the *Oilweek* lead feature included a look back twenty years to Leduc No. 1 and a look twenty years into the future, based on an interview by Gray of Imperial Oil President W. O. Twaits. It was revealing that neither Gray nor Twaits made any reference to the environment or agriculture.

When the NEB's Report to the Governor-in-Council arrived, the St. Valentine's Day hearing dissolved into pure bile. The words of Francis Bacon seemed very appropriate: "Hope is a good breakfast, but it is a bad supper." I had been sustained by the expectation that the board would act decisively on my ten points and make them conditions for future construction. Instead, the board chose to ignore my concerns and authorized construction without the safeguards requested.

I wrote to McKinnon that "I have entertained the belief that the National Energy Board was composed of honourable men who had remained in ignorance of the conflict between the farmers of Canada and the utilities which receive authority from the board. . . . The board has sent to cabinet an extremely biased and inaccurate document." Copies of that letter went to scores of federal and provincial politicians and to farm leaders across Canada, but heading the list, was the Right Honourable L. B. Pearson, prime minister of Canada, who was to be asked to make the NEB reopen hearings.

The NEB was to find that it had to reopen hearings into a project to which both the board and the federal cabinet had given approval. It is logical that such a major change could have been made only with the authority of the prime minister.

Subsequently, when the Law Reform Commission of Canada issued its report on the NEB, it noted that "our observation of how the Board considered one citizen's complaint suggests that the attention given is likely to be proportional to the potential for embarrassment should the Board fail to act and the complaint turn out to be justified." And Bob Burgess, who had rhetorically asked, "Where is the Federation?" was soon to find out.

Ray McDougall was one of those dairy farmers whose well had been drained by the pumping of the London Public Utilities Commission (PUC). Ever since, he had been active in the Middlesex Federation of Agriculture in matters of land use. McDougall and such other federation stalwarts as Ron White spearheaded a joint approach of the Middlesex, Ontario, and Canadian Federations of Agriculture to Jean-Luc Pepin, minister of Energy, Mines and Resources. The brief endorsed my points and deplored the decision of the NEB.

On April 19, 1967, The London *Free Press* (and who knows, possibly the *Afghanistan Times*) included a legal notice that on May 3, the NEB had ordered a hearing into Interprovincial's application to lay its second pipeline. There was no reference to the irony of a board's ordering a hearing into something it had already decided was a fait accompli; but then, the advertised hearing, while ostensibly ordered by the NEB, must have resulted from a decision of a disturbed federal cabinet. Democracy, if not well, was at least alive.

CHAPTER 9

Rural
Revolt

I am in earnest. I will not equivocate; I will not excuse; I will
not retreat a single inch; and I will be heard!
—WILLIAM LLOYD GARRISON

I t was teeming with rain on the afternoon of
May 2, 1967, the eve of the reopened NEB
hearings scheduled at the Federal Building in
London, Ontario. A couple of automobiles pulled into the laneway of
Larigmoor Farm, and out clambered the passengers, all dressed in rub-
ber boots and raincoats befitting a wet day in the country. They marched
up the laneway, led by the stocky figure of Douglas Fraser wearing a
sou'wester above an engaging grin.

The NEB had not only acceded to requests to hold a meeting in a
farming area to facilitate the attendance of rural people; they had also
accepted the challenge to visit affected farmers enroute to the hearings.
The mountain had come to Mohammed. This was to be no routine NEB
hearing; in fact, it was unlike any that had gone before or any that were
likely to come. In a face-saving mood, the NEB had attempted to camouflage the reasons for the hearing. It was ostensibly called for Interprovincial to be granted "Leave under the provisions of Section 76 of
the National Energy Board Act to carry four portions of its pipeline
across certain highways et cetera, et cetera." This served only to encourage participation of numerous reeves and other township officials
from the municipalities all along the proposed routing. Many of them
knew that the London hearing was due to the NEB having been caught
with its pants down in the aftermath of the St. Valentine's Day hearing in
Ottawa. Farmers and farm organizations had not been duped by the
camouflage. They had heard farm broadcaster George Atkins and others
alerting rural people to the hearing—and the unusual circumstances in-

volved, including an about-face by the government of Canada, which had already rendered a decision.

When Douglas Fraser, as chairman of the panel, (assisted by Maurice Royer and H. L. Briggs) called the hearing to order, there was not an empty seat in the court. Apart from a large media contingent, most of the people in the crowded courtroom had come not just as observers but as participants. They echoed the clarion call of William Lloyd Garrison, "And I will be heard!"

One of the ironies of the three-day hearing was that one man in the audience (who followed everything with rapt attention) was never heard from, directly. He was the Honourable William A. Stewart, minister of agriculture in Ontario. A man from whom a lot was heard was Robin Scott, Q.C.; he was there through the good offices of Bill Stewart and represented the minister of justice and attorney-general for Ontario — and the outraged rural people of the province. Also there, at Stewart's bidding, was the acknowledged Canadian drainage expert Professor Ross Irwin, who is the drainage specialist in agricultural engineering at the Ontario Agricultural College. OAC had finally become involved, and, in passing, it can be noted that Bill Stewart, having retired from politics, was a chancellor of the University of Guelph, which embraces OAC.

Bob Burgess was there, by then a queen's counsel, flanked by fellow lawyers Gordon Sheasby and D. L. Mathieson. This hearing was also different in that it had attracted active participation of members of Parliament from both sides of the House of Commons. Although they were of different political persuasions, they were united in recognising that the unfair and archaic legislation that surrounded the NEB must be changed. I don't think that any of the M.P.'s had any personal antipathy to Interprovincial; they were there because they knew of the problems their constituents continued to experience as a result of archaic legislation. It is a continuing mystery why Burgess went to such lengths to alienate members of Parliament, to treat them to such boorish rudeness in front of their constituents. Hell hath no fury like an M.P. scorned! The metamorphosis of Jim Lind, the then Liberal M.P. in East Middlesex, has already been noted. Now Burgess went out of his way to offend Bill Thomas, the Progressive Conservative M.P. representing West Middlesex. "As a member of Parliament, surely to goodness he understands English!" declared Burgess.

Bill Thomas had more than a nodding acquaintance with the English language, having spent a lifetime as a high school teacher. In his latter years, as a member of Parliament, he devoted a great deal of his time and energy to the eventual reform of legislation, and in particular the change that gave gravity tile drainage priority over pressure pipelines.

The hearing had opened with a flag of truce from the NEB and an olive branch from Interprovincial. In his opening statement, Fraser revealed that the NEB had appointed a drainage inspector "whose responsibility it will be to be present when the construction operations of Interprovincial are conducted; to record the cutting or interruption of drainage facilities; to ensure that such facilities are repaired, restored or replaced in a proper manner; to ensure that the pipeline construction is conducted with due regard to the existing and planned drainage facilities and with minimum interference with such facilities."

Fraser went on to compliment Interprovincial for its support and cooperation, and revealed that "the company has, since that hearing [on St. Valentine's Day], indicated its willingness to alter the level of its pipeline where such alteration is necessary for the efficient operation of an approved municipal drainage system."

But this was too little too late. Again in the words of Garrison, "I will not excuse."

As Fraser asked the numerous intervenors to identify themselves and their affiliations, there were reminders that the controversy had festered too long. Declared Wilfred Bishop, secretary of the Oxford County Federation of Agriculture: "Our brief is a reiteration of the precedents established ten years ago when we appeared before the Board of Transport Commissioners relative to the protection of farmers' interests in existing drainage and future drainage plans."

The day evolved as a rancorous one, one that was neither completely satisfactory nor conclusive for any party. For instance, there were confirmations by the engineer that there had been changes in the plans of several municipal drainage systems to accommodate Interprovincial's pipelines. These included the O'Reilly drain and its monstrous siphon on the Tilden farm and the elevated gradient on the Needham Municipal Drain from the westerly line fence of Larigmoor Farm. An unwavering requirement of Interprovincial is that its representatives be alerted and present whenever there is a crossing of its pipelines by drainage equipment; notwithstanding this rule, Burgess adamantly held that IPL knew nothing about the changes that had been made in our municipal drainage systems.

At times, the hearing degenerated into an ugly mood. At one such juncture, John Martens, his voice shaking with emotion, said, "If anybody stands up and says something, everybody is hateful." Fraser was visibly shaken by the sincerity of John Martens. From time to time, Fraser tried to restore decorum. For instance, "Just let us cool down here right now. I think we are all going to take five minutes to cool out. This hearing is not for the purpose of having a dogfight."

But if it was to be a dogfight, Fraser had to look no further than himself and his fellow board members for the cause. Fraser knew first-hand that rural people had recorded the litany of their concerns to his board and its predecessor, largely without success. Now he faced what amounted to a rural revolt. Despite the fact that late April to early May is the seedtime that must precede any harvest, farmers had neglected their customary spring work to prepare briefs they hoped would sway the NEB.

When the sessions resumed the following morning, the 153-page transcript of Day One was available. Fraser delicately referred to the "difficulties yesterday," which required some amendment and clarification in the transcript. These were amicably taken care of. It was then that Bill Thomas stated that anyone not in possession of a transcript operated at a serious disadvantage. Responded Fraser: "I appreciate this difficulty, Mr. Thomas, but if we were to ask the Treasury Board to supply free copies to anyone, we would be told the contract regulations prohibit this. No copies are free. The National Energy Board pays for its copy; the applicant pays for its copies at a different higher rate. The general public is free to buy the transcript on the same terms as does the applicant."

When pressed by Thomas for the cost, Fraser said that the rate was 40 cents per page. As the final transcript was to run to 468 pages, it was obvious that being a part of the democratic process was an expensive privilege. Representatives of corporations and boards routinely have access to such essential transcripts; the representatives of corporations and boards are paid for the time they spend perusing such transcripts. Contrast this with the situation of the farmer who intervenes. He is not paid for his participation. In fact, he may suffer significant loss through neglect of his farming business. And then he has to pay for such essential tools as transcripts to participate on anything approaching equal terms. This is not to argue that the intervenor should be subsidized but to point out that this is yet another of the factors that distort the scales of justice. Notwithstanding the length of the transcripts, they still do not convey the total weight of evidence given the company and the board. Many of the intervenors, including Robin Scott, preferred in the interests of time to read excerpts from their briefs and lodge them in their entirety with the company and the board.

On the second day, Robin Scott led Ross Irwin through the labyrinth of Ontario drainage technicalities. Irwin noted that 40 million feet of tile were then manufactured annually in Ontario and that 75 percent of it was installed in the counties of southwestern Ontario, the very area most noted for its conflict of drainage and pipelines. The board accepted as exhibits a veritable library on drainage law, benefits, and costs. The short course on drainage concluded with the luncheon recess.

When the hearing resumed, it became evident that by resorting to the subterfuge of convening a hearing allegedly on road crossings, the NEB had inadvertently laid itself open to interventions from an even wider spectrum of concerned parties.

The brief of the corporation of the township of East Williams:

> Requests that the board [NEB] issue orders that the Interprovincial Pipe Line Company shall be held liable and responsible for the proper repair and maintenance of field tile lines cut by the installation of the carrier pipeline. The Corporation submits that when it is found that there is not sufficient cover to facilitate the drainage of adjacent lands without the drainage works being routed over or under the pipeline, the Interprovincial Pipe Line Company shall be bound at its own expense to make the necessary alterations and alignment.

My neighbour and township councillor Ron White made it plain that London Township intended to flex its muscles. "The Corporation of the Township of London contends that the granting of any right to any corporation or body to cross any road allowance or property belonging to the municipality is a right which should be at the sole discretion of the municipality." He then went on to detail numerous conditions that would hamper the activities of IPL; included were load limits for trucks loaded with pipe and equipment crossing some township bridges.

"I wonder if you would be able to answer this question, Mr. White," said Burgess. "Why does this township council think that their municipal elected people are in any way superior to the members of the federal Parliament who are elected from the same area?" To this, White responded with quiet dignity.

> Basically, sir, we feel as local representatives we represent the people on a grass-roots basis. We are the most approachable government body. I believe that municipal government is the place where the people get the first chance to speak, and therefore we feel we have a responsibility. We find in our work that people will come to us first, before they go to other levels of government, particularly in the matter of drainage, because the municipality acts under an act set out by a higher level of government.

But White had not finished. He donned another hat and presented a brief on behalf of property owners and farm tenants in the Township of London. This opposed the IPL application:

> We are not asking for anything more than that to which we are entitled. We think that it is within your power to see that the farmers' interests are protected. We are most concerned with drainage, and we ask the board to conduct a survey of the Interprovincial pipeline easement in Ontario, in order to determine any conflicts of level which may exist and resolve them in favour of gravity drainage systems. . . . [The NEB] can protect the rights and privileges which we should enjoy in this country. We do not wish to inhibit progress. Gentlemen, it is a fact that everyone involved in this application will benefit to some extent from the laying of this proposed pipe, except the property owner. The federal and provincial governments will gain some taxes, municipal governments will get increased assessment and Interprovincial will profit. Unless we the property owners are given the security and concessions for which we are asking, we shall again take a loss at the benefit of everyone else.

This proved too much for Bob Burgess, who denounced White's "ridiculous statements" and attacked him for not having the requisite number of copies of his brief. Said Burgess: "Mr. White is not a neophyte in these hearings. He is not an innocent first-time farmer."

Responded White: "I assure you that I am most innocent. We are sincere and conscientious people, wishing only to be left alone or dealt with as respected citizens."

It was a case of mistaken identity. Burgess had mistaken White for some adversary of yesteryear. When convinced that they had never met before, Burgess was prompt to apologise, saying, "I am terribly sorry. I will retract those remarks."

Finally, when questioned by Fraser, White made a last telling point. "There surely must be some other means whereby we can have these matters rectified, problems removed, without having to go to a court of law." White and many other farmers were concerned that when the board abdicated its responsibilities, farmers were left at the costly mercy of unsympathetic courts.

The wording of the legal notice of the hearing had left the door open for the township of West Nissouri to raise such hoary concerns as the O'Reilly Municipal Drain and IPL's noisy Bryanston Pump Station.

Throughout the afternoon, there had been a lot of flack, and Lamar conceded somewhat ruefully, "I had better start thinking."

Just when the NEB thought that it had finished with municipalities, I rose on behalf of the corporation of the Township of Beverly, near

Hamilton. This occasioned some laughter in what had been a rather tense courtroom. Gordon Jamieson, the reeve of Beverly, had not been able to stay overnight in London and had asked me to present his brief, which included the request that "the National Energy Board require pipeline companies to remove and replace topsoil in agreement with the landowners at no expense to the said landowners."

When Fraser invited the input of members of Parliament, it became evident that Bill Thomas had done his homework thoroughly. He made reference to eight professional and farmer organizations. He included a cross-indexing to Robin Scott's brief, which read: "The Minister of Justice and Attorney General for Ontario supports the principle of the pending Bill sponsored by Mr. W. H. A. Thomas, M.P. Middlesex West, to amend the National Energy Board Act in respect of drainage rights."

Thomas then put C. P. Corbett on the stand. He qualified as a consulting professional engineer and an Ontario land engineer entitled to practice municipal drainage. Under oath, Corbett conceded that he had changed the publicly agreed specifications of various municipal drainage systems when he found a conflict of level with pipelines. This precipitated a rebuke from John Walker Elliott, one of the farmers who had contributed to Corbett's fees but had not received the drainage works for which he had been assessed. Snapped Elliott: "I figure my money was wasted in hiring you." Although the involved municipality hires a consulting engineer, it is the landowners who pay the engineer.

Corbett was also obliged to admit that he had changed the specifications of the drainage system for the western half of Larigmoor Farm and those of some of our neighbours. Once again, he had found a conflict between a pressure pipeline and a farmer's gravity drainage system. "We did not probe this pipeline. This may have been an error on our part as it turned out later, but we had an understanding . . . we had understood that an effort . . . " Whatever it was that Corbett "understood" was not clarified.

It had been another long day, but a revealing one. Farmers had documented some of their concerns, concerns they had not previously been able to prove in a court of law. It had also been a day relieved by snatches of humour. When Don Middleton spoke on behalf of the Ontario Federation of Agriculture, he zeroed in on IPL's damage release form, which had been a cancer of concern among farmers for years. Said Middleton: "It would be a glorious thing to have your mother-in-law sign if you didn't want to see her come back again! It is that broad."

Fred Lamar got into the act when he said, "I cannot resist telling a very brief story. I found it necessary to go to the washroom, and while I was there, a citizen, completely unconnected with this hearing, said, 'Say, what's going on down there at the end of the hall?' I said, 'Well, the National Energy Board is having a hearing down there, and we are getting representations from citizens.' 'Oh, is that what it is,' he said, 'I thought it was a centennial project.' " And perhaps, in its own way, it was just that. What better way to celebrate the centennial of Canada than for citizens to insist upon their rights in a parliamentary democracy?

What was to become the third and final day of the hearing had its own, different character. It was a day primarily concerned with the presentation of briefs from the Middlesex County Farm Management Association, the Middlesex County Federation of Agriculture, the Middlesex County Soil & Crop Improvement Association, the Drainage Committee of the Ontario Land Surveyors Association, and the brief of the Canadian Federation of Agriculture.

Involved in the briefs by farmers were some of the best practitioners of the art of crop and livestock production in Canada, farmers like Ray McDougal, Ken Patterson, Lorne Dodge, and John R. Stewart. It was a storehouse of information on how modern farming interfaces with modern energy conveyance. Unlike the preceding two days' events, a great deal of light was generated and very little heat.

However, as I was the only farmer who had participated in both the February and the May hearings, I could not resist making a link between the two in concluding my brief. "During the course of the February 14 hearing I was asked if drainage tile are laid on the surface of the ground or whether they were subterranean," I recalled. "As drainage tile are customarily buried in the ground and cannot be viewed by the board I would like to file as an exhibit this clay drainage tile." It was symbolic of the hearing, which had included all the variety of a Gilbert and Sullivan production, that Exhibit 43 was incorrectly identified in the transcript as "clay file." Fred Lamar had thought it was something else. For three days, he had watched me carry the tile, concealed in brown paper, into the courtroom. He had been reminded of a classic legal case in which a man stood charged with the murder of his estranged wife and only some of her dismembered remains had been found. When the prosecution daily brought a brown paper parcel into the courtroom, there had been the inference that the lost had been found.

And then, towards the end of the lengthy transcript, there is a gap. I had asked the NEB if I could censure them for filing a false and misleading document with the federal cabinet. Fraser promptly called a recess to consider the point. On his return, he questioned the propriety of such a statement. He cited such authorities as the speaker of the House of Commons, who held that members might not debate a report or decision of a judicial tribunal. He turned to Fred Lamar for advice. "I think that legitimate criticism of any judicial or quasi-judicial decision is acceptable in the broad sense," advised Lamar. "The point I believe Mr. Lewington is trying to make is that in his view, the report was misleading, and he enumerates the reasons why he believes that this is so. I don't think anything really would be gained by Mr. Lewington in reiterating his belief about the misleading nature of the report, in that the report, or, as I call it, a decision, is not a finished, completed matter."

It was far from finished. It would not be considered finished until the Supreme Court of Ontario completed its end run around the NEB fourteen years later.

CHAPTER 10

Pyrrhic Victory

It was the best of times, it was the worst of times. . . .
It was the spring of hope, it was the winter of despair.
—CHARLES DICKENS

Pyrrhus, King of Epirus, was a great Greek warrior three centuries before the birth of Christ. In 280 B.C. he defeated the Romans, and he gave them another trouncing the following year at Asculum. But those victories had been won at heavy cost, prompting Pyrrhus to conclude, "One more such victory and I am lost." So was born the concept of a Pyrrhic victory, a victory whose cost has been too high.

Interprovincial was not exactly the Roman Empire, and the farmers who opposed them, although the underdogs, didn't fit the mold of Greek warriors. Nevertheless, the analogy is apt in that it had been a victory for which a high price had been paid. Those who have not been engaged in such battles may underestimate the cost, a cost in which the cash for such things as hearing transcripts are only the tip of the iceberg.

It would all have been worthwhile had there been some visible evidence that some of the philosophies that motivated farmers had rubbed off on the NEB and IPL. If only Interprovincial, having made contact through the May 1967 hearing with such farm leaders as the president of the Ontario Soil & Crop Improvement Association, had followed through with some funding for things like compaction studies. It would have been bread upon the water.

Despite his abrasive attitude in court, Bob Burgess was an agreeable fellow offstage. No one could question his dedication to his company. But was it misplaced? The hard-liners in the energy business tend to think of farmland as something between pump stations. And farmers? Well, they tended to fall into one of two categories: the compliant ones who signed virtually anything placed before them or that smaller group of activists who were more likely to be viewed as anarchists.

The gregarious and honest Jean-Luc Pepin was probably the minister of Energy, Mines and Resources who had the best grasp of what concerned farmers. In 1967, in the House of Commons, he observed that "there is no doubt that the hearing which took place in London at the beginning of May has been enlightening." If the hearing had been enlightening, the aftermath was to be even more so. Instead of the new era of understanding and cooperation, it turned out to be a very mixed bag.

There were many indications that it was the best of times. No longer could the company or the board kid themselves that they faced, in the words of *Oilweek,* "a disgruntled farmer." Now they knew of the broad-based opposition to their policies. The board, and the companies it regulated, could no longer plead ignorance of any relevant aspect of agriculture. The briefs of farmers had covered the abuse of expropriation, outdated legislation, drainage law and practice, and some of the skills required to survive and prosper in a highly capitalized agriculture.

A significant improvement in company-farmer relations was the appointment of Gordon Frew as Interprovincial's liaison in the field. He was visible, he was identifiable, and he willingly let it be known where he might be reached by telephone. This was the first time, in my experience, that there was a responsive and responsible person who could be contacted about problems. And during the May hearings, when Bob Burgess had led Roger Clute through his testimony, he had been at great pains to be precise that certain changes were now established as company policy. These related to stripping of topsoil and the resolution of conflict of level between gravity drainage systems and the company's pipeline that was to go in the ground and those which were already there. And most importantly, it looked as though the work would be done in midsummer when there was less risk of damage to the soils.

Jim Lind, M.P. for our riding of East Middlesex, gave repeated indications in the House of Commons debates that he had neither forgiven nor forgotten his experiences at the London hearing. Having read the board's order of May 30, 1967, which gave Interprovincial the looping rights it had asked for, he said in Parliament:

> The company [Interprovincial] failed in the past to make complete and adequate compensation to the farmers for damage to crops and existing drainage systems and has refused to compensate the individual farmers for their losses. I would appreciate it if the minister would give the farmers of Middlesex County his assurance that the Interprovincial Pipe Line Company will be fair and not take advantage of them. These people are the

backbone of our society and they have every right to demand fair and equitable treatment. . . . Mr. Minister, all I am asking is that you insist that the National Energy Board see to it that these farmers are justly and honestly compensated for the inconvenience caused by the laying of the pipeline.

To this, Jean-Luc Pepin replied:

It is often said that ministers should not be technicians. Tonight I wish I knew more about the law, about farming, and about pipelines in order adequately to answer my friend the Honourable member for Middlesex East. . . . When damage occurs, there is recourse to the courts of this land. I understand however that the legal procedure may be time-consuming and expensive and consequently I think my Honourable friend is right in attaching a great deal of importance to the conduct of the pipeline company. The Honourable member has said that the company has accepted, recently, more responsibility than perhaps it had in the past. . . . With respect to past damages, the NEB has no jurisdiction to reopen cases, but it considers that it can act as an intermediary between the farmers concerned and the company.

And still another harbinger that this was to be the best of times was the appointment of a drainage inspector by the board. In choosing Vincent Moran, of Oil Springs, Ontario, they had found a man of considerable experience in municipal affairs and one who appeared acceptable to all parties.

In the face of all these encouraging developments, how could the summer of 1967 degenerate into the worst of times? Readers may recall the comments of Douglas Fraser in the London hearing when he announced that "the Board has appointed a drainage inspector whose responsibility it will be to be present when the construction operations of Interprovincial are conducted; to record the cutting or interruption of drainage facilities; to ensure that such facilities are repaired, restored, or replaced in a proper manner; to ensure that the pipeline construction is conducted with due regard for existing and planned drainage facilities and with minimum interference with such facilities." The realities made it plain that the high-sounding promises of the NEB were not worth a pinch of snuff. The pipeline looping occurred at different spreads on the long route from Sarnia to Port Credit. Over a distance of some 150 miles, several pipeline construction crews concurrently installed the pipeline. In the face of this concurrent construction, the appointment of a single, however well-meaning, inspector made this board concession another Pyrrhic victory.

And what of those categorical promises to dig up and relocate the pipeline where it conflicted with a farmer's drainage? This had seemed to the farmers attending that May hearing a clear and unequivocal obligation. In my case that promise appeared relevant because it had been substantiated that our westerly outlet, the Needham Drain, had indeed been changed to accommodate Interprovincial. Despite all that, the company found an easy escape clause. The land tenure and the topography of southern Ontario are such that the municipal drainage systems that serve a watershed involve the lands of several, even numerous, farmers. The point of conflict of the pipeline and the Needham Drain was not on Larigmoor Farm but on that of a neighbour two farms away. Bob Burgess rigidly clung to the view that it was an impertinence for farmers to expect to be paid for crop damage in the event of pipe relocation. This intransigence effectively ruled out relocation. It has been said that one can exist without friends, but not without neighbours. How could I possibly live in the community if I inflicted the awesome damage on a neighbour's farm that would inevitably follow pipeline relocation? This is a crucial rural dilemma that urban people are unlikely to encounter.

I had hoped that after all the static Interprovincial and the NEB had received from me, when it came time to install the pipeline through Larigmoor Farm, at least this would be done with due care and attention. By now, the Lewington Drain was part of IPL's corporate history, and the company could no longer plead ignorance or heavy rain when it blundered into the aquifer.

The huge trenching machine clawed its way across the farm and didn't even slow up when it chewed through the Lewington Municipal Drain. When it was last repaired, the tile had been lodged in a split steel pipe to keep it in some semblance of the correct level and grade. The steel was no match for the trenching machine, and on either side, the pipe spiralled to the heavens like so much candy floss. The trenching machine, like some giant juggernaut, proceeded serenely on its way to the terminal on the shores of Lake Ontario. The aquifer was breached again, and once again there was soupy slurry in the trench. Because of the tangle of the steel, it was hard to plug the exposed ends of the tile drains; the slurry was allowed to silt our expensive and vital drainage system. It was all very sad and stupid, and clearly avoidable.

Doing battle with farmers and stickhandling its way around NEB regulations are relative sideshows for a major pipeline company. Its priorities are the installation and operation of a large and complex system. This must involve expertise in many areas; the record clearly shows

IPL to be a well-managed and profitable system. For virtually every year of its history, Interprovincial has made some extension to its pipeline system. This must necessitate planning to an inspired degree. While there was systems planning, farmers were not part of the system.

There is no indication that Interprovincial neglected to order turbines for its pumping stations or to alert the steel companies that it would be in the market for pipe. But farmers' fencing was something else again. Fence posts had not been on the Interprovincial shopping list, and once again IPL representatives gave the limp excuse that no decent fence posts could be found. In one of its briefs submitted to the NEB and IPL, the Middlesex Federation of Agriculture had requested that "where fences are erected, suitable anchor and brace posts must be equipped with proper fastenings in order that the original tension will be maintained. Whenever, or wherever openings in the fence are necessary, adequate gates must be constructed." Even if the fence workers had been provided with adequate fence posts, they would not have known what to do with them. In the interests of harmony, Ron White and I spent the better part of a day, unthanked and unpaid, training the workers hired by IPL in the art of farm fencing.

Gordon Sheasby was then moving up the corporate ladder and taking more of the legal load from Bob Burgess. I invited Sheasby to come to Middlesex and meet with farmers in an effort to resolve outstanding problems. It was a very civil meeting, and after it ended, I brought Gordon back to Larigmoor Farm for a late dinner before he set out on his way back to Toronto. While it was a civil meeting, he made it plain that he still held all the trump cards, either through legislation or as a result of expropriation. IPL owned the necessary easements. They had now been granted the certificate to proceed. Farmers could not regard the company request for additional working rights as a bargaining tool; if the working rights were not voluntarily surrendered, at a pinch, IPL claimed, the construction could be done within the existing easement. This was an effective but specious argument. If the contractors did stray beyond the easement, they would be long gone before the farmer could do much about it.

It had been the spring of hope in London, Ontario. Now, with the passing of summer, we entered the winter of despair. For the next decade, it seemed that Sheasby had been right.

And then it became apparent that there was one vital card in the deck that even a compliant NEB could not give the company. When it came time for a third pipeline in 1975, there was still room for a larger-diameter pipe within the easement, but there was not room to install it without, heaven forbid, having the construction equipment operate above the existing pipelines. It was evidently one thing to operate heavy equipment over clay, concrete, or plastic tile drainage systems, but it was not to be condoned over the generally deeper and certainly stronger steel pipe.

That fall, when John Brownlie on behalf of IPL confidently demanded in Judge McCart's court the knee-jerk approval of working rights, times had changed from the lopsided victories of Arthur Pattillo a generation before. McCart clearly believed that the law he was obliged to uphold was signally lacking in fairness.

While the centennial year of 1967 had witnessed a kaleidoscope of spring hope and winter despair, the efforts had not been entirely wasted. The paper trail had been extended. It was to lead to law reform. Ultimately, for the first time, it was to create a Hobson's choice for utilities. They would have to choose between implementing good practices or paying for them on default.

CHAPTER 11

The Lewington Drain

A court may not permit one litigant to sit and compel the other to stand, one to speak all he desires and the other to be brief.

—THE TALMUD

The contributions of some of the architects of our world are recognized by place names. For Vancouver, a beautiful island and an exciting city; for Champlain, a lake; and for Humboldt, an ocean current. I must be content with a drain—the Lewington Municipal Drain. And even as drains go, it is not a very big one. It is fed by the tile systems on some five hundred acres of fertile land. It was designed to take any surplus water that would inhibit maximizing crop production and send it on its way to the Medway and Thames rivers, and finally to the Great Lakes. While it is a small drain, it is not your average drain. It has played a part in reforming some Canadian laws that affect landowners and the takers of land.

How important is tile drainage? Well, without it, farmers would find that some of the best land in the world would not be economic for crop production.

Ontario is a leader in drainage legislation that enables landowners in a watershed to take their requests for drainage improvements to their own municipal council. The council acts as the hinge between the provincial government and ratepayers. Council retains an engineer to bring in a report that includes drainage specifications and the estimated costs. This is debated before council, and on reaching agreement, tenders to construct the drainage works are advertised. Comparable procedures are followed in all of Canada's ten provinces, where drainage works can benefit some 10 million acres. There is a complex ritual to be followed, and the plans are modified in the light of public debate. Affected farmers have their say in a local forum in which they can feel comfortable. Because the creation of an outlet and the actual drainage benefits are unique to each farm, the costs are prorated by an agreed formula.

The Lewington Drain is a minor footnote in history because it tangled with North America's most extensive pipeline system. It served to expose the gaps between federal and provincial legislation that could cost farmers dearly. It figured in the evidence before legislative committees and the courts. It was part of the challenge to acts affecting expropriation, the NEB, railroads, and pipelines. After a century of Canadian history, a small drain was to help change some of the most unfair and antiquated laws of the land.

With the impressive benefits of a federal charter and a compliant Board of Transport Commissioners, Interprovincial did not feel constrained by provincial drainage legislation. Despite the two-year-long paper trail of the Lewington Drain, Bob Burgess had advised the board that the drain was "a figment of his imagination." It is indicative of the way the scales of justice were then weighted that the board obligingly accepted Burgess's figment as fact. My requests to the board at least to check with London Township were ignored.

In 1957 the nine farmers between Redwater, Alberta, and Port Credit, Ontario, who went to court to protect their drainage rights fared no better. Snapped Middlesex County Court judge Ian McRae: "Do you wish to continue with this discussion of drainage to the point where you make me cross? Drainage is of no concern of this court." A consensus of legal experts is that Judge McRae was technically correct; but he could have exhibited some concern, and he could have exercised the latitude inherent in our legal system. Ideally, laws are not etched in stone but modified by precedents. However, his attitude was in keeping with the times.

The pace of creating a drainage system is deliberately slow to ensure that all the viewpoints are adequately explored. The concept of the Lewington Drain was born before any of us had even heard of Interprovincial, but the drain was still only an engineer's blueprint when the ditching crews came through our line fence. The planned location and depth of the Lewington Drain were clearly marked on stakes, and the pipeline crews were alerted to them. But the contractors from the arid southwestern United States had other priorities than concerns for a picayune drain. The key player, Interprovincial, was conspicuous by its absence, as was the "impartial" referee, the Board of Transport Commissioners.

When the pipeline was lowered into the soupy slurry created by construction through our aquifer, it was quickly lost to sight. The foreman of the pipeline crew nonchalantly assured me that there would be no conflict of levels. But as the pipeline could not be seen, this could not be easily confirmed. I stripped off and swam in the trench until I could locate the pipeline. With the aid of my neighbour Albert Townsend on dry land, we checked the level. Sure enough, the pipeline had usurped the level required for our gravity drain.

The consequences were not what they should have been in a democratic society. The hard-nosed attitudes of the pipeliners made a mockery of Ontario drainage legislation and all the checks and balances it incorporated. After a stormy session with us without the aid of anyone from the municipal, provincial, or federal levels of government, the pipeliners agreed to pump out some of the slurry and weight the pipeline so that we could still have a drainage outlet.

It was the following spring before the drainage contractor, hired by London Township, arrived to install the Lewington Drain. As I worked a nearby field prior to corn planting, I watched the drainage machine serenely installing the tile. And then, the intersection with the pipeline passed, there was a departure from the routine.

As required by law, IPL had been alerted and was represented at the crossing to ensure that there was no damage to the pipeline. In normal practice, the spoil, or dirt removed from the trench, is backfilled by a bulldozer. But in an age of mechanization, the pipeline crew had suddenly reverted to manual labour. Their enthusiasm did not permit awaiting the arrival of the drainage contractor's bulldozer; instead, the shovels flew as they covered up the tile by hand. Curious, I went over to have a look; and there, on the upstream side of the intersection of the tile drain and the pipeline, there was water — where it should not have been. I found that at the insistence of Interprovincial, the drainage contractor had been ordered to elevate his machine over the pipeline, which had floated up to once again usurp our drainage level. Contrary to the law of gravity, Interprovincial was content to let our drainage water flow uphill!

For two days of bitter controversy, the trenching machine remained stalled at the pipeline. Ultimately, we reached a compromise. The company dispensed with the traditional twelve inches of soil between a pipeline and a tile, and the Lewington Drain was bedded down touching the pipeline. They were to prove to be uneasy bedfellows.

With the installation of IPL's second line, the poor old Lewington

Drain got clobbered again, as noted in the preceding chapter. On Albert Townsend's farm, which is downstream from us, the tile repairs were made improperly, and the catch basin was broken and never repaired. The problems were aggravated by carelessness in construction, which allowed silting. In his absence, I could only write to the NEB's drainage inspector, Vincent Moran, that "I am disappointed that no one was on duty when the tiles were cut, no attempt was made to plug the tiles to avoid debris entering and that backfilling was done when it was known that I was unavoidably away from the farm."

Because Larigmoor Farm is located at a watershed, the easterly half is drained by the Lewington Drain, while the westerly half is served by the Needham Drain. The vintage Needham was shallow and ineffective as it had been installed as an open ditch in an era of horses and scoop shovels. The Needham and Lewington drains had something in common; each of them had to cross IPL's pipeline at two places.

When it came time to modernize the Needham Drain, I endeavoured to prevent the conflicts that had marred the Lewington Drain. As always, there was a paper trail. I wrote to thank the clerk-administrator of the township of London "for your very painstaking and comprehensive review of the correspondence in regard to the Needham Municipal Drain. I telephoned Mr. C. P. Corbett [the engineer retained] and he assures me that the plans forwarded to the Board of Transport Commissioners are in complete accord with those submitted to council. Further, that representatives of the Interprovincial Pipe Line Company have probed the pipeline; where it will be crossed by the proposed drain, it is at a depth which will not interfere with our outlet." Chapter 9, "Rural Revolt," details how Corbett told an entirely different story when he testified before the NEB.

The Needham Drain was to be constructed as an open ditch that ended at our line fence where it would provide the outlet for our proliferating installation of tile systems. I was dismayed to find that the ditch, as constructed, bore no resemblance to the agreed and approved specifications. I complained to Corbett's assistant and a fellow professional engineer who was supervising the construction, and he blandly told me, "You were not supposed to know that the specifications had been changed." The estimates of cost had been computed on the removal of x cubic yards of dirt. By raising the level of the ditch at the intersection with the pipeline, the elated contractor found that he would be paid for work he didn't have to perform. The farmers got much less than they had paid for.

The ensuing years saw a great deal of fruitless effort to achieve justice. I spent many a long night arguing with London Township councillors, but they chose not to fight vigorously on behalf of farmers against the entrenched odds of a powerful company and the federal government. In comparison with the vast revenue that pipelines were by then generating for the municipality in taxes, my concerns must have looked rather small. Pipeline taxes are now the largest source of cash for the township of London, so there is a conflict of interest.

Earlier, it was noted that Ron White had spoken of municipal government as the one closest to the people, but pipelines had polluted even that. I was advised by the clerk-administrator that under the Municipal Act, I could not have direct access to the Needham drainage file. When I visited the township office, the deputy reeve, Graydon McRoberts, asked the clerk, "Have you finished editing the Needham Drain file?" The answer was in the affirmative, and I was given the file — less whatever documents had been removed.

We had reached an impasse. I received a visit from a Mr. Gibson, of IPL, who didn't like the impasse any more than I did. He agreed that the fairest solution would be for IPL to install a pumping system, just as one finds in Ontario's Kent County or in Holland. I still have Gibson's plan of how it would all be accomplished, but I never saw Gibson again. If a farmer is successful in negotiating progress, the company representative is likely to be spirited away by the winds of heaven.

Having tried every possible effort to redress an intolerable situation, I took my concerns to the Court of Revision sitting in the township office at Arva. The court could find no weakness or inaccuracy in my case, but, as I was to read in the *London Free Press,* the court found against me. No reason for this decision was given.

Jean and I discussed this further reverse at length and decided not only to appeal to the county court but to make the appeal on a point of principle. I sought a reduction in our assessment of $1.00, on the grounds that pipeline construction had adversely affected our drainage systems and our ability to farm profitably. The notice of my appeal came from the very official of the township of London who had cited chapter 249, section 216, subsection (1) of the Municipal Act to deny me free access to the relevant files. While this was technically correct, I was left with the feeling that the courts and the municipality were one. A more impartial system would have obliged the county court to issue the notice. It must be conceded that comparable procedures are used at the federal level; from the published legal notices, it is difficult for a farmer to know who is calling the shots, the company or the NEB.

While I had prepared assiduously for the appeal, I was not prepared for Judge R. J. Cudney. He was in a foul mood. He behaved like one of those fireworks, modelled on Vesuvius, that emit smoke, sparks, and flame at frequent intervals. It was my first and only meeting with him. Judge Cudney alleged that the time of his court was being wasted over a single dollar. When I tried to point out that the issue was not a one-dollar bill but a point of principle, he flailed away with his gavel and threatened me with fines and contempt of court. A *gavel* is defined as a "small mallet, as used by a judge." Cudney used his gavel as an intimidating weapon. In the witness box, I was treated like a criminal judged guilty of the most heinous crime. The judge was a willing party to any sleight of hand. For instance, the assessment commissioner for London Township asked me about our corn yields. I routinely record such information and could give him a precise answer. I was then forced to read from the Agricultural Statistics for Ontario. As our corn yields were higher than the provincial average, Cudney concluded that there could be no adverse effects from the pipeline. This "logic" ignored the fact that the provincial corn average was just that; it included the corn yields in the majority of Ontario, which is less favoured with heat units and soil. The issue would more properly have involved a comparison of our actual and potential corn yields.

It was a terrible experience. On the one hand, I had my own municipal officials digging traps for me, while my every response precipitated new hammering outbursts from the judge. Eventually, it was my turn to ask the questions. Having assembled my documents and thoughts, I phrased my first question. It seemed innocuous enough, but it precipitated the most violent hammering yet of the judge's gavel. "I will not have my court treated with this discourtesy! You will stand if you have anything to say," declared Cudney, his face flushed with fury.

And that is why I prefaced this chapter with a quotation from the Talmud. For hours, my opponents (I now had to think of my own municipal officials as such) had remained seated when they questioned me as I stood in the box. Now, as our roles were reversed, Judge Cudney moved the goalposts, changed the rules of the game. Not only did I have to stand, but every word precipitated new charges of contempt of court and threats of fines.

Finally, it was all over. Judge Cudney had brought his gavel down for the last time. Free from his fury, I could contemplate the impact on the observers in the courtroom. Some were actually weeping. Others came up to shake my hand, commiserating that they never thought such a thing was possible in a Canadian court. Some were friends, and some were complete strangers who had dropped in to experience the administration of justice.

I never heard from Cudney or his court again, but I did receive a registered letter from the Township of London, dated the day of the appeal: "Please be advised that your appeal against the 1967 assessment was dismissed by the judge of the County of Middlesex." Cudney had clearly not found it necessary to dwell very long on the evidence before reaching his decision.

I was down, but not out. I wrote to the Honourable P. E. Trudeau, who was then Canada's minister of justice. Having detailed eleven areas of concern, I concluded my letter: "That I should lose an appeal when the stakes were one dollar can be regarded, in these times of inflation, as a matter of small moment. That a court should be conducted in such an arbitrary manner strikes at the very roots of Canadian justice. I trust that you will deem it to be a matter of utmost gravity to investigate the conduct of Judge Cudney."

Trudeau did not reply, but his deputy minister did. "I am sure you will understand that, under our system of law, the executive branch of government has no authority to interfere or to attempt to control a judge's conduct of his judicial duties and that the independence of the judiciary is a most important part of our legal system. It is with regret, therefore, that I have to advise you that I am not aware of any way in which we can be of assistance to you in connection with this matter." Once again, we were thrust into that unreal world of *Alice in Wonderland*. Government used the privilege of power to appoint judges but eschewed responsibility for their competence or the consequences.

The indefatigable Jim Lind was still beavering away, this notwithstanding the fact that he was a Liberal backbencher in a Liberal government. He wrote in support of my concerns to both Trudeau and his cabinet colleague Solicitor General Larry Pennell. Pennell, incidentally, is now a judge of the Supreme Court of Ontario. Back from Pennell, via Jim Lind, came the word that nothing could be done, although it was readily conceded that the calibre of some judges was appallingly low. While I endorse judicial independence, such independence ideally requires that judges are appointed on merit.

The score was now game, set, but not yet match. I found that I had the option of appealing Judge Cudney's decision to the Ontario Municipal Board (OMB). With Jean's dedicated help and three month's lead time, I felt that I was well prepared to make a strong case before the OMB. I also had some excellent help from our son Roger, who was then in grade 12 at Medway High School. We both thought that his exposure to the legal process would benefit his education more than a few hours in school.

The appointed hour came and went without any representatives appearing from either London Township Council or the Middlesex Assessment Department. The OMB panel, led by R. M. McGuire, silently retreated to chambers in the Middlesex County Court Building. I explained the significance of this to Roger. "That's a big plus in our favour. One can't treat a court with such discourtesy." A search party eventually located my adversaries, who arrived very late. They were led by lawyer John Gillies, who for many earlier years made the job of reeve of London Township his personal fiefdom. Roger and I waited expectantly for McGuire to rebuke Gillies and his colleagues for their rudeness to the court and to us.

"Hi, John! Long time no see," said McGuire from the bench. Gillies was equally pleased to see McGuire, and they had an animated conversation, which excluded any consideration of Roger or me. It was an omen of what was to come.

Gillies explained, in increasing detail, what he alleged had happened in Judge Cudney's court. I repeatedly tried to tell the OMB that as Gillies had not been present in Cudney's court, there had been no transcript of the proceedings, and there had been no written reason for Cudney's decision, anything Gillies might say could only be at best secondhand. It could be only hearsay and should not be admitted as evidence. My objections were brusquely overruled. Everything Gillies said had occurred in Cudney's court was accepted by the OMB as fact. Everything I tried to introduce was irrelevant or out of order.

It was all contributing to Roger's education, but not in the way I had anticipated. There was not even any cliff-hanging suspense. McGuire didn't find it necessary to recess to consider a decision. My appeal was not only dismissed, but for good measure, I was assessed costs. It was yet another irony that when the invoice came from the OMB, it was over the signature of Robin Scott, who had appeared on behalf of farmers before the NEB in the May 1967 hearing. This was a bitter pill, and it ended all appeal procedures. It was not the end of the matter, even though many of my friends advised that I would feel much better when I stopped banging my head against the wall.

The paper trail continued with extensive but fruitless initiatives with the NEB and a succession of federal ministers of Energy, Mines and Resources. I also seized the opportunity to document my concerns before the select committee of the Ontario legislature, appointed to examine agricultural land drainage in Ontario. Despite the reality that affected farmers slipped into an abyss between federal and provincial legislation, the committee's report noted that it was "pleased that the Board (NEB) has developed the positive policy towards land drainage that it presently observes and hopes that this enlightened policy will continue." But by then, the select committee was already facing a crisis of credibility. Its dedication to research had included an all-expenses trip to West Palm Beach, Florida, while Ontario shivered in a brutal cold wave. Commented James Bulbrook, M.P.P. for Sarnia, in a scathing judgment of committee chairman Lorne Henderson: "You're the biggest drain in this province" (in reference to the expenses that then exceeded $200,000). Henderson was later a director of Union Gas.

Interprovincial had not been neglected. There was a continuing exchange of correspondence with Gordon Sheasby, who was now general counsel for Interprovincial and on his way to a vice presidency.

And finally, my neighbours and I spent another $32,000 to improve the Needham Drain. That some progress had been accomplished could be seen in the financial contribution of Interprovincial in rerouting the Needham Drain to avoid the pipeline conflict.

It had been a long and expensive learning experience. Along the convoluted trail, every base had been touched on the way to our eventual goals. It had been a circuitous but essential route on the road to yet another new era—the Trudeau years and their catchphrases of "participatory democracy" and the "Just Society."

CHAPTER 12

A Journeyman in the Just Society

Government, even in the best state, is but a necessary evil; in its worst state an intolerable one.

—THOMAS PAINE

In 1968, we entered the Just Society, eloquently espoused by Pierre Trudeau, Canada's sometime minister of justice and the man destined to become the most influential and powerful prime minister in Canadian history.

I was at the base of the pyramid of power. I was one of the citizens of Canada invited to participate in democracy, not that I ever understood the need for the phrase "participatory democracy." After all, democracy is defined as government by the people in which the supreme power is vested in the people and exercised by them. How could they aspire to do all that if they did not participate? In any event, it sounded good, and I was ready to welcome the Just Society, a society which I had been seeking for so long. A journeyman is one who has served his apprenticeship. By now, I could qualify as having done my apprenticeship in democracy; I was ready to enjoy its benefits as a journeyman in the Just Society.

Mr. Trudeau had invited my participation. After so many years spent banging on closed doors, it was a joy to learn that one had swung wide open with a fanfare of welcome. So I wrote to him.

Dear Mr. Trudeau,

The enclosed correspondence will indicate the shoddy treatment which has been accorded farmers and Canadian agriculture.

You may recall that when you were Minister of Justice, I kept you fully informed on the farming and legal problems which plagued farmers who had suffered the first two Interprovincial pipelines.

I trust that you will act with speed and vigour to bring us the integrity and participatory democracy which you have promised.

And in similar vein on December 11, 1972:

Dear Mr. Trudeau,

I would like to draw your attention to a long-standing dispute which I have with the federally chartered Interprovincial Pipe Line Company. As a direct result of company policy I have been denied the opportunity to adequately drain my farm.

It does not seem reasonable to me that a federally chartered company should be permitted to continue to impair the effectiveness of a farmer to work his land.

Having explored every other possible means of reaching an equitable settlement with the company, I have taken this opportunity to apprise you of the injustice perpetrated by the Interprovincial Pipe Line Company.

It was shortly thereafter that Rudy Platiel, a thorough, painstaking, and well-respected reporter with the *Globe and Mail* dropped in for lunch. I don't recall all that we talked about because the dining room at Larigmoor Farm had become a debating forum in which participation was encouraged. I think the central topic was water quality. We were concerned over the threat to the quality of the tiny Medway River and had developed a philosophy that I believe is the only one that offers much hope. People can relate to water quality at the local level and should be encouraged to believe that they are both part of the problem and the solution. This is not a popular philosophy; a preferred one is to send the wastes further downstream and point to somebody else as the cause of the problem.

Perhaps we discussed the Just Society and participatory democracy. In any event, Rudy asked to take copies of several documents and letters with him. I had no idea what he might want them for. I found out on the morning of November 3, 1975, when our son Roger telephoned to say, "You are the subject of the *Globe*'s editorial today!" That editorial was short and very much to the point.

REST EASY

From a letter signed by Peter Lewington, Larigmoor Farm, Ilderton, Ont., to Prime Minister Pierre Trudeau:

"Your staff promised that my concerns relating to agriculture and the Sarnia–Montreal pipeline would be brought to your attention. The result? Silence from you, and expropriation proceedings by your National Energy Board. . . . I trust that I may receive your informed response. . . ."

Response, signed by a correspondence assistant in the Prime Minister's office:

"This is just a note to acknowledge and thank you for your letter, and to assure you that your further comments on the subject of land expropriation for Pickering Airport have been noted."

Noted, obviously, with care and deep concern.

This promptly triggered a telegram that came via CNCP Telecommunications:

I have been apprised of the regrettable mistake made by one of my assistants in handling your September 8 letter to the Prime Minister and wish to sincerely apologize on his behalf and on mine. We were actually flooded with mail concerning Pickering Airport at the time. On behalf of the Prime Minister, I wish now to inform you that your September 8 correspondence is immediately being transmitted to the Honourable Alastair Gillespie, Minister of Energy, Mines and Resources, for careful consideration and further response. Claude Desjardins, Correspondence Secretary to the Prime Minister.

The *Financial Times of Canada* had done some research on the operation of the prime minister's office. It was then operating on a budget of $19 million annually and employed 468 people. When the prime minister appeared before a committee of the House of Commons, he provided additional information. Half of the people on his staff were employed in answering the 300 letters he received daily. The *Times* worked this out to an average of 1.28 replies per employee per day.

If the prime minister's office was not yet efficient, efforts were made to achieve that laudable goal. Trudeau's principal secretary alerted all secretaries involved: "Would you please make sure that the top margin of the second or third page of letters is sufficiently low (no less than 1¾s to 2 inches in depth) so as to permit the Prime Minister to read his correspondence with ease and without having to pull out the letter from the signature book. It is sometimes difficult to see the first few lines of the second page of a letter."

It transpired that a lot of people had no difficulty in reading the "Rest Easy" editorial. I received tear sheets in the mail from the *Calgary Herald* and the *St. Thomas Journal,* which were among the Canadian newspapers to reproduce the editorial. Grant Webber, one of the farm specialists with Ontario Hydro, tacked it on the notice board at Hydro headquarters on University Avenue in Toronto. It was a popular conversation piece and stayed up there for six weeks.

But it didn't do much to advance the cause of participatory democracy in the Just Society. On January 30, 1976, I wrote to Mr. Trudeau for the last time:

> I have repeatedly brought to your attention my concerns for agriculture threatened by the lack of research and sensible policies relevant to pipeline construction through the good farmland of Canada. Repeatedly, I have been assured by your staff of your interest and that I may expect to hear from you. All that has emerged from the spate of letters is the fatuous confusion with Pickering Airport.
>
> You cannot expect to enjoy credibility with the electorate if you continue to surround yourself with a huge and incompetent staff and totally ignore the documented concerns of Canadians.

My experiences had fallen far short of the expectations raised in a manifesto of the Liberal party of Canada, entitled *The Just Society.* It had promised that "above all, it is our determined wish to give our citizens a sense of full participation in the affairs of government."

Doris Shackleton, in her book *Power Town — Democracy Discarded,* came much closer to recognising reality.

> We have less knowledge, less power to control or direct our government than at any time in our remembered history. The paralysis grows. We are accepting what we should resist — the secret conduct of what can scarcely be called public affairs, since the public now suffers the results without being taken into the confidence of those who govern. We have an unhappy sense of having been vanquished within our own country by our own leaders. We have begun to believe there is nothing we can do to resume democratic control.

In a similar vein, the *Financial Post,* in a front-page feature: "Secrets are for Ottawa to know . . . and for the public to guess. For too long the public's right to know has run a poor second to the government's need for confidentiality in its deliberations." The Law Reform Commission of Canada had provided a useful service when it documented some fifteen thousand hidden powers possessed by the federal government and its multitude of agencies.

The man who in my experience most enjoyed the exercise of many of those powers was Donald Macdonald. And as federal minister of Energy, Mines and Resources at a time when energy was central to the government of Canada, he had lots of opportunities. He laid his heavy hand on Judge Thomas Berger during the latter's study of the then-proposed Mackenzie Valley Pipeline. His letters often include a hectoring and bullying tone, and his nickname "Thumper" appears to have been honestly earned.

For instance, he straightened up Roberta Tilden in a hurry when she had the temerity to complain about Interprovincial's Bryanston Pump Station, which is located just a few yards across the county road from her farm home. Macdonald dismissed her concerns on the ground that she lived ten miles from the pump station. It is not known whether Macdonald "researched" this fact on his own or relied upon someone trained in the prime minister's office. Someone had evidently looked at the map, located the village of Bryanston, and noted that Roberta had a Thorndale address; ipso facto, she was ten miles from the pump station! The reality is that Roberta lives on a rural route served by the Thorndale post office and is equidistant from Thorndale and Bryanston, right across from the pump station. It began to appear that in the Just Society, citizens could approach the pinnacles of power but that the rewards were no greater than shouting into the wind.

If there were no tangible rewards, at least the paper trail continued. For instance, I wrote to Macdonald, complaining about "your decision to withhold documents, your covert meetings with Interprovincial Pipe Line officials during the National Energy Board hearing adjournment and statements which prejudiced the NEB hearings. You have emasculated a willing NEB. . . . Justice has neither been done nor seen to be done. . . . There is a world of difference between alluding to issues and dealing with them." I don't know what other mail Macdonald received, but I know he got a lot from me.

The voters of Middlesex tend to be a rather fickle lot and variously send a Liberal or a Progressive Conservative representative to Ottawa. Regardless of his or her party affiliation and whether the party was in or out of power, each successive member has taken up the cudgels on behalf of farmers. For instance, the Commons debates of March 6, 1974, related to the concern of farmers of southwestern Ontario about the route of the proposed oil pipeline extension. Our member, Bill Frank, a Progressive Conservative, asked, "In view of the concern recently expressed by farmers that the proposed route of the extension of the oil pipeline will result in the rape of prime agricultural land in southwestern Ontario, can the minister tell the House whether he has received direct representations from these farmers or by farm organizations on their behalf in recent weeks?"

To this, Energy Minister Macdonald replied briefly, "If by direct representations, the Honourable member means representations to me, the answer is no."

It was to prove yet another unsatisfactory duel. Frank's supplementary question drew the admission from Agriculture Minister Eugene

Whelan, "We have had correspondence about it between ourselves."

Frank then referred to his question, which had included the words "directly or indirectly," and he then asked, "Who are the farmers to believe?"

This was the sort of unsatisfactory conduct of "public" affairs that caused Gordon Hill, as president of the Ontario Federation of Agriculture, to make the unprecedented move of seeking dismissal of a cabinet minister—the Thumper.

While I had the utmost difficulty in getting straight answers from Macdonald, there was no equivocation in his November 19, 1974, letter to David Waldon, Interprovincial president. "It is the policy of the Government of Canada that pipeline facilities should be promptly constructed to enable Western Canadian oil to be supplied to refineries in the Montreal area." It was this sort of directive that made it very difficult for anyone appearing before the NEB to know the point and substance of such hearings—when the outcome had already been decreed by the minister to whom the NEB apparently felt responsible.

There were other factors that marred the lustre of the Just Society. Another of Macdonald's responsibilities was to be the Liberal party's patronage boss in Ontario. It was also during the years of the Just Society that there seemed to be a scandal a day. There were confirmations that cabinet ministers had telephoned judges during the hearing of proceedings affecting fellow cabinet ministers, and there was even the admission of the solicitor-general that he had forged a document. It was hard to equate any of this sleazy conduct with concepts of the Just Society or participatory democracy. But there was some comfort to be found in the Canadian Bill of Rights; it boldly affirmed the freedom of speech and the right of the individual to equality before the law and the protection of the law.

None of this seemed to equate with my frustrations before various boards, courts, and commissions or the fruitless exchange of correspondence with a wide variety of federal ministers. But suddenly there was a beacon of hope. The Ontario Law Reform Commission advertised for briefs to be presented during public hearings relating to the administration of Ontario courts.

On the appointed day, I appeared at Osgoode Hall in Toronto where the commission was conducting its hearings. Jean and Ann were along for valued moral support. I could have brought the population of London Township, so large was the amphitheaterlike lecture hall. It was only when we got there that I was advised by the commission's counsel, Ron Atkey, that I would have just fifteen minutes to make my presentation.

Neither was the setting conducive to making one comfortable. The commission chairman, Allan Leal, was flanked by Commissioners the Honourable James C. McRuer and the Honourable Richard Bell, and lawyers Gibson Gray and Bill Poole; they were seated at a well-equipped dais. The supplicant had to work from a pint-size lectern and peer up at the panel of lawyers.

Leal was in a chatty and expansive mood. As one petitioner after another endeavoured to maximise his or her allotted fifteen minutes, much of their time was eroded by Leal's comments.

Initially I fared no better than my predecessors. To make matters worse, Leal began cracking jokes in Latin, a language in which I failed miserably during my school days. And then we reached a wonderful watershed. McRuer, who had been quietly watching, now interjected that "I have always held the view that if a man cannot make himself understood in English, he does not have the right to resort to Latin. This man has not been listened to in fifteen years. That will be our assignment this afternoon."

And listen they did. The constraint of fifteen minutes was ignored. When it came time to recount my disaster before Judge Cudney, I called for an end to the political patronage appointment of judges. I pleaded for appointment on merit, so that incompetent judges would not have the opportunity to downgrade the administration of justice. The panel was split. Leal had relapsed into unaccustomed silence following McRuer's rebuke. Bell and Poole, as Progressive Conservative activists, were outraged by my criticism of patronage appointments. However, they were overwhelmed by Gray and McRuer, who asked for additional information. Their interest and friendly demeanour made the pilgrimage to Toronto worthwhile. Incidentally, Gray is now a judge of the Supreme Court of Ontario.

Finally, it was all over. Suddenly, down from the top row of the amphitheater where he had been sitting unobserved came a gaunt and striking figure dressed in a long black cloak. He strode down to the dais with a long boney finger outstretched as he cried, "You have heard the truth today!" It was a dramatic moment, one not lost on the commissioners. Lawyer Ron Atkey, on behalf of the commission, went trotting after the stranger to find out his name and why he was there. But the only response was "You have heard the truth today."

Ann was then working as a planner in Toronto, so we set off by car for her apartment and a cup of tea after the afternoon's excitement. We had been keyed up prior to the presentation and had left elated. They had listened! The euphoria was short-lived. Absorbed in reliving the events of the afternoon, I had driven through a stop sign at one of Toronto's quieter residential streets, and right there was a policeman who gave me a $20 ticket! But even that was worth it. My appearance before the Ontario Law Reform Commission sparked an invitation from the commission's federal counterpart to participate in their investigations.

That, as has been noted, contributed to the reform of some of the more archaic laws of Canada. Everything changes and nothing changes. The scoreboard is still somewhat mixed and confused. While there has been some tangible progress to report, there are other areas in which the system still does not work.

When they were in opposition, the Progressive Conservatives rightly censured Liberal cabinet ministers for their indiscretions when matters were before the courts. No one had been more righteous or censorious than the New Brunswick M.P., Elmer MacKay. With the landslide victory of Brian Mulroney, MacKay, who had surrendered his safe seat to Mulroney prior to the election, was back in the House of Commons. He was solicitor-general; he was also to admit to private meetings with a prominent fellow New Brunswicker and premier of the province, despite the fact that Premier Hatfield was then before the courts charged with possession of marijuana.

And the political appointment of judges? Well, the swan song of Pierre Trudeau did nothing to buff the tarnished image. Before surrendering power, Trudeau demanded and received the written assurance of his successor as prime minister, John Turner, that patronage appointments would be made on the grandest scale. There were numerous judicial appointments, including cabinet ministers Mark MacGuigan and Bud Cullen to the federal court (and salaries of $91,000) and former M.P. Bob Daudlin to the Kent County Court (at a salary of $82,000). I am personally aware of some "patronage" judges who are a credit to the Canadian judiciary. But I fervently believe that the time is long overdue for appointment on merit exclusively.

Tradition dies hard. At the end of the last century, Sir Wilfrid Laurier elevated his sometime law partner to the Quebec Superior Court; the real reason was that the judge's wife (Laurier's girlfriend) would then be conveniently domiciled at public expense across the river from Ottawa in the city of Hull.

From time to time throughout this narrative, there have been numerous links, or bridges, connecting people and events. McRuer served as chief justice in Ontario; he had some vigorous input to the Ontario Law Reform Commission and had earlier been commissioner of the Ontario Royal Commission Inquiry into Civil Rights. Having examined the role of the ombudsman in Sweden and Denmark, and the role of parliamentary commissioner in Great Britain and New Zealand, the McRuer commission, in 1969, issued its extensive report on the pros and cons of an ombudsman for Ontario.

McRuer noted:

> An Ombudsman is not a substitute for a proper legal framework which provides adequate, substantive and procedural safeguards for the rights of the individual. Much that has been said and written about the Ombudsman as a protection of the rights of the individual is misleading to the public and goes far beyond any claims that are put forward at the office by those who occupy it in any country. The real safeguards of the rights of the individual lie in good legislation and good rules of procedure designed to guide and direct those who make decisions in the administrative process of government. Rules that give a right to be heard before decisions are made affecting the rights of individuals and the right of written reasons for decisions when decisions are made, together with the right of appeal or review by a superior body having power to correct errors wherever practical, are fundamental rights for which an Ombudsman is no substitute.

Well, in 1975, Bill 86 received a third reading in the Ontario legislature, and Ontario was on its way to its first ombudsman. As McRuer had foreseen, it was not the all-embracing ombudsman that existed in popular imagination. It was in fact "an act to provide for an ombudsman to investigate administrative decisions and acts of officials of the Government of Ontario and its agencies." Stu O'Neil and I were among the first to see what the ombudsman could do for us and Ontario agriculture in general. We were on the scene early before the first ombudsman, former colourful criminal lawyer Arthur Maloney, had even completed setting up shop across from Toronto's dramatic City Hall. Our file with the ombudsman was number 34, and it was to become a very fat file. But it was never to become a dramatic or productive file.

It had seemed to us that the terms of reference of the ombudsman provided the latitude to assist Ontario citizens who were denied some provincial rights through the exercise of federal powers. We were caught between a rock and a hard place, and hoped that the ombudsman, even if he could not devise a solution, would forthrightly address the issue. Despite return visits to the ombudsman's office, long sessions with researchers on the ombudsman's staff, and extensive correspondence with Maloney and his successor, Donald Morand, Stu and I had nothing tangible to show. One more harbinger of the Just Society had turned out to be just another cul-de-sac.

The journey through the Just Society had been largely disappointing. There had been repeated rebuffs from cabinet ministers who obstinately refused to recognise our concerns. But the concerns were real. Recognition came from an unexpected quarter. In an off-the-cuff remark during debate on the Mackenzie Valley Pipeline, Jean Chretien, then minister for northern development conceded, "The developments would be pursued in the North, but not with the environmental damage that has been inflicted in Southern Canada. We need pipelines — but not at any price." Chretien is now leader of the Liberal opposition in Parliament.

If we were to enjoy the Just Society, we would have to try a different tack. It turned out to be one that had been clearly foreseen years before by McRuer.

In parts of our world, food is a luxury, while in other parts, abundance is regarded as a God-given right. With world population growth of ninety-five million per annum, wise land use becomes a necessity. Through careful crop and animal husbandry and the use of improved seeds and technology, we made three ears grow where one grew in 1952, the year we purchased Larigmoor Farm.

A well-proven maxim is "look after the land, and it will look after you." It was a shock to hear the senior lawyer for the largest pipeline system in North America declare in court, "We can go into Class I farmland [which has no constraints on productivity] and make a wasteland if we want to." (Photo by Roger Lewington)

Our children, Ann, Jennifer, and Roger, all learned to swim in this pond at the edge of our bush. It is probably fed by our aquifer and remains pure. It took thirty years to convince the pipeline industry that the conservation techniques we devised for pond construction were equally applicable to pipeline construction.

For many summers, that pond, which was securely fenced, provided water for our Holstein dairy herd. Cows promptly learned to pump their own water with a Dutch pump.

Jean stocks another pond on our farm with large-mouth bass. The ponds, together with a variety of shrubs, trees, and hedges of cedar and multiflora rose, contribute to attracting nearly sixty bird species.

What became an expropriated and drastically disturbed pipe-line corridor was earlier used for agronomic demonstrations and won for us the first prize in the Middlesex County Pasture Competition. (Photo by Jean Lewington)

Agronomist R. A. Woods taught us how to grow weed-free bird's-foot trefoil. This highly nutritious legume, unlike clover and alfalfa, does not cause bloat in ruminants. Our pedigree trefoil seed became an important cash crop. Bob is now chief executive officer of Garst Seed Company, based in Coon Rapids, Iowa.

Less-labor-intensive beef cattle replaced our dairy herd so I
could cope with additional writing demands—and court appearances.

Our herd sire Banderante was a seven-eighths Simmental. He
achieved an average daily gain that was twice the provincial
average in the Ontario testing program and transmitted that
phenomenal growth to his offspring. (Photo by Jean Lewington)

Everything changed at Larigmoor Farm with the arrival of the first pipeline trenching machine. The trench sides quickly cave in when an aquifer is breached, in the absence of conservation measures.

For weeks, elevated welded pipe formed an impenetrable banner through the middle of our farm. Our lawyer, Geoff Bladon,
referred to it in court as "a belt stretched too tightly."

A "bridge" was built by pipeline contractors when I requested
access to harvest the ripening grain. The bridge might have
been negotiated by nimble mountain goats, but not by modern harvesting equipment.

Failure to separate soil strata negated nature's bounty, which had been evolving since the Ice Age. The damage was compounded by bulldozing material back into the trench when it was far too wet. The predictable result was chaos.

At age ten, our elder daughter, Ann, discovered the ceramic qualities of the material left in place of topsoil. Ceramics formed part of Dr. Norman Pearson's testimony before Judge Killeen some thirty years later.

As editor of *Drainage Contractor*, I was privileged to travel to many parts of the world. Information gleaned from these travels, together with our own practical farming experience, made it possible to survive without legal counsel for thirty years before courts, boards, and commissions.

Jean helped me gather erosion-control information in Brazil.

The Incas of Peru perfected both irrigation and drainage, and they successfully cropped steep mountainsides with their terraced agriculture. Five hundred years later, the legal counsel for the National Energy Board (NEB) of Canada, which authorized pipeline construction crossing the United States or provincial borders, asked me, "Is the tile drainage to which you refer some form of subterranean structure or doth it lie upon the surface of the land?" The NEB now has an excellent environmental department and rates the protection of farmland as a top priority.

Agriculture Canada scientist Dr. A. D. (Al) Tomlin, *left*, takes delivery of soil samples that Jean and I gathered in South America. A sample taken at Porto Alegre, Brazil, resulted in the find of a species of mite new to science, and it is now part of the Canadian National Collection in Ottawa. (Photo by Jean Lewington)

This causeway protects the lowlands of Holland from the ravages of the North Sea. Having reclaimed their most productive farmland, the Dutch have a reverence for land and water management. Our hosts explained how to install a pipeline through an aquifer without environmental damage; unfortunately, that expertise has yet to be applied in North America.

Following intervention before the International Joint Commission, I was invited to cruise the Great Lakes aboard the *Martin Karlsen,* the research ship of the Canada Centre for Inland Waters. This generated more useful environmental expertise that contributed to reform.

When I visited U.K. drainage contractor Dick Dottridge, *left,* one of his eighty-six pieces of major drainage equipment was at work on the dairy farm of Robert Quartly. There is much that North America can learn about land-use planning and conflicts from such densely populated countries as England.

The Land Improvement Contractors of America (LICA) and such Canadian organizations as the Ontario Farm Drainage Association helped popularize the plowing in of plastic drainage tubing.

Despite earlier documented problems, severed drainage tile were left open during the third pipeline installation at Larigmoor Farm.

The expertise from Holland was ignored, and the breached aquifer caused the pipe to float to the surface. (Photo courtesy of Dr. R. M. Quigley)

The size of this deliberately ignited oil spill from the Bryanston Pump Station near our farm can be appreciated by the huge backhoe, which looks like a toy.

The fire destroyed my neighbor's white-ash grove, but the picture contributed to convincing the National Energy Board that vastly better oil-spill policies would have to be developed.

Prime Minister Lester Pearson acceded to my request to reopen a National Energy Board (NEB) hearing. When it was reconvened in London, Ontario, the participants included, *back row from left,* Conservative Member of Parliament Bill Thomas; Robin Scott, Q.C., representing the minister of justice and attorney general for Ontario; Liberal Member of Parliament Jim Lind; *front row from left,* Fred Lamar, NEB counsel; Bill Stewart, Ontario minister of agriculture and food; and leading Middlesex farmers Ray McDougall, Ken Patterson, and Lorne Dodge (*back row, far right*).

Former Ontario Chief Justice the Honourable James C. McRuer, throughout a long and productive life, made many improvements to justice, including such areas as civil rights and expropriation powers. His spirited support made my involvement with the Law Reform Commission of Canada possible. (Photo courtesy of Paul J. Lawrence)

This was one technique we used to authenticate the date on which a picture was taken.

A Drastically Disturbed Lands Conference at Ohio State University and visits to open-pit coal mining sites confirmed that a resource can be mined and the land restored to former productivity, providing the soil strata are segregated and a restoration program is prepared in advance. The restored land may be even more productive if changed gradients preclude a repetition of former soil erosion.

John Wise, a former dairy farmer, as a backbencher in the House of Commons and subsequently as minister of agriculture, provided crucial support that led to environmental and legal law reform. (Photo courtesy of Agriculture Canada)

In my work as a farm writer, I had known Gaetan Lussier in his various careers, which included the fertilizer industry and deputy minister of agriculture in the Province of Quebec. When he became deputy minister of agriculture in Ottawa, he swiftly made public the previously secret funding by Agriculture Canada of the chief witness who appeared in the courts against us on behalf of Interprovincial Pipe Line, Ltd. (IPL) and its contractor, the multinational giant Bechtel.

Following breaching of our aquifer, construction equipment created a quagmire. The restoration techniques of Interprovincial Pipe Line/Bechtel included dumping a proprietary brand of cement and aggregate in the heart of Larigmoor Farm in a desperate attempt to stabilize the soil. When the concrete set, it was used for a base to replace the Lewington Drain—without the use of any device to install the drain at the correct level and gradient.

Churned by construction equipment to a consistency of cake batter, the soil crusted and fissured as it dried. This restricts root development of all crops, but especially the white or navy bean. These two white bean plants were growing just ten feet apart. The plant grown off the disturbed area had multiple pods, which add up to profit. The other plant, denied a normal growth pattern as a result of pipeline construction, represents economic loss. (Lower photo courtesy of Dr. R. M. Quigley)

Larigmoor Farm had been virtually stone free. Pipeline construction brought stones to the surface. Stone is bad news for combine harvesting, especially the white bean crop. We now grow white beans in rotations with wheat, red clover, and corn.

When the Interprovincial Pipe Line drainage contractor was asked in Judge Killeen's court whether he had made a mess of Larigmoor Farm during repairs to our drainage system, he simply answered, "You're damned right." (This is confirmed by reference to page 1470 of the official court transcript, which, together with our other documents, is stored in the Weldon Library at The University of Western Ontario.)

Our own easterly main drainage outlet was installed under ideal conditions.

Norman Pearson, our planning consultant since the early 1960s, parlayed the experience into a Ph.D. Judge Gordon Killeen decided that there would have been no need for a court case if Pearson's timely planning advice had been heeded.

Dr. R. M. (Bob) Quigley, a graduate of the Massachusetts Institute of Technology, is director of the Geotechnical Research Centre at The University of Western Ontario in London. He combines dedication to meticulous research with rare expertise in solving complex soil problems.

The University of Western Ontario research team sampled the soil to a depth of 18 inches with Shelby tubes to determine the depth and quality of our topsoil. Sampling was done according to a prearranged grid so that any previously disturbed land, where drainage tile had been installed, was avoided.

Dr. Quigley, *left*, supervised a drilling company retained by The University of Western Ontario. Auger boring and soil sampling off the right-of-way established the stratigraphy—or bedding sequence—of the glacial soil system to a depth of 98.4 inches. The scope of this research far exceeded anything conducted in Canada by either the oil industry or government.

Gordon Killeen, senior district court judge in Middlesex County, had said exuberantly, "We're on an archeological expedition!" As archeology has been defined as a discipline that attempts to reconstruct human events and history, he was dead-on. He listened intently to the relevance that Dr. Quigley attributed to the era of glacial formation of farmland, and he was sufficiently part of the twentieth century to question the archaic nineteenth-century Railway Act that caused so many of our problems when the Canadian government applied it to pipelines and agriculture.

Dr. Quigley helped mix bentonite balls to pack into the bore holes to seal a piezometer installed into our aquifer.

Measurement of the in situ density of the topsoil zone by nuclear method was part of the The University of Western Ontario research, which the courts subsequently found to be both complete and accurate.

One of my National Energy Board exhibits was provided by Dr. Quigley. It could be used to demonstrate a total lack of effervescence by topsoil when contacted with dilute hydrochloric acid; this distinguished topsoil from the highly reactive carbon-rich subsoil.

Our stalwart friends and neighbors Stu and Jocelyn O'Neil took soil samples for analysis at the University of Guelph. Our credibility in the courts was enhanced by the presentation of all research data.

This grid was established by our plant ecologist, Dr. Roy Turkington, and his graduate students in plant sciences at The University of Western Ontario. The precision and counting of beneficial plant and weed species may be judged by the size of a rubber-topped pencil in the middle foreground.

Jim O'Toole, head of the agronomy department at the Centralia College of Agricultural Technology at Huron Park, Ontario, obtained his own subpoena so that he could appear before Judge Killeen as our expert agronomist.

Dr. Angus MacKenzie, *standing,* and his bearded student Alec Ramsay, who is now Interprovincial Pipe Line (IPL) chief of right-of-way, scraped away the snow in preparation for soil studies without consulting our tile-drainage map. While Dr. MacKenzie, with the benefit of funding from IPL/Bechtel and Agriculture Canada, has been published widely on agricultural and environmental issues arising from pipeline construction, Judge Killeen found him "unpersuasive."

The effectiveness of the Interprovincial Pipe Line expert witness on real estate was impaired when it was revealed that his was a "windshield" appraisal, made without stepping on Larigmoor Farm.

Ian Goudy, who farms across the road from The University of Western Ontario research farm, displays a copy of Judge Killeen's arbitration decision. Goudy already has three provincially chartered gas pipelines on his farm, and a fourth is imminent. He said, "I wish that every farmer could have been in Judge Killeen's court. The integrated agricultural information was fascinating and changed my outlook on both farming and conservation."

H. A. (Bud) Olson, a former minister of Agriculture Canada, was appointed to the Canadian Senate, where he played a key role in reform of antiquated expropriation laws. (Photo courtesy of Agriculture Canada)

John Robinette, widely regarded as the dean of Canadian lawyers, combined consummate legal skills and knowledge with a warm personality and a sense of humour as he successfully defended three challenges to the arbitration decision in the Supreme Court of Ontario. Further appeal to the Supreme Court of Canada was denied, and a new agricultural/environmental era dawned. (Photo courtesy of McCarthy and McCarthy)

CHAPTER 13

Nature Makes One Inch of Topsoil Every Thousand Years

Pipeline installation invariably disturbs the natural soil profile and its contained ecosystems. The extent of the damage and the subsequent effects on farm productivity relate directly to the care taken during and after construction to return the land to its original use.

—DR. R. M. QUIGLEY

T he invoice from London lawyer (now judge) John Kerr read, "Perusing transcripts, reports, discussions with you, letters to Interprovincial Pipe Line and to Donald C. Macdonald, Minister of Energy, Mines and Resources and including all telephone attendances." There wasn't much to show for all that effort and expense, unless it was measured in futility and frustration. While that is so often par for the course in doing battle with entrenched interests, it could be recorded that all avenues of hope had been explored. Nonetheless, it had been another $300 down the drain; mostly down the Lewington Drain.

What we did get was a piece of good verbal advice. Said Kerr: "I can't help you. All of the precedents and all of the weight of legislation are against you in your efforts to reform the law and encourage pipeline practices which will mitigate damage to farmland. All I can suggest is that you make friends; that you try and find people with the professional skills and the expertise which pipeline companies, energy boards and the courts will have to take seriously."

Implementing that advice proved to be very difficult yet ultimately

131

rewarding. For starters, we had to have a champagne taste on a beer budget. We had to attract the best people in their fields of expertise, and we had only our very limited personal resources. We embarked on the first interdisciplinary research involving pipelines and agriculture, to our knowledge, in the world. It was certainly a first for Canada.

The initiatives we planned would have to be in virgin territory. Any reports or recommendations would have to compare favourably with anything relied upon, or generated by, federal agencies such as the NEB. Any research would have to be perceived as more thorough and relevant than anything that might be presented by such corporations as Interprovincial and Bechtel. We had to surmount the barriers of over a century of prejudice against agriculture and the environment. Such a struggle is, on the surface, clearly an unequal one. There is an additional factor that makes it even more unequal. Precedents of any sort, and especially environmental precedents, are fought vigorously by interests that have enjoyed permissive legislation and compliant courts for their entire history.

To be effective, the conclusions of our consultants would have to be perceived by the most independent and objective legal minds as issues of landmark significance. And that's a tall order, even on a champagne budget! An analogy might be the relative chances of success for a highly organized attempt to scale Mount Everest and one dependent on running shoes and some plastic rope.

The great equalizer proved to be commitment. As Interprovincial's president, David Waldon, conceded under oath, his company had done no environmental-impact studies in its quarter century of operation. And when the company did hire professional people, they all too often acted in an unprofessional manner.

Our terms of reference were very simple. We wanted the best people we could find, and we wanted them to live comfortably with the implications of any conclusions. We didn't want any professional guns for hire; we aspired to commitment because the individuals would then consider the issues to be of social and environmental significance. In our largely crass, commercial, and cynical world, it was a wonderful experience to find that such people existed — people dedicated to the reform of archaic systems.

The conflicts between utilities and farmers had festered in the absence of planning. It was only natural that our first thought was to find someone with appropriate professional and practical experience in planning. I first met Norman Pearson when, as president of the Bruce Trail Association, he addressed the annual meeting of the Federation of Ontario Naturalists on the merits of a Bruce Trail. One of the many aesthetic and geographic virtues of Ontario is the unique limestone formation that runs from Queenston on the Niagara River through some of the most scenic parts of southern Ontario to culminate in the rugged grandeur of the Bruce Peninsula beside Georgian Bay and finally the giant flowerpots nature has sculpted over the millenia. Pearson is not only a highly qualified planner but one with a social conscience and an awareness that society can be changed.

Norman and his wife, Gerda, became frequent visitors at Larigmoor Farm. A summer visit often included planning to avoid the cow-pads in the pasture during an impromptu baseball game. Afterwards, there was animated conversation. It had all seemed so natural for Norman to be our consultant during the 1967 pipeline installation. He developed a very useful report, which was typed by Gerda. It didn't do much to change the way the pipeline was installed because the archaic system had handed Interprovincial a deck of cards of aces. However, the whole exercise proved to be a prelude to the more ambitious report needed prior to Interprovincial's third installation in the late 1970s.

To reproduce Norman Pearson's curriculum vitae in its entirety would be a chapter all its own. He continues to be the busiest, most productive, yet charmingly relaxed person I have ever had the privilege to know. Pearson's academic qualifications now include a Ph.D. (on the impact of pipelines on farming in southwest Ontario) and a master's degree in business administration (on a new concept in the management of urban development in Chinguacousy Township and the new town of Bramalea, areas northwest of Toronto that have had to adapt to some of the fastest population growth in North America). His initial planning degree related to problems associated with coal exploitation in northeastern England. He added to this experience of energy and the environment while working with the National Coal Board in the United Kingdom. On emigrating to Canada, he obtained further broad planning experience, the most relevant as director of planning for the Hamilton-Wentworth Planning Board in Ontario. Its jurisdiction includes part of that Golden Horseshoe bordering the western end of Lake Ontario, where numerous pipelines had been installed. It includes Beverly Township, referred to in Chapter 9.

Norman's career is an unusual blend of the academic and the practical in areas of planning. He has lectured on planning at McMaster University, Waterloo Lutheran University (now Wilfrid Laurier University), and the University of Waterloo. He was later chairman and director of the Centre for Resources Development at the University of Guelph and was a professor of political science at The University of Western Ontario. Throughout, he could draw on a uniquely broad experience and a gift for stimulating students.

His energies embraced cooperative work on four books relating to resource management and planning. He authored some 75 articles in refereed academic and professional journals, over 200 in other journals, and a further 100 newspaper articles and book reviews. Along the way, he became a Life Fellow in such diverse organizations as the American Geographic Society and the Royal Economic Society. He somehow made the time to serve as a trustee of the National and Provincial Parks Association of Canada and as a member of the Conservation Council of Canada.

And there in the curriculum vitae, among some selective consulting and professional practice experiences, is this item: "1974–1982 consultant to Lewington and O'Neil Farms (Ilderton, Ontario) in the case Lewington et al. vs. Interprovincial Pipe Line Limited (Impact of pipeline development on farmland)."

Norman Pearson's specific assignment was to provide a professional opinion on pipelines at Larigmoor Farm that I could present to the National Energy Board and Interprovincial in the hope of encouraging pipeline practices that would mitigate damage during the projected installation of Interprovincial's third pipeline. The purpose of the report was "to present a consultant planning and land economist's opinion for the owner of Larigmoor Farm with respect to the application of Interprovincial Pipe Line Limited to the National Energy Board, dealing with the pipeline extension, from Sarnia, Ontario, to Montreal, Quebec."

Some paraphrased excerpts from that report:

•On either side of the easement, the material is friable, workable, and characteristic of Class I and II soils under good farm management.

•The material on the right-of-way is a much less useful material, and while it might be useful for ceramics, it is not Class I or II soils.

•It reminds me of the experience with open-cast workings (stripmining) and construction works in which the topsoil is either buried or removed, or destroyed by mixing or erosion, and in which the nonhumus subsoil material is inverted and left on the top.

•It is clear that the problems could have been averted in part by location changes and in part by better practices of construction, such as more careful stockpiling of the topsoil and replacement later.

•When there is a combination of disturbance, subsoil inversion, drainage interference, and loss of topsoil, the result is a permanent dis-advantage and a quite unnecessary adverse impact that is a permanent loss for all practical purposes.

•There should be, as a precedent condition, a proper environmental-impact assessment and much tighter control of the actual operations.

The Pearson report demonstrated a good practical knowledge of the impact of pipelines on agriculture. Of even greater significance was its conclusion that with common sense and planning, much of the adverse impact of pipelines on agriculture could be avoided.

Perhaps the most extraordinary aspect of the entire saga of utilities and agriculture is that the concept of mitigating damage was new and revolutionary. In the absence of environmental-impact studies and good pipelining practice, the inevitable damage was inflicted, and then farmers had to seek compensation. If the NEB and Interprovincial were ready to listen, the Pearson report would go a long way towards reaching a consensus that prevention was the desired route because there could be no cure for profligate damage.

What we desperately needed to complement the Pearson report was the opinion of a soils expert. It would have been relatively easy to find someone with the qualifications to explore the productive potential of soils on and off the right-of-way. This would probably involve soil analysis for such nutrients as nitrogen, phosphate, and potassium — N, P, and K. But this was not what I needed. What I felt was essential was somebody qualified to explore all the ramifications of the inversion of the soil profile, the importance of topsoil, and what happened to soil compacted through the use of heavy equipment or construction equipment during wet soil conditions.

I had looked sporadically for one and a half years for someone with this very specialized expertise. The search had been unproductive, and I was becoming resigned to the probability that no one existed who might fill the bill. And then came a phone call from one of the many people who had very kindly extended the search, like ripples on a pond. The caller was Dr. Bill Chefurka, a research scientist with Agriculture Canada at the London, Ontario, Research Centre. "I have found your man! That's Dr. Bob Quigley, and he is right here at The University of Western Ontario!" I had neglected to check the faculty of engineering science and specifically the soil mechanics section. That was home to Dr. R. M. Quigley, a Ph.D. from the Massachusetts Institute of Technology and one of those rare soils experts who can explain how a tragic mudslide occurred in Quebec and confirm that a complex of skyscrapers can be safely built on a specific soil—one deeply versed in the myriad implications when soil is compacted.

I telephoned Dr. Quigley, who listened with interest to the problems I described and the urgency of a soils report because the NEB hearing was imminent.

"Come and have lunch at the Faculty Club, and we'll talk it over" was Dr. Quigley's immediate and most welcome reaction. So began not only a fortuitous association but an enduring friendship. The first tangible benefit came within days when Bob Quigley analyzed soil samples from Larigmoor Farm and prepared a professional report that I could present, all being well, at the NEB hearing scheduled for the following week.

A concurrent letter from Bob Quigley provided the title for this chapter. "Since the oxidation and leaching processes that form topsoils are very slow processes, topsoils and soil profiles take hundreds or thousands of years to develop. In the case of Southern Ontario, the topsoils have been developing since the retreat of the last glaciation 8,000 to 10,000 years ago. All construction through the productive farmland should therefore include provision to strip, store and replace topsoils."

The depth of topsoil is influenced by many factors. In parts of Larigmoor Farm, the topsoil extends to an unusual fifteen inches because of the deposits that first accumulated when the area was a glacial lake. In parts of Ontario where sheet erosion has taken place, the topsoil may have been lost entirely or reduced to a fraction of the original deposit; in many areas, the topsoil is about eight inches; that means that it took nature a thousand years to accumulate just a single inch of topsoil. That fact alone should be enough to confirm that the preservation and conservation of topsoil is an economic, social, and moral responsibility.

In future years, Norman Pearson, as noted, expanded his interest and involvement into his Ph.D. dissertation. Bob Quigley's interest also continued to expand. We coauthored various articles. One of these, published in *Geoscience Canada,* stated that "topsoil is a very precious, nonrenewable resource which all too frequently is wasted and buried at depth by pipeline contractors unless they are subjected to strict environmental controls. Since pipeline easements are some 90 feet wide, some four acres of a 100-acre farm may be adversely affected." Larigmoor Farm became a practical laboratory for students in various disciplines, from soils to plant sciences, from political science to environmental studies.

Bob Quigley is a disciplined and precise specialist in his chosen field. He also has a broad interest in what goes on around him and wants to find out how his discipline interfaces with those of other professionals. It was through Bob Quigley that Dr. A. D. Tomlin, a research scientist with Agriculture Canada in London, became involved. His research was to take that of Bob Quigley's to a new dimension; Al Tomlin's speciality is exploring the soil to see what compaction does to the populations of fascinating creatures that inhabit the soil. But that dimension belongs more properly in a later chapter, "Soil Isn't Just Dirt."

As John Kerr had advocated, we had made friends — wonderful friends. Armed with the reports of Pearson and Quigley, I set off for the NEB and Ottawa to sell the virtues of common sense and the mitigation of damage during pipeline construction. In my baggage were some soil samples and the chemistry I hoped to use in a demonstration designed to convince the NEB members of their responsibilities. In Bob Quigley's laboratory at UWO the addition of 10 percent hydrochloric acid to subsoil caused it to fizz dramatically, while the carbonate-free topsoil remained dormant. Would these and other initiatives put some fizz into the NEB, which, from the farmers' viewpoint, was dormant?

CHAPTER 14

A Majority of One

Mr. Lewington will have to be kept within strong confines.
—J. H. HENDRY
NEB legal counsel

I t was May 1974, and the NEB had settled at posh and spacious quarters in the Trebla Building, close to Ottawa's Parliament Hill, surroundings fitting for one of its more significant hearings. On several counts, this was to be a watershed in both energy policy and the exercise of democratic rights.

The Borden Line, named for Henry Borden whose commission led to the creation of the NEB, established that west of the Ottawa Valley, energy requirements would be filled by western Canada resources, while east of the capital would be served by imported oil. OPEC changed all that. The government of Canada, primarily through Energy Minister Macdonald, was determined to expand the Interprovincial pipeline system with a 30-inch-diameter pipeline stretching from Sarnia, Ontario, to Montreal, Quebec.

In the seven years since I had first asked the NEB to implement a policy of alerting landowners to hearings that affected them, the system remained unsatisfactory. I wrote to Marshall Crowe, then NEB chairman, and now an Ottawa consultant: "Dear Sir, Does your board intend holding hearings affecting my farm? Yours truly." The response came by telegram on April 25, advising that the hearing had been delayed and would begin on May 14. I was able to qualify as an intervenor but had to face procedural requirements designed for large corporations. Fulfilling those requirements was both difficult and expensive. In the face of yet another postal disruption, various air-express and courier services had to be used to ensure delivery of some thirty copies of my brief. Distributing the brief was also very much a family affair. Our daughter Ann and some of her friends did yeoman service by delivering copies in the various cities where they worked.

To preclude any misunderstanding of my intent, the brief was labelled "Opposition and Intervention." It referred to the issues that I hope are now familiar to readers. They ranged from the failure to protect prime agricultural land; the absence of policies to mitigate damage; the burning of oil spills; secrecy surrounding the Sylvain Cloutier Report to the NEB, which was said to recommend the route through southern Ontario; to the concluding paragraph, which read, "The onus is clearly on the NEB and IPL to adopt responsible and retroactive policies. Any further pipeline construction must be vigorously opposed, pending sweeping changes in the policies of both the NEB and such federally-chartered utilities as IPL."

As the signs pointed to a protracted hearing, I tried by telephone, without success, to determine when I might speak.

Subsequently, on May 10, I sent the following telegram to Crowe: "My earliest intervention requested May 14. Urge priority on grounds of my seniority of opposition to IPL, damage to my farm, personal costs attending hearing, and livestock and cropping demands here." There was no response, but I went to the Ottawa hearing anyway. The NEB fielded a panel with the customary homogeneous background. The chairman, W. A. "Bill" Scotland, is an engineer who had worked variously on the Athabasca Oil Sands Project with Texaco, and then Energy, Mines and Resources. Jacques Farmer, another engineer, spent most of his working life with Hydro-Quebec, Quebec Natural Gas Corporation, and Gaz Metropolitain. The third panelist, Ralph F. Brooks, was still another engineer, with a career with electrical power companies.

Interprovincial was there in strength, led by President David Waldon. Gordon Sheasby was assisted by fellow lawyers C. D. Gonthier, Q.C., and M. G. Van Vliet. In addition to IPL staffers, the company drew, for the first time, on environmental consultants.

The provincial governments fielded an array of legal talent. Ron White led the group from the Ontario Federation of Agriculture. For the first time, the National Farmers Union was there; President Walter Miller had the support of farmers, including John Martens. As this was a hearing with significant implications, the other intervenors ranged from TransCanada Pipe Lines to the Committee for an Independent Canada.

With such a crowd at the starting gate, Scotland was fully aware of the importance of allocating the order of priority. He established that this would be provincial governments, municipalities, federations, asso-

ciations and companies, and finally individuals. To ensure that the as-
pirants were actually there, he initiated a roll call. For instance, "Mr.
Chairman, my name is Pierre Fortin, and with me is Mr. Jean Piette. We
are both solicitors for the government of Quebec, and we both represent
the attorney-general for Quebec."

When my turn came, I advised the board that I appeared on behalf
of my wife, Jean, and myself, and protested relegation to the lowest
priority, despite being there at my own expense and injuriously affected.

The federal courtroom was sufficiently large that I could not identify who advised the panel that "individuals are not necessarily put at the
bottom of the list; however, in Mr. Lewington's case it may be that we
feel it wise that he be so placed." The speaker turned out to be J. H.
"Jim" Hendry, one of the board's internal legal counsel.

Scotland softened to the point where he said, "Mr. Lewington, if
you can make arrangements with other counsel to have you placed earlier in the batting order, we will look forward to that type of motion
being made as we proceed." To this I responded, "I don't know the
counsel present today, so I wonder if they might indicate whether this
would meet with their approval to make such a change in the order of
appearance."

Scotland called for an oral reaction, and we all got a surprise! In
every case, the provincial governments' representatives offered to surren-
der pride of place. With such a beginning, nobody else was prepared to
object, nobody except Hendry, who said, "This submission is nothing
but a lot of vague, unsupported, and in my opinion, apparently un-
founded charges. Mr. Lewington will have to be kept within strong confines."

Scotland then read Hendry a little lecture on the law, observing that
"the subject of the discussion is not what Mr. Lewington is going to say,
but when he is going to say it." He then asked for my reaction, and I
said, "I did not like the sound of being put in strong confines, unless this
is going to be some general ruling of your court."

And so, for the first and only time to my knowledge in the history
of Canada, an individual won the right to take priority, even over the
provinces, in a federal court. This was more than just a legal precedent;
it proved to be the turning point. It was the end of the beginning and the
beginning of the end.

The precedent allowed me to be the first to cross-examine IPL,
following its evidence-in-chief. By winning priority among the intervenors, I was able to make my presentation on the fourth and final day
that I could afford to stay in Ottawa. Had I not been given priority, I

either would not have had a turn at bat or would have been obligated to make several return visits to Ottawa as the on-again, off-again hearings dragged on until October. And that would have been beyond my budget.

In refusing to submit to Hendry's strong confines, I could look back in history to that gentle naturalist Henry David Thoreau whose essay "Civil Disobedience" inspired such remarkable people as Gandhi. Said Thoreau: "Any man more right than his neighbours constitutes a majority of one." Thoreau was not being arrogant but expressing his belief that if you are convinced of the rightness of your cause, you don't have to wait for the approbation of your peers or succumb to opposition.

To mix metaphors, I had won my spurs but was still a burr under Hendry's saddle.

But the early stages of the hearing were dominated by Interprovincial, as Sheasby for IPL led his technical witnesses. They began with some number crunching. The capacity of crude oil from western Canada was established at 2 million barrels daily. The capacity for the proposed expansion ranged up to 690,000 barrels per day. IPL preferred the southern route through farmland rather than a route through rocky northern Ontario. Farm organizations had favoured the northern route and had been backed by several Ontario cabinet ministers, including agriculture's Bill Stewart. Their rationale was the protection of farmland and the economic impetus that the pipeline would give to the North. In rejecting the northern route, IPL witnesses estimated that $125 million would be added to the cost and also that the project could not be completed in the established time frame laid down by government. Once again, Energy Minister Macdonald, though not present at the hearing, was effectively calling the shots. (The Thumper is now Canadian high commissioner to the Court of St. James in London, England.)

Interprovincial's engineers reported that the pipe would have a wall thickness of ¼ inch through farmland, would increase to 9⁄32 inch in urban areas, and would be ½ inch under all water courses flowing into the Great Lakes and the St. Lawrence Seaway. The sophisticated technology would include the x-raying of all welds, and the pipe coating materials were designed to protect against external corrosion.

The man most responsible for Interprovincial's engineering criteria was C. H. Bucklee, who was my first cross-examination target. On behalf of Roberta Tilden and John Walker Elliott, who lived on farms right across from the Bryanston Pump Station, I inquired about the potential for even higher noise levels than those that had bothered residents up to a mile from the station. Ron White effectively pursued the problems of noise pollution. Bucklee conceded that everything possible was being done to reduce the noise to an acceptable level and acknowledged that noise was a factor in the selection of equipment for the proposed expansion. White fared less well on planning procedures that could obviate drainage conflicts.

As Sheasby led his several panels through their paces, it was asserted that "throughout twenty-five years of construction and operation in various environmental settings the Applicant [IPL] has developed and maintained standards of construction and procedures to minimize environmental damage and to ensure the functional integrity of the pipeline system. As part of the overall plan to minimize the environmental impact of the proposed extension the Applicant retained consulting firms to make an environmental assessment of the proposed route in the provinces of Ontario and Quebec." An environmentally sensitive area was Lake of Two Mountains, Quebec, which is a major source of drinking water for the city of Montreal. Interprovincial reiterated its willingness to strip topsoil above the trench area and to install remedial tile drains. On oil spills, the board was reassured that "the recovery factor of all oil spilled or released from the pipeline system has been about 80%." Regarding damage releases, it was revealed that Interprovincial had changed its policy to read to the date of signing. This too was progress.

However, when I had the opportunity to cross-examine IPL staff and the company's environmental consultants, some disturbing facts came to light. No soil specialist had been involved in any way. In its entire twenty-five-year history, Interprovincial had done no environmental impact research on the changes its pipelines caused in the disturbed soils of easements.

In documents filed by Interprovincial it was noted that "the tiled, fine-textured soils of Southern Ontario are particularly vulnerable to disturbance." However, my cross-examining of the "experts" further confirmed that there had been no soil studies, no soil samples, and no comparison of soils on and off the existing right-of-way. In addition, there were no compaction or soil-permeability studies and no studies on how the pipeline might affect natural subsurface drainage.

Perhaps most revealing of all was the admission that "we did not do any fieldwork on the ground . . . we covered the whole line by aircraft."

When I inquired about the variation in soils along the route, it turned out that the research had been restricted to examining maps because "the soil was covered with snow at that time."

With the benefit of three years of hindsight, the Law Reform Commission of Canada, in its report *The National Energy Board,* noted that "despite his lack of barrister's skills, his tendency to wander, and Sheasby's rattling objections, Lewington's cross-examination was fairly effective, bringing to light such matters as Interprovincial's lack of knowledge of the effects of pipelines on soil drainage patterns and casting doubt on the company's past record in predicting and avoiding environmental damage."

When the hearing adjourned at 5:00 P.M., Jim Hendry had reappraised his position. Beginning that evening, he became my much appreciated legal coach. Following adjournment each evening, he would generously spend an hour or so on rules of procedure, what was admissible in the questioning of witnesses, and how one's own testimony should be given when the time arrived.

On Day Two, D. H. Rogers, representing Ontario's energy minister, exposed during his cross-examination further environmental hazards and the absence of research or even detailed consultation with logical sources of information. This led to the admission that "certainly, further investigation is going to have to be made in certain areas." These included sensitive marine clays and groundwater problems.

Rogers referred to Interprovincial's brochure *On to Montreal* and observed that it was an inspiring title. It was also inaccurate in that it referred to "the pipeline" when in fact granting an easement involved pipelines (plural).

Jean Piette pursued the hazards of oil spills with Interprovincial's witnesses. He noted that just the day before, ten thousand gallons of crude had flowed from Westcoast Transmission's pipeline into the Fraser River. His concern was with the safety of the water intakes for the city of Montreal. In cross-examination, he drew from Interprovincial's Owen Linton that the company's research had located only three or four of the twenty-one water intakes! This was all the more astonishing in that Linton had been designated as the project manager for Interprovincial and manager of the Sarnia to Montreal Pipeline Project.

In his extensive cross-examination, Ron White drew the admission that in the event of wet soils, construction should be delayed but that there was no firm policy and no autonomy granted environmental consultants in halting construction.

Linton was still being pursued on oil spills by the Committee for an Independent Canada when Day Two ended.

Interprovincial's Linton didn't fare much better as Day Three dragged on. Responses to questions on the problems of oil spills were inconclusive. For instance, Hendry asked Linton, "So, even a leak of considerable size, from your experience, could be cleaned up satisfactorily?" To this Linton replied, "Yes. I mean, especially where . . . the answer is especially where it is hard to relate volume to the damage." I still don't know what that means!

Scotland queried Linton on the size of spills and learned that the figure of 250 barrels per spill mentioned in the documentation was not the upper end of the scale. Spills were measured in thousands of barrels. However, IPL's consultant D. H. Duncan reassured the board that "most of this material is either picked up, and what is left is biodegradable."

When IPL president David Waldon (later a director of Union Gas) was questioned by the Committee for an Independent Canada about leaks in IPL's Lakehead system in the United States, he said, "We didn't lose too much oil . . . about six thousand to seven thousand barrels out of the line. . . . In 1973, we had two big ones. . . . Nineteen thousand barrels got out of the system, and we recovered all but three hundred barrels, and one where seventeen thousand barrels were estimated to go out of the system, and we recovered all but fifty . . . which I find a little hard to believe. I think somebody must have got some water in that deal."

At the end of another long day, Scotland asked me to elaborate on oil spills, and I observed that all of the extensive evidence had been totally devoid of any reference to burning spilled oil.

After years of inconclusive responses from people at different levels in the IPL hierarchy, it was a welcome change to be in the position of leading the cross-examination of Waldon. He conceded that since 1950, IPL had installed over five thousand miles of pipelines, at least two-thirds through agricultural land. This had been done at a cost of millions of dollars, but in the complete absence of any environmental-impact studies. IPL still had no one on staff with any agricultural or environmental expertise. While his subordinates had referred to "sound pipelining practice," there was nothing written down that one might see.

It was a hearing singularly lacking in even the wriest of humour. However, Waldon did confirm his signature and that he wrote wishing me a happy Christmas in 1972. "Perhaps, I should withdraw it," he said.

Many of the responses and reactions of David Waldon went a long way to explain the company's hard-nosed attitudes. He grudgingly conceded that possibly some soil research might be beneficial. "If a pipeline is going to be constructed, it is going to disturb the soil."

In many areas of this saga it has often been confusing to determine the role of companies, regulatory agencies, and government. This became evident when I pressed Waldon about the time constraints on construction that could (and subsequently did) contribute immeasurably to environmental damage. "If the line is to be completed on schedule, and that has been indicated to us as important by the government, it is entirely possible that certain environmental repercussions are going to have to be waived," responded Waldon.

Rereading the nearly one thousand pages of transcript of that single hearing, the ambivalence of Interprovincial becomes apparent. It comes through clearly as a company that is soundly financed and efficiently managed. It could spend upwards of $200 million — much of it borrowed — to complete the extension from Sarnia to Montreal and profit from a tariff of just 28 cents a barrel. However, when it came to corporate policies relating to agriculture and the environment, the company was strictly out to lunch.

In my view, the hearing had also exposed the limitations of an NEB panel drawn from such a narrow spectrum of society. They lacked knowledge of so many ramifications of Interprovincial's application that it was largely left to intervenors to expose the weaknesses. Sadly, even when those weaknesses were exposed, the board failed to act.

For instance, Exhibit 25 is entitled "photograph taken January 1970 of oil being destroyed by fire." Exhibit 26 was another view of the oil burning in the vicinity of the Bryanston Pump Station. They were dramatic colour pictures and measured nearly two feet square. I can still see Scotland propelling his caster chair across the dais in his eagerness to see pictures of something IPL had spent three days ignoring. As late as 1985, the board had taken no action on the burning of oil spills, and had neither initiated nor encouraged alternative forms of remedial action and cleanup.

On the evening of the third day, I had my customary legal tutoring from Jim Hendry. My major concern was that the following morning was the last I could afford to spend in Ottawa, and I did not know how to ensure that our consultants' reports would be accepted as evidence. I knew that ideally a lawyer and one's consultants should be in attendance. Such an ideal situation is beyond the resources of most individual intervenors, especially when there is no indication of the date they will actually be called upon to testify.

"All you have to do is to ensure that Gordon Sheasby has had an adequate chance to read your consultants' reports," advised Hendry.

The next morning, I was up at 5:00 A.M., having established that Sheasby was staying at the Skyline Hotel. I got a bleary-eyed Sheasby out of bed. He said he neither wanted nor needed any papers and would see me in court at 9:30. Not so, I countered. "You now have four hours to read the reports," and I thrust them into his hand.

When questioned by Scotland on the admissibility of the reports, Sheasby very fairly said, "Mr. Lewington, I know, wishes to have these reports submitted for the board's information, and I have absolutely no objection to his filing them on that basis." Hendry was also affirmative when he said, "This board wants to obtain all the information it can."

• Exhibit 30 was the report by R. J. "Bob" Milne, the most experienced drainage consultant with the Ontario Ministry of Agriculture and Food. It may be recalled that Bob was our consultant two decades earlier when Arthur Pattillo had tried to lure him to his room at the Hotel London.

• Exhibit 31 was the report by Professor (now Doctor) Norman Pearson entitled *Pipelines and Larigmoor Farm, May 11, 1974.*

• Exhibit 32 was the report from Dr. R. M. Quigley dated May 7, 1974, and entitled *Preliminary Soil Analysis, Pipeline Easement in Larigmoor Farm.*

• Exhibit 33 was a further report by Dr. Quigley dated May 1974 and entitled *Site Visit and Soil Analyses, Larigmoor Farm.*

When I look over the transcript, I find that Gordon Sheasby's objections and comments took up rather more space than my own presentation. "I would like to register my objection," said Sheasby at one point. "If we look at Mr. Lewington's intervention, the thrust of it, firstly, as in past interventions relating to the same problem, dating back to 1967, whereby he attacks in general shotgun fashion the federal government, this board, the courts, and Interprovincial, and I submit that this particular hearing should not be used as a forum once again for this purpose."

I thought that that was a very reasonable and succinct summary. Gordon Sheasby had listed all of the organizations that to that point had been noted for their black hats. I should perhaps clarify that. Reference to the "board" refers to NEB members and not the staff whose job it is to carry out policy. I have reason to appreciate the expertise of board staff, and certainly Hendry's tip to get Sheasby out of bed!

Bill Scotland, in accepting our consultants' reports, had said, "The board will give them the attention that they deserve." That was a somewhat ambiguous statement. It turned out that the reports were ignored by both the board and Interprovincial. Fortunately for us, and for agriculture, the courts were to take a very different view. The evidence the NEB chose to ignore Judge Gordon Killeen was subsequently to elevate to the starry status of "prescient information."

CHAPTER 15

Creativity
of an
Unusual Degree

... And that you [IPL] put down all resistance and opposition [of Peter Lewington] thereto, taking with you sufficient assistance for that purpose.

—JUDGE J. F. McCART

B ecause of the complexity of the issues and the ever-increasing cast of characters, it may be helpful to pause and interject a note of continuity.

The events of May 1974 in the previous chapter were followed by the September 1975 Sarnia NEB hearing described in Chapter 2. This sequence was used to introduce such significant players as Stu O'Neil.

As a result of the two hearings, IPL got the green light, despite the absence of any acceptable oil-spill policy and failure to implement construction policies to mitigate damage. What the NEB could not give Interprovincial was the requested additional thirty feet of working rights. Only the courts could do that, using the expropriation powers of the National Energy Board Act and the Railway Act.

Several references have been made to some unnecessary confusion in the affiliation of some of the cast of characters. On October 25, 1975, I was served with a legal notice that IPL would seek expropriation through the county court of the county of Middlesex. Delivery was made by a Mr. Bentley of Bechtel, who had no identification. That legal package included two affidavits — one by Ronald Richardson, a London, Ontario, realtor, the other by President David Waldon on behalf of IPL. The latter's argument for expropriation included the following: "I know that the immediate possession of the said lands . . . is necessary for the construction. . . . Unless the applicant is granted such immediate possession and the power to exercise immediately the said right and licence consisting of temporary working rights, serious loss, damage and delay will occur in the construction of the said pipeline."

I did not accept Waldon's affidavit as persuasive; he, and his predecessors, had had more than adequate time to implement environmentally sound practices over some twenty-five years.

As IPL had largely ignored the agricultural and environmental issues, I telephoned John Brownlie, of Blake, Cassels and Graydon, that when the case was heard, I would seek an adjournment. Brownlie broke into wild laughter. The prospect of being thwarted was clearly ludicrous after a century of unbroken successes in issues involving the Railway Act.

When I entered the impressive new County Court Building in London on the morning of November 7, 1975, I was greeted by Stu O'Neil and lawyer Geoff Bladon, whom he had retained the night before. Geoff was to acquit himself nobly over the next few years, but at that stage there had not been time to brief him adequately. Consequently, the O'Neils and ourselves agreed to split all legal costs equally; however, I would continue to take our own case until Geoff had had an opportunity to become acclimatised. To Brownlie's chagrin and our delight, Judge McCart ordered an adjournment so that we could question Waldon and Richardson under oath.

The confidence of IPL was evident in the fact that the long lines of construction equipment were already poised at the westerly line fences of the O'Neil and Lewington farms. During the hours of darkness, the armada was moved, via public roads, to the easterly line fences. We did not relish this wasteful exercise, but justified it on the grounds that the long-sought reforms were still not in place.

Five days later, Geoff, Stu, and I, on the one hand, and David Waldon, Ron Richardson, and Brownlie, on the other, appeared before A. C. Devenport, a special examiner, in his chambers adjacent to the office of the Ontario Ombudsman in Toronto. While he qualified as a realtor and appraiser, Richardson ventured into areas where he had no demonstrated expertise. He gave the unqualified opinion that crop damage would be restricted to two years as a result of construction, even in a worst-case situation. Richardson conceded that he stayed in the car when he visited Larigmoor Farm. He evaluated Larigmoor Farm from the vantage point of the Middlesex County road on the southerly farm boundary. He admitted that he had no knowledge of soils and had never taken a soil sample. Richardson also stated that he had been kept in ignorance of the reports of Pearson and Quigley.

When Waldon was in the hot seat, both Brownlie and Bladon gave some scintillating displays of their talents on behalf of their respective clients. Bladon would press for information, and Brownlie would object. At one point, Waldon said that they did not have a copy of a requested report, but "if you ask Mr. Lewington, I am sure he has one." (On returning home that night, I checked the bulging files, and there it was!)

Geoff Bladon explored the area of greatest concern to us. With winter imminent, would the construction be done under conditions of wet soils that could contribute to maximizing damage? David Waldon's response was less than reassuring. "In most any condition, if you bring in sufficient riprap [stones, debris] sufficient to work with, it can be done. . . . Riprap would be put in to support the equipment, and it would be moved as soon as we could take it out, which would be in the spring."

Prior to my education into the ever-increasing ramifications of pipelines and agriculture, I had thought that Latin was a dead language. Now I learned a new term: *amicus curiae*. Brownlie had been curious about the legal relationship of Geoff and me. Geoff explained that he was acting as amicus curiae, a "friend of the court," to give me legal advice, during a brief recess.

We reappeared before Judge McCart on November 17, after the twelve-day adjournment. Brownlie was equally prepared and aggressive; after all, his client faced the intolerable situation of investing some $200 million in a pipeline that which had two sections missing!

Throughout the day, the two lawyers sparred as they picked over the Devenport transcripts and sought to breathe relevance into bygone cases under the Railway Act. Brownlie had a winner in *McCarthy v. Tillsonburg Railway* (1910), but Geoff noted that this was all about vacant land, whereas the current issue was prime farmland. Volunteered McCart at one stage: "I am at a loss to determine what the damage will be."

Geoff Bladon drew McCart's attention to the Pearson and Quigley reports, which had been accepted by the NEB. "Pearson and Quigley are as knowledgeable as anyone in the world. What they say is that the kind of construction practiced causes permanent damage. If you will read these affidavits carefully . . ." To this McCart reacted testily: "I read everything carefully!"

During the afternoon the mood became more fractious. Geoff Bladon merely stated that he was doing his best, to which McCart responded, "And it's not good enough." It was then nearing the time for the evening adjournment, and we retired to the judge's chambers to determine when I might go to bat.

I told McCart that I would prefer to start fresh in the morning, and he agreed to this. I thought I knew what was bothering the judge. He was caught in a cleft stick. Under the law, which he was obligated to uphold, he had very little latitude. He had exercised some of that latitude in authorizing the adjournment to cross-examine Waldon and Richardson. Now he had very little manoeuvering room left. Brownlie had told him, "You shall grant us a warrant. We can go in and make a wasteland of these farms if we want to." McCart knew this to be the literal truth.

Everyone appeared refreshed the next morning. I began my presentation by filing a letter from the chairman of the Law Reform Commission of Canada as an exhibit. Patrick Hartt, now back as a justice of the Supreme Court of Ontario, had urged that due to the archaic nature of the legislation, a judge hearing our case should use "creativity of an unusual degree."

Judge McCart gave me an excellent hearing, and my comments evoked only minimal objection from John Brownlie.

In his written judgement in 1975, McCart observed:

> The evidence adduced on behalf of the respondent, essentially related to the damage to the land in 1957 and in 1967 when the first two pipelines were installed and it was established to my satisfaction that substantial damage resulted. While such damage may not be permanent it will certainly be many years past the life expectancy of the respondents before the soil returns to its original fertile state. Unfortunately, the statutory provisions under which I am acting prohibit me from taking such damage into account, except in so far as I am required to order security to cover the probable compensation. . . . The evidence also established to my satisfaction that construction methods will probably leave the temporary working rights as well as that portion of the easement which will be dug up for the new line in no better condition than resulted following the installation of the two previous pipelines. Mr. Waldon admitted that the applicant had no contingency plan for the mitigation of damage to the land. The applicant intends to work through the winter, if necessary, and construct a line regardless of the weather, and will then consider what will be done on the farmer's behalf with respect to damages. In my view there is a substantial probability of severe damage to the land of a lasting nature.

As security, Judge McCart ordered Interprovincial to pay into court some $27,000 on behalf of the O'Neil and Lewington families, a decision generally regarded as of landmark significance. It was published in its entirety in *Dominion Law Reports,* which go to most lawyers and many real estate appraisers in Canada.

But the realities of Judge McCart's decision continued to escape the Interprovincial-Bechtel twins. They arrived at Larigmoor Farm to announce that the construction equipment would be coming through the westerly line fence. When I asked them if they had been issued a warrant by the court, having paid into court the required funds, they hit the panic button. A courier had to be sent to Toronto to acquire the funds, pay them into court, and obtain the court warrant quoted at the start of this chapter.

I cannot hold Judge McCart responsible for the wording of that warrant; he was merely the victim of what Mr. Justice Hartt had called "archaic" legislation. However, I found it repugnant to receive a warrant that authorized a commercial company to take with them sufficient assistance to put down all resistance and opposition. Did that include goons with baseball bats and heavyweights with side arms? Throughout the long struggle, we had stayed scrupulously within the law despite the inadequacies of the law and all of the avoidable frustrations and damage which flowed from laws inappropriate to the twentieth century.

Notwithstanding the misgivings of Judge McCart and his valiant efforts to stave off the inevitable, Interprovincial was in a legal position to implement John Brownlie's reference to making a "wasteland."

CHAPTER 16

A
Higher
Duty

Because of the complexity of this and other cases, injustice would clearly be done if a claimant would be limited to three experts in all the factual issues. I have a higher duty and that is to arrive at the truth. I will allow the evidence!
—JUDGE GORDON KILLEEN

D raw near and be heard. God save the Queen!" cried Assistant Sheriff Ross Hodgins. The court of Judge Killeen had convened to hear our claims against Interprovincial for the damage caused by the third Interprovincial pipeline in 1975.

While it was now December 9, 1976, the threads could be traced all the way back to the mid-1950s. Despite all the complexities and the diversions, it was all of a pattern, all of a piece.

Declared Geoff Bladon: "The overriding issue in these proceedings is that we have on the one hand a need for energy represented by the interests of Interprovincial Pipe Line, and on the other hand there is the need to preserve our farmland in order that its production, high production in these two instances, can continue unimpeded. Those interests are represented by O'Neil and Lewington."

John Brownlie again represented Interprovincial. We might instead have been facing Jake Howard, who with Arthur Pattillo came to Larigmoor Farm two decades earlier to witness our practical demonstration on how a pipeline could be installed without environmental damage. Howard had subsequently risen to star status with Blake, Cassels and Graydon, but had recently been injured when thrown from a horse. Brownlie, Howard's replacement, was assisted by G. W. Gee and law student Gary Joseph.

A crucial thread running back to the 1950s was the provision of the Railway Act that restricted the number of witnesses. How would Killeen react to a challenge to that apparently impregnable legislation with its century of precedents?

For us, Judge Killeen was an unknown quantity. All we had to go on was Geoff's comment that "we are lucky to have him; he won't make any mistakes in law." And that was really all we could ask for. In retrospect, I wonder whether we could have dredged up the physical, mental, and financial resources to go through the whole debilitating legal process again in the event of a mistrial.

It soon became apparent that Killeen was briskly in charge of his own court. He allowed considerable latitude in the introduction of evidence but did not tolerate sloppiness or ambiguity. He treated the opposing lawyers with no apparent bias. When he sought clarification from a witness, it was evident that he had been listening intently. He took copious notes, but his thoughts remained a mystery. He would make a formidable poker player! When Stu and I felt that a bolt from the heavens should strike down a witness for failure to tell the truth, the whole truth, and nothing but the truth, the expression on the judge's face never changed.

A rare change in the judge's demeanour occurred at the start when a third applicant, Irwin Lunn, was discovered sitting in the prisoner's box. Killeen promptly ordered more suitable accommodation and had to be reassured that Lunn had all that he needed in the way of paper and ballpoint pens. He then ruled that Lunn, though not represented by counsel, would be privileged to be part of our case and to benefit from all that we had done. This was discouraging, as Lunn's only expressed intent was to increase damage payment; he had demonstrated no interest in reforming the system. I wondered if Killeen thought Lunn was the only real farmer in the court. He was disarmingly simple and as cunning as a fox. He talked about "yoes," which was interpreted to Killeen as ewes. Lunn was to get a free ride all the way to the Supreme Court of Ontario. Brownlie had wanted Lunn included so that he didn't have to go through the whole procedure again, and Killeen responded by saying, "I'll see that your case is properly put before me. I will decide what evidence is common and what is relevant to each of three individual properties."

In challenging the Railway Act, we had handed Geoff Bladon a hot potato. In very little time, he had, all on his own, to become conversant with some nine disciplines, several of them incredibly complex. He had to decide on the order of the witnesses, bearing in mind that on the count of three, no additional witnesses might be allowed. He had to tread the delicate path between keeping the judge sufficiently well informed to reach a decision while avoiding an excess of minutiae that might try his patience and endurance during what would certainly be a lengthy trial.

Geoff chose to lead with Stu O'Neil and to paint the broad picture. This was an inspired decision. Stu had graduated from the University of Guelph in agronomy, was head of the Science Department at London's Banting Secondary School, and together with his sons Barry, Steve, and Brian, cash-cropped 250 acres of land. Stu had a very extensive background in documenting his farm management and cropping practices. He had become increasingly involved in the issues of pipelines and agriculture.

Stu O'Neil has the professional training and the keen eye of a good farmer to relate such things as the pollination of corn and the uneven maturity of white beans to agronomic practices — or pipeline construction. He had assembled some two hundred colour slides and a great deal of detailed information on each one. At slide number 177, even Killeen wavered when he asked, "Have you not run out of slides?" But those slides were successful in putting the judge in the picture. Together with such other exhibits as a map showing the township of London and the various pipelines that laced it, the judge had a framework into which he could slot all of the subsequent evidence.

John Brownlie was evidently still feeling the reverses he had suffered before Judge McCart. He subjected Stu to some tough interrogation and demonstrated that he was very alert; for instance, he pounced when he, alone in the court, realised that a single slide had been incorrectly identified.

Differing philosophies were evident in the opposing lawyers. When Bladon referred to the substantial and emotional involvement of his clients, Brownlie responded that "we are here for compensation only. Any pictures showing fallen-in caverns are not relevant." Killeen reacted by saying, "It's always relevant to see the site. I participated in many cases of expropriation, and it is always important to see the site in photographs. It is not going to inflame me. We are on an archaeological expedition."

If you looked at the stoney face of the judge and read the nine volumes of the transcript, you could still get an erroneous impression. When Stu had launched into his testimony and slide show, Killeen had kindly called for a chair for Barry, who was running the slide projector.

In Dr. Bob Quigley, who testified next, Geoff had a perfect witness — and a problem he shared with his legal opposition. Quigley had impeccable qualifications for the task at hand: a master's degree from the University of Toronto in geological engineering, with emphasis on glacial geology and soil mechanics. On graduating with a Ph.D. from the Massachusetts Institute of Technology, he spent several years with Geocon, a soils consulting organization. He then moved to The University of Western Ontario (UWO) and became head of the soil mechanics section of the faculty of engineering science. His broad interest in his field of geotechnical engineering extended to involvement with the International and North American Societies of Clays and Clay Minerals, membership on the National Research Council of Canada's Earth Science Granting Committee, and contributing to professional publications and discharging the responsibilities of editor of the *Canadian Geotechnical Journal.* Quigley also had a demonstrated interest in interdisciplinary research. He was concurrently lecturer in the department of geology at UWO and liked to rub shoulders with other scientists, including Agriculture Canada's Dr. Al Tomlin.

In his preamble, Bladon said, "Your Honour, Dr. Quigley has done a substantial amount of research. . . . I have a great deal of difficulty trying to understand all of it." Responded Judge Killeen, in wry humour: "Is that supposed to be a criticism of you or the witness?"

Bladon readily conceded that this was intended as self-criticism. It was the problem he was to share with Brownlie and his legal associates. Quigley's testimony was to stretch the minds of all those in the court and lead the judge to comment, "I wasn't far wrong when I said this would be an archaeological expedition."

During the three-week trial, Geoff visibly lost weight. While the rest of us had luncheon at nearby restaurants, Geoff restricted himself to a coin-operated confectionary machine in the County Court Building and worked right through every recess. Each evening after the court adjourned we had a council of war. Still later, Geoff would visit with our various expert witnesses to prepare cross-examination for the next court session. Brownlie's role was less demanding, but he cited his own difficulties, which were compounded by being "just a city boy."

Dr. Quigley's evidence involved a whole lexicon of technical terms seldom used outside his area of expertise: *Hydrogen ions, carbonate leaching, X-ray diffraction traces, piezometers, Shelby tubes, capillary rise capacity, Atterberg Limits test, Smectite clays, goniometers, anonymously alkaline, logarithmic scale,* and such sundry other terms as *montmorillonite,* many of which had to be spelled for the benefit of the court reporter.

But Quigley is not one to use a ten-dollar word where more simple terminology will suffice. He was merely using the precision essential in the presentation of such technical work. Geoff's agriculturally oriented education had exploded at an exponential rate. Together, Bladon and Quigley managed to give the court a unique insight into what a soil specialist could discern on the impact of pipelines on farming. John Brownlie was apparently awed by much of this and was restricted in the interjections and questions he was competent to frame.

In matters of fact he couldn't lay a glove on Quigley. When he suggested that Quigley might have extrapolated on his admittedly "limited" research, he touched a raw nerve. It is all a matter of relativity. While Quigley might categorize his efforts as limited, most everybody else would have viewed them as complex and nudging star wars technology! Quigley was able to sharply rebuke Brownlie that the work he had done was more comprehensive than anything previously attempted in Canada. His soils initiatives on the Lewington and O'Neil farms exceeded any comparable efforts by all levels of government and the entire oil industry in the Dominion of Canada. It was symptomatic of Quigley's modest professionalism that he alluded to his work as limited.

Throughout Dr. Quigley's evidence, Brownlie's cross-examination, and Bladon's reexamination, there had been an ongoing battle of wits that was probably lost on many of the observers in the court. I would not have appreciated the significance of that battle had I not been privileged so many years before to watch Arthur Pattillo destroy an expert witness, lured beyond the area of expertise in which he had qualified. Quigley stuck to the mandate under which he was retained by us as a consultant. Like our other witnesses, he remained in a watertight compartment, declining all entreaties to elaborate on areas in which he was not qualified. For instance:

•When asked about the significance of particular tills in crop growth, he replied, "The plant uses all the elements I have referred to. It probably uses many more which I don't know anything about."

•When asked to elaborate on a technicality of drainage tile, he replied simply, "Ask somebody else."

•Asked Brownlie, "Just tell me again, the significance of a low-carbonate level or higher-carbonate level in the rectangular trough and its effect on plant growth." Quigley cautiously replied, "You realise this is just an opinion."

•When pressed to comment on possible crop damage, Quigley replied, "I have presented a factual resume of the damage to the components in the system. I cannot assess the crop damage."

•Agronomy and the management of a beef and seed farm were not his specialities. Quigley merely said, "We have people who can talk about that. I cannot answer that question."

•Again, in the knowledge that our team included a plant ecologist, he declined to be drawn into a discussion of weeds with the comment "That is not my business."

•On a question relating to possible financial loss as a result of pipeline construction, Dr. Quigley said, "I know almost precisely what has been caused in terms of facts and information I have given. I do not know the consequences of that kind of damage to his [Lewington's] financial yield for that farm."

•When pressed further on farm crops, he responded, "I can offer you opinions, but that is all they would be, all general ones."

•Quigley was also careful to avoid any assumptions or projections that were not confirmed by his actual observations and research data. When asked about drainage problems at Larigmoor Farm, he replied, "I cannot speak with authority as to whether it was a problem before the pipeline went through."

•And sometimes there was even a dash of humour. Brownlie had asked, "Did you have any direct evidence yourself? You spoke of the figure of soil, topsoil being created at one foot per ten thousand years. Do you have any direct evidence of that yourself?" To this Quigley replied, "I have only been here for forty-two, but if you measure the topsoil and bear in mind that the land has been developing for approximately ten thousand years, then you can calculate about an inch and a quarter per one thousand years." He went on to refer to indirect evidence of the much smaller thickness of topsoil covering Indian archaeological sites abandoned some four hundred years ago.

So much for what Quigley didn't know and didn't do. When Quigley refused to be drawn into areas beyond his professional competence, he reinforced his positive testimony and gave a splendid example to our other witnesses who were to follow. Despite all the entreaties and temptations, not one of them was lured into the quicksand.

Now let's see what Quigley did during his scientific investigations. First, he carefully examined the site and all factual material we could bring before him, and then drafted a scientific plan. The first physical objective involved the use of Shelby tubes to obtain soil profiles three inches in diameter and to a depth of eighteen to twenty-four inches. The locations were selected following consultation of our drainage map, so that areas disturbed in tile installation would not distort the evidence. Each location from which a profile was taken was then recorded on a chart drawn to scale. Bulk-density evaluations were conducted, both on and off the right-of-way, to compute soil compaction. One of the more expensive field activities involved the sinking of bore holes and the installation of piezometers to track the movement of water in the soil. At long last, the significance and complexities of a stratigraphic system that included an aquifer or aquifers were being examined and evaluated by someone who appreciated their importance. In a word, Quigley found it interesting; he was involved in a site that had many interesting characteristics, stemming from the Ice Age.

Quigley's conclusions were unequivocal and could not be challenged. He concluded that pipeline-installation practices had been detrimental. He referred to the plastic subsoil material left on the surface, which visually had no organic matter whatsoever in the germination zone where seeds are placed in planting operations. He also noted that on the surface were a large number of old boulders that must have come from the glacial till and have now been mixed by process of three construction intervals and contaminated the present topsoil. He pointed out that the construction techniques used had aggravated erosion. "If this had been on a hillside, it would have been extensively eroded as subsoils disappeared." "I know enough about clay mineralogy to speculate that there are other problems that haven't even yet been considered in this testimony."

And finally, a solution? "I don't know what it would cost for a farmer deliberately to go about trying to improve that soil. I suspect that it could be cheaper to bring in four acres [the width of an easement across a 100-acre farm] of topsoil one foot deep. That is just wild speculation, but that is the only way you are going to recreate the soil to the way it was. Preferably the pipeline contractors should properly store the topsoil and replace it, without contamination. It would seem to me this would be a logical, not only logical, but a very profitable thing to do. Encyclopedias list topsoil as a nonrenewable resource. If you take care of your topsoil, it tends to regenerate itself. Topsoil is such a valuable commodity. This is why our land is so fertile."

Throughout Dr. Quigley's testimony there were students in the audience from high schools, colleges, and universities representing many interests and disciplines. More on that later.

As Quigley was winding down, Judge Killeen queried whether his evidence would be applicable to Lunn, who had been hung round our necks like a dead albatross. The court rippled with laughter as it was discovered that Lunn was fast asleep. In dozing off, he had missed the key that Dr. Quigley had given as a solution, a solution that Killeen seized upon and the Supreme Court of Ontario was ultimately to confirm.

[In the fall of 1990, there was a restructuring and the Supreme Court of Ontario became the Ontario Court of Justice (General Division).]

CHAPTER 17

A Question
of Credibility

"Who do I believe?" asked Judge Killeen. There was no response from IPL's battery of lawyers. Geoff Bladon responded, "Just read your notes Your Honour; it's a question
of credibility."

As the days of the trial grew into weeks, Stu
and I ruminated on the possible costs. We
began to conclude that in the event of
failure, even second and third mortgages on our farms would not keep
us out of the poorhouse. It was a spooky feeling and one which our
families bore with commendable good humour.

Towards the end of another long day, after working through the
complexity of Quigley's evidence, Bladon had to change gears. He had to
be knowledgeable about plant ecology and how it interfaced with Quigley's world of soil mechanics. Fortuitously, I had found Dr. Roy
Turkington, who was doing postdoctoral research in plant sciences at
The University of Western Ontario. He was, and is, the only Ph.D. plant
ecologist I know. He has now returned to teach at the University of
British Columbia, following a sabbatical at University College of North
Wales.

Roy, in his early thirties, came on strong in the witness box and
exhibited a tremendous enthusiasm for his work, which was detailed in
his engaging Ulster accent. He described how he first came to Larigmoor
Farm with his graduate students as part of his postdoctoral program in
plant ecology at UWO. He described how "we designed a very simple
survey of the vegetation on and off the right-of-way. Our purpose in
being there [as consultants] was to see what was on this disturbed habitat, irrespective of what caused this disturbance."

While Killeen was ever careful to avoid changes in expression that might betray his thoughts, he had hung on every word of Quigley's. He evidently found Turkington of comparable interest.

When Turkington filed as evidence a typical six-week-old plant of bird's-foot trefoil, Killeen exclaimed, "Would somebody tell me where that name ever came from, bird's-foot trefoil?" To this Bladon replied: "Mr. Lewington can explain that, and it has to do with the shape of the pod, which is in the shape of a bird's foot." This satisfied the judge, who observed that it was "just as simple as that!"

Earlier, Quigley had modestly referred to his work as "limited"; now Turkington described his as "simple." It was, in reality, incredibly complex and unbelievably painstaking. It involved executing a precise plan and identifying every single plant in grids assigned to representative areas in accordance with accepted scientific principles.

Turkington and his assistants were there to identify crop species and weeds. He acknowledged that it was difficult to define a weed.

It is largely a psychological thing. The weed is a different thing to different people. For example, let's take a cabbage, and let's take a dandelion. Let's say they are both growing together in your cabbage patch. Let's say both of them, again, are growing together in the middle of your lawn. In your vegetable patch that cabbage is a vegetable. In your vegetable patch that dandelion is a weed. Take the same two species growing on your lawn; both of them are weeds. By definition, a weed is any plant growing where you don't want it to grow. Compare the dandelion and the cabbage and how you dig them up. You pull a cabbage out of your lawn, and it is not going to grow again. It doesn't tend to proliferate. But you can have weed species that do tend to proliferate where you don't want them. The dandelion is a typical case. You break the root system, and dandelions can regenerate from tiny pieces. Many weed species have a tendency to proliferate both vegetatively and by seeds.

While Turkington had no firsthand knowledge of Larigmoor prior to pipeline construction, we did have material that indicated some of the then-prevailing conditions. Since we were members of the Canadian Seed Growers Association, our registered bird's-foot trefoil seed had been both field- and sample-inspected by Agriculture Canada and found to be very pure and free from weed seeds. As some seeds are very difficult to extract from a bird's-foot trefoil sample, the inference was that the crop had been relatively weed-free prior to pipeline construction.

Turkington explained how desirable species and competing weeds vie for such factors as light, space, soil, fertility, and moisture. He explained the importance of ecological maturity, which could give weed species a head start in disturbed soils because weed species tend to be very competitive.

To illustrate his work, Turkington used charts and slides. Sometimes Killeen was first to identify a species, as when he explained, "Yes, that looks like lady's thumb!" Turkington explained the significance of such terms as *noxious weeds* and how even alsike clover could be regarded as a weed if it was a contaminant in a sample of bird's-foot trefoil. Turkington explained how the weed species could have become a problem on the right-of-way when he said, "If you dug below this courthouse, you would probably find weed species. You might even find species that had been there for two thousand years." The testimony tended to confirm how soil disturbance could produce new weed problems and how the existence of a right-of-way through a farm can create management problems far beyond the right-of-way.

Brownlie could find little to quarrel with in the authenticity of Turkington's presentation; in fact, cross-examination merely provided additional information.

For a change of pace, G. W. Gee then called Ron Richardson on behalf of IPL. Richardson qualified his position by saying it involved an evaluation of the affected farms rather than a full appraisal. This shortcut left Richardson vulnerable to Bladon's cross-examination. But what really damaged Richardson's credibility was his confusion and his failure to rationalise his current testimony with that which had been recorded under oath during the adjournment from the court of Judge McCart.

Gee next called H. H. Todgham, holder of a bachelor's degree from the University of Toronto in civil engineering and a licenced Ontario land surveyor. Gee was quick to produce a document entitled *Report to the National Energy Board re. Peter Lewington and Interprovincial Pipe Line Company, Todgham and Case Limited, November 9, 1973.* This disputed report related primarily to the Lewington Drain. The *Todgham Report* had been circulated despite the fact that my lawyer at the time, John Kerr, had disputed its validity and had been promised a hearing by Energy Minister Donald Macdonald, a hearing that never occurred. The *Todgham Report* concluded that the pipeline had no measureable effect on Larigmoor Farm drainage, and it also included a request for more such work from the NEB! Todgham had noted that "he [Lewington] should be looking elsewhere than to the National Energy Board."

Brownlie had been exuberant at finding Todgham, but that enthusiasm had completely evaporated when Bladon concluded his devastating cross-examination. Bladon had questioned the reliability of the *Todgham Report* and "thirdhand hearsay"; Brownlie promptly qualified this to "secondhand hearsay." Todgham then volunteered that when he wrote his report, he did not anticipate it being presented in court. He added, "I believe even tenthhand information is worth looking into." Belatedly realising what he had blurted out, he left the witness stand in confusion. Killeen watched him go without any indication of what he might be thinking.

Geoff Bladon next called Murray Maltby, a graduate of OAC and a teacher of biology at Westminster Secondary School. His testimony was succinct and lacking in controversy; it related to the assistance he had rendered his friend Stu O'Neil in measuring crop yields and drying seed samples. Drying seed samples to a uniform moisture content is the standard procedure used to make meaningful yield comparisons.

When Geoff began my own examination-in-chief, he had his usual personal touches. The court learned that Larigmoor Farm was named for a beautiful spot in Scotland where Jean and I had spent our honeymoon. I will make only fleeting reference to my examination-in-chief because many of the points have been made in previous chapters.

Geoff elicited from me that for nearly thirty years I had followed twin careers in writing about agriculture and farming, with Jean and I doing most of the physical work. I was questioned on the farm management, the improvements that had been made to the farm, and, of course, the problems of pipelines and agriculture. Among many other things, I was asked to describe the drainage repairs made after the third installation.

> Well, I saw them installed. I have seen a considerable amount of drainage work done in different parts of the world, but I have never seen anything that could be remotely construed to have any comparison with what was done. The area under the Lewington Drain was very unstable. In fact, I think, Dr. Quigley in his testimony said he didn't venture to walk out there. It was a serious, hazardous thing. Our dog would bark in an agitated manner because she felt this was a pretty hazardous thing and had almost disappeared into this churned-up material.

With the introduction of numerous enlarged photographs and reference to my diaries, I could respond with some precision to Bladon's questions. One such response related to the "restorative" initiatives of IPL and its agents in, of all months, January 1976. A huge bulldozer appeared, pulling a hydraulically controlled ripper, a large steel knife that it dragged through the easement, slicing through all of the tile that had been repaired the fall before!

Geoff then logically followed through to the time when in the late spring of 1976, Ken Acton, the IPL drainage contractor, came to repair the drainage system — once again. I mildly observed that "it was at this time the conclusion was reached by Mr. Acton that my concerns about what the ripper had done were effectively borne out."

To this, Brownlie said: "I object to him coming to state to this court Mr. Acton's conclusions." (Brownlie came to regret even more that he called Acton as an expert witness. When Acton was asked whether he did any damage at Larigmoor Farm during his "restorative" initiatives, he replied, "You're damn right!")

I detailed some of the problems of farming in the aftermath of a pipeline — how debris discarded during construction could kill a cow or damage farm equipment; how the shoddy fencing repairs had led to two of our good Simmental heifers being bred by a neighbour's scrub bull. Adding up the time spent in giving evidence and being cross-examined by Brownlie, I found that I had spent nine hours in the witness box. When I queried Geoff why he had not come to my defense during many of Brownlie's rapier attacks, he replied, "I didn't think you needed any help."

Jim O'Toole, it may be recalled from the Preface, had sought his own subpoena so that he might appear. As head of the Agronomy Department at Centralia College of Agricultural Technology and a nationally recognised expert in the use and limitations of herbicides, he was a crucial witness. We were once again grateful to Judge Killeen for admitting our entire roster of expert witnesses. When Brownlie had complained that the hearing was taking too long and that a soil expert was a soil expert, the judge had clearly understood that there were many entirely different disciplines involved under the umbrella of soils. Killeen evidently understood that many disciplines had to interface before he could determine the facts.

While Jim provided some additional evidence, his prime function was to augment and complement all of the testimony that had gone before. He could confirm and elaborate the practical farming problems and opportunities referred to by Stu and myself. He provided a very effective link between Drs. Quigley and Turkington, and he did it all within the confines of his own area of expertise.

Bladon next called Karl Stumpf, one of our neighbours, who was a member of the Middlesex Farm Management Association, which had produced such an effective brief before the NEB back in 1967. Karl had come from Germany as a displaced person and had built up one of the most successful farming operations in the province before expanding into a farm-supply and elevator business. Having for years purchased some of Stu's crops, he was able to state that "the O'Neils are in the top ten percent of farmers." Karl provided some effective mortar to hold together the edifice Bladon was building. Stumpf was listened to by the court because of his authority and reputation. In addition to being appointed to the influential Ontario Corn Committee, which evaluates new hybrids for possible licencing, he had fulfilled speaking engagements such as that before the World Congress of Agricultural Economics in 1975.

At Bob Quigley's suggestion, Geoff called Dr. James E. Zajic. The ever-meticulous Bob had felt that some issues should come before the court that were beyond his own expertise. These related to the importance of soil microbes, and Zajic had a Ph.D. in microbiology from the University of Wisconsin. Indeed, this area is so relevant that it has been allocated a subsequent chapter, "Soil Isn't Just Dirt."

It was now Monday, December 20, 1976. I realised that despite the reference to topsoil by both Quigley and O'Toole, Judge Killeen had no good costings. I had driven the previous Friday evening to see Harry Loyens, founder and secretary-treasurer of Walloy Excavating Limited at Elginfield. It is illegal in many municipalities to sell topsoil, except that which is stripped during such construction as the building of a new street. The Walloy business interests spanned gravel, ready-mix concrete, and subdivisions, consequently the availability of topsoil. From our point of view, Harry made a perfect witness. He knew his name, his business affiliation, and the price of topsoil, delivered and spread. End of message. Killeen now had a figure upon which to make his award if he subsequently cared to do so. It worked out to $8,600 per acre to replace topsoil on an easement.

For their final expert witness, Gee introduced IPL's big gun, Dr. Angus F. MacKenzie, who qualified as an expert in agronomy, being chairman of the department of Renewable Resources at Macdonald College at Ste. Anne-de-Bellevue, Quebec. Macdonald College is affiliated with McGill University in nearby Montreal and enjoys an excellent reputation as a teaching and research institution, a leader in many areas of animal science, in soil compaction studies, and in the development of drainage techniques in agriculture. MacKenzie had been retained by Interprovincial to prepare a program in concert with Bob Dunsmore, IPL's right-of-way chief, to "restore the productivity of agricultural land on the right-of-way." Also involved was Earl Stobart, of Bechtel. MacKenzie had as his assistant his former student, S. Alex Ramsay, who is now IPL's right-of-way chief.

My first reservations about MacKenzie and Ramsay had appeared the preceding fall. They wanted to take soil samples but were unable to explain what they wanted them for. In this regard they differed dramatically from our own consultants, such as Bob Quigley who had a detailed research project that anyone could examine. Also, MacKenzie came late on the scene. He could not develop the before-and-after data essential to his mandate.

My reservations about MacKenzie were justified early in his direct examination by Gee. He filed as evidence a form that he said had come from the Ontario Soil Testing Laboratory at Guelph, to which he had sent the Larigmoor Farm soil samples. The alert Jim O'Toole noted that the form, as handed to the judge, was the wrong shape. When Geoff was subsequently able to find out why the form was the wrong shape, MacKenzie had to admit that he had photocopied only part of the soil report, thereby omitting data essential to its completeness and accuracy.

When MacKenzie introduced evidence from Saskatchewan and referred to chernozem soils, the significance escaped everyone in the court except Quigley and O'Toole. They promptly passed notes to Bladon that this would bear looking into. By the next day, they had armed Geoff with such publications as *Vegetation of Soils and World Picture,* by Ayer, and *Soil Conditions and Plant Growth,* by Russell. The latter book included the following definition: "The chernozems, or black earth, to give the English translation of the Russian word, are so-called because of their black colour. This black layer is one metre in depth, although the colour lightens with depth."

It transpired after pages of cross-examination that the pipeline trench in Saskatchewan was much smaller than that through Ontario. The diameter of the pipe was not given but was referred to as "small," the overall inference being that the pipeline installation had been carried out in topsoil. If so, the mere aeration of the topsoil could have accounted for any increase in productivity. It was not your average pipeline. It was one of those rare instances when research had been funded by a pipeline company. But it was hard to comprehend reference to pipeline-agricultural research done with a trench eighteen inches wide and thirty-six inches deep, especially if the topsoil was thirty-nine inches in depth!

It was not explained why MacKenzie strayed into pipeline work on the Prairies and refrained from any reference to the significant and relevant work in soil compaction and drainage being done by his own colleagues at Macdonald College. Early in MacKenzie's testimony, Bladon had questioned the introduction of evidence that was not under

MacKenzie's supervision. Judge Killeen had specifically said, "I will allow it in."

All in all, it was not an edifying sight to see a Ph.D. and university department head conduct himself under oath in such a manner. He had left himself vulnerable to some damaging exchanges such as Bladon's question: "Have I got the complete document here this time?" To this, MacKenzie responded: "Yes, as far as I am aware, yes."

Logically, Geoff might have used Norman Pearson in his capacity as a planner early in the proceedings. But Norman was involved in an Ontario Municipal Board hearing in Barrie at the start of the hearing and was then struck down with the flu. On the last day before Judge Killeen, Norman manfully struggled from his sickbed to keep his commitment. Even a sick Norman Pearson is an impressive wind-up man on anybody's team. It took some time for Geoff Bladon to introduce the versatile Pearson, whose credits included everything from national and international planning affiliations to writing a film script on the Great Lakes. But before he could utter a word in evidence, Brownlie rose to object, and the judge, anticipating the objection, ruled that the Railway Act notwithstanding, he would hear the witness.

Bladon was content merely to bring to the court's attention the thrust of the *Pearson Report,* the report that had apparently been gathering dust at the NEB and IPL. The report had listed not only the problems but also opportunities for avoiding them. Recalled Pearson:

> The material now on the right-of-way is a much less useful material, and while it might be useful for ceramics, it is not Class One or Two soil. . . . Well, what I found on the Lewington property reminded me of some of the bad practices which were originally carried out historically in Britain, which were replaced by a much more advanced method, where in fact there was much greater care taken to remove the topsoil. They sort it very carefully, to remove the subsoil and then deal with the problem of pipeline displacement by either bringing in new topsoil, if there was a loss, or making sure that the soil was put back in a sensible and proper order with the topsoil at the top, as it should be, and with, of course, drainage and fissures dealt with over a rehabilitation period. . . . My finding is, despite the change in practice, that the end result appears to be substantially the same [in 1976] as that which I examined in 1967, with the difference that it is both wider and more extensive, and there appears to be a very considerable mixing of materials to produce a very similar result. In my opinion as a planner and geographer, it's perpetual.

Brownlie moved quickly to cross-examine, having discerned a chink in Norman's armour. Was this guy qualified to comment on the ceramic qualities of soils? Responded Norman: "Yes, I have worked in coalfield areas and other areas where fire clay and various similar materials are mined."

Norman was our closing act, and Brownlie brought the curtain down in fine style. His cross-examination was much longer than Bladon's examination-in-chief. Every time Brownlie asked one of his repetitive questions, more damaging testimony went into the transcript. Topsoil should be replaced in an area larger than the easement and temporary working rights. The damage is more extensive.

> The opportunity which I indicated in my report on page twenty-nine has been lost. . . . It seems to me fairly obvious that if you trench for a large pipeline and you don't have the kinds of measures which I am suggesting, you are liable to dig up parent material or lower-horizon material and mix it, and I think that is what occurred. . . . I'd move the topsoil carefully and segregate it, and move that before I touched the ceramic material. Then I would go in and deal with the ceramic and other material, then rehabilitate from the topsoil and try to remove the displaced material. . . . For the drainage condition I'd need engineering advice. . . . All I can say is, looking at the end result, something sad and drastic happened. . . . If you take a pipeline across municipal drains at the point where the headers are joining, you will be risking a very serious drainage condition. . . . I am saying as a planner I would never recommend anybody to put pipelines across that kind of location.

At one stage, the stuck-phonograph-needle syndrome sparked Killeen to say, "Mr. Brownlie, he's said that three or four times." But Brownlie would not be dissuaded and gave Norman the opportunity to elaborate even further: "it [the right-of-way] was in terrible condition. . . . It could be a relatively perpetual condition, . . . as I described, a very considerable evidence of erosion."

And then finally Brownlie threw in the towel. "All right, I won't pursue it any longer." Next he tried to breathe life into the *Todgham Report,* only to find that Pearson was not "a drainage expert, sir, I can't comment."

Despite the Railway Act, Judge Killeen had heard no fewer than nine witnesses on behalf of Lewington and O'Neil. None had been found wanting, and none had strayed beyond his area of expertise. Arthur Pattillo would have wondered what the law was coming to!

It was now the eve of Christmas Eve 1976, the day allocated by Killeen to hear the argument of counsel. The spirit of Christmas was already in the air, for when I stepped into the elevator at the courthouse,

I was greeted by a prominent local lawyer with, "Good Morning, Your Honour!"

Brownlie, Gee, and Bladon picked their way through the testimony in search of gold nuggets and rattled the bones of old legal cases for some grist for a particular mill. Brownlie, in a rare moment of generosity, said, "I concede that Lewington and O'Neil are doing this out of deeply held conviction, but they are turning it into a cause célèbre. Right or wrong, a pipeline company can go into a property and turn it into a wasteland."

And of course it had been that sort of concern that had got Bladon so involved in not just winning a case but winning a war. He told Killeen, "Your decision may well have far-reaching effects. Your judgment, based on the evidence, will either be a landmark decision to protect our environment, or it will be regarded as an expression of approval for the buccaneering practices of pipeline construction."

Bladon then alerted the judge to the evidence that had shown that our strong allegations had not been refuted by IPL personnel. Bladon then quoted Conan Doyle's famous fictional character, who was asked by the police inspector what could be curious about a dog not barking in the night. To this, Sherlock Holmes replied: "The dog was not heard from in the night. . . . That is the curious thing." Continued Bladon: "It is curious indeed that we have heard nothing from the people who have built three pipelines across these properties."

Judge Killeen complimented all counsel for their very careful presentations and for the excellence of their arguments. "I promise that I will be working on the judgment over the holidays and will have a decision for you by January 14, 1977."

But what was a mere wait of three weeks when the battle had lasted into a third decade?

CHAPTER 18

Of a
Prescient
Character

His [Norman Pearson's] report, if followed, would have
eliminated, in my view, most of those issues now before
me.

— JUDGE GORDON KILLEEN

The crescendo of anticipation built to a climax by January 14, 1977, but it turned out to be just another day. As the ensuing months went by without any decision from Judge Killeen, there was no slackening in my own search for information. We could not anticipate what the judge might decide and had to be prepared for any eventuality. One scenario could have been a judgment against us and then perhaps our appeal.

During 1976 there were some encouraging reports published in the *Canadian Bar Review*. "Many environmental lawsuits do require the services of more than one expert witness. They contain a range of technical issues much broader than the range of competence of any one expert." Another crucial issue was that of credibility, and this had been addressed by reference to "the use by the expert of dubious testing equipment or procedures."

In the spring of 1974, I had checked with the Soil Research Institute of Agriculture Canada in Ottawa. I specifically asked the director, Dr. J. S. Clark, about "any work of your institute which relates to the structure of soils and how they influence the need for, and success of, open ditch and tile drainage systems." I was directed to an Ontario government publication because "we have no additional information to send you."

In the aftermath of the third IPL construction and the making of the wasteland, I telephoned Dr. Clark to learn whether he had any new and relevant information. He could point to very meagre pickings. Apparently to justify the role of his institute, he let slip that they had funded an outside researcher to explore agricultural-pipeline problems. Even this belated initiative began when half of the construction was completed; disturbingly, the initiative had come from the NEB and not from Agriculture Canada.

Who could that researcher possibly be? We already knew that someone must be at work because of a casual comment of Dr. Angus MacKenzie when asked if he knew of any other pipeline-agricultural work apart from the instances he had cited on the Prairies. He had replied, "I think that there is a girl doing some work somewhere." After considerable digging, I was able to establish that the "girl" was none other than MacKenzie's Ph.D. student!

And that opened up a whole new can of worms, one that involved Eugene Whelan as minister, Agriculture Canada. I had had a long and convoluted association with Gene Whelan, which can be best described as one involving love-hate. When he entered the federal cabinet as minister of agriculture in 1972, I wrote to congratulate him, to thank him for his past involvement in drainage-pipeline disputes, and to alert him to outstanding issues. He replied, "The National Energy Board should become more responsive to the public. . . . I very much appreciate hearing from you on these matters and hope that you continue to let me know your views."

And then Gene blew it. On learning that I intended to oppose the IPL application in the May 1974 NEB hearing, Whelan wrote, "There was no need to generate your own representation. . . . I am very sorry that you've gone ahead and expended your finances to travel to Ottawa to attempt to develop an agricultural policy in relation to pipelines and initiate research. Perhaps a bit of patience would have spared you the unnecessary expense." What irony! The details of that hearing are recorded in Chapter 14, and there was of course no discernible involvement of Agriculture Canada. In retrospect, what makes Whelan's position even more untenable is the fact that the hearing turned out to be the fulcrum; with the acceptance of the Pearson and Quigley reports, we began the long route out of the valley of despair.

Throughout much of 1975, Whelan's position was somewhat ambivalent and included letters to me that stated, "The public owes people like you, the Ontario Federation of Agriculture, and other farm groups a lot for exposing the problems and damage that the laying of pipelines can cause. You do have my support in your campaign to stand up for your property rights and your rights as an individual. . . . Farmers like yourself must be protected from any possible damage that a pipeline could cause."

An intriguing vignette occurred when Whelan and I were both on the program and addressed a seminar sponsored by the Ontario Society of Farm Managers and Rural Appraisers. Whelan had been eyeing me in the audience as he made his own presentation. He then made a departure from his speech, which had nothing to do with pipelines. He said, "I want to tell you that Peter Lewington is one hundred percent right." He then resumed his speech without any elaboration, thereby mystifying most of his audience.

Having established that MacKenzie was concurrently being paid directly by Interprovincial-Bechtel and indirectly by Agriculture Canada, the next step was to establish MacKenzie's terms of reference and funding agreements made with Agriculture Canada. The funding of MacKenzie's students with taxpayers' money should have been readily available public information.

The exchange of letters with Whelan became more acrimonious as I noted, "I am deeply shocked that you confirm and condone and fund the pipeline consultant whose testimony against farmers is still before the courts." Whelan replied that "I can assure you that Agriculture Canada has not provided any funds to the chief pipeline witness against farmers."

A logical source of definitive information would surely be Dr. E. J. Leroux, the guru and assistant deputy minister of Agriculture Canada's research branch in Ottawa. My telephone notes of November 1977 record that I requested the terms of reference and any reports completed by MacKenzie under Agriculture Canada funding. The spokesperson in Leroux's office responded, "May I ask who is calling? He is going to be tied up all day." My inquiry about when he might be untied drew the information that he had "an awful lot of meetings" ahead. I never heard from Leroux but could understand his departmental nickname of "the Silver Fox."

The response from the Soil Research Institute continued to be negative. None of this sat very well with Al Tomlin. He was disturbed for the overall integrity of Agriculture Canada in which he has justifiable pride. He received the endorsement of his director at the London Research Centre to pursue the search for the MacKenzie funding information. Dr. Tomlin was advised by Dr. Al MacLean of the Soil Research Institute that the "public" information must remain secret because "we don't want it to get into the wrong hands."

I tried another tack. The then secretary of state, John Roberts, advised that the federal government intended setting up a new information agency to make sure that the public got the good news about the government. I thought that the good news might include the still covert MacKenzie information, but once again I was proven wrong.

I was to fare much better with Gaetan Lussier, then Whelan's deputy minister, having entered the civil service following a distinguished career in the fertilizer industry. My first approach to Lussier was made on November 13, 1977, and culminated in his letter of February 27, 1980, stating that "I have asked the Director, Land Resource Research Centre to forward a copy of MacKenzie's last report on the pipeline study." The institute now had a new title, but it still hadn't done much for farmers such as Stu and myself, caught in pipeline conflicts.

Yet another concurrent effort to get the information was made through John Wise. Wise was then a backbencher in the House of Commons. He was promoted to agriculture critic and has twice succeeded Whelan as minister. The file involving Wise is a fat and productive one. It includes telephone notes, our exchange of letters, and letters involving Stu O'Neil and Gene Whelan. With all of the many avenues to the MacKenzie data closed to us, Wise publicized the issue on the floor of the House of Commons on October 27, 1977. The *Commons Debates* records:

> Time does not permit me to deal tonight with such a problem as the explosive situation that exists in the dairy industry, or the ridiculous granting of precious and shamefully inadequate research funds to a former employee and consultant for The Interprovincial Pipe Line Company to do a study on the "effect of pipeline construction on the productivity of soil in Western Quebec and Eastern Ontario." Although such a study is necessary and we would support it without question, this is a scandalous appointment at a cost of nearly forty thousand dollars. How can one possibly accept the credibility of the results when the engineer who was hired would testify in court and supplied information to the courts which has been used against farmers? It is a clear conflict of interest and another prime example of bad judgment and poor judgment on behalf of the government. Peter Lewington, an Ilderton farmer and writer, sums it up accurately by saying, "It's like letting the fox mind the chicken coop."

Finally Geoff Bladon was able to write to me on February 14, 1978, that he now had in his possession all of the documents which we had been seeking for so long. At my insistence, and against his better judgment, Geoff advised Judge Killeen and Interprovincial that "I have been instructed to bring an application for leave to reopen the applicant's case."

"The girl who was doing some work somewhere" turned out to be Denise Neilsen; her professor was none other than Dr. MacKenzie, and their joint reports were developed "in response to questions raised concerning the effects of the Sarnia-Montreal pipeline on agriculture production." By working both sides of the street, MacKenzie had created a cloud over any research done by his students on the impact of IPL's third pipeline; that cloud had grown to cumulonimbus proportions by the protracted, and eventually futile, attempts to keep the federal funding secret. The academic and intellectual hazards were most evident by omissions. The Neilsen-MacKenzie reports could make no bibliographic references to the most relevant research, namely, that by people on our team, including Drs. Quigley and Pearson. Omissions caused concern in various reports and professional publications, which quoted MacKenzie and his students without flagging attention to MacKenzie's concurrent roles on behalf of IPL and the government of Canada.

Perry Mason might have viewed favourably our sustained efforts in assembling all the relevant documentation, but more important, what would Judge Gordon Killeen think? It was two years to the day since we had concluded our case before him. It was now December 22, 1978, and in those two years we had had no indication of how the judge was getting along in sifting all of the evidence before him. How would he react to still more testimony?

The judge was restrained in his enthusiasm at seeing us once again and asked somewhat testily, "What's this all about?" To this, Geoff Bladon responded: "More sophisticated evidence is now available, which was not available during the original trial." Geoff then made reference to *An Environmental Study of the Interprovincial Pipe Line Limited Sarnia-Montreal Extension,* dated October 1978 and published by the Ontario Ministry of the Environment. Geoff read some excerpts from the report, including:

> On a number of occasions, the excavating or trenching crew opened an area well in advance of the welding and pipe-laying crew. The infiltration of ground water that resulted over a period of time was sufficient to fill the trench with water and to initiate the collapsing of banks. . . . The overlap of topsoil and subsoil piles occurred frequently. . . . Heavy farm equipment experienced difficulty in crossing the construction ROW [right-of-way] on occasion, . . . a continual use of vehicles on wet right-of-way causing mix-

ing of the subsoils, with potential for changing the soil structure. Disturbance resulted especially from vehicles, such as pipe-stringing trucks. . . . It has become clear from these investigations that to avoid the type of problems identified in this report, the National Energy Board and pipeline companies must, in future applications, consider changes to present policy, procedure and practice.

Bladon then introduced the MacKenzie reports, which had been acquired by us with such difficulty. "The point is," said Bladon, "if you compare the evidence MacKenzie gave at the trial and the research referred to in these reports, you will find a number of inconsistencies. I would like to cross-examine him again."

Geoff had anticipated that the application to reopen the case would take half a day, but Judge Killeen brought it to a swift conclusion, and I dashed out to telephone the news to Jean, who had stayed home to look after the cattle. "What would you like first, the good news or the bad news?" I asked. Replied Jean, "I'll take the bad news." "The bad news is that Judge Killeen refused to reopen the case, and we have been assessed costs," I said. Jean wondered, given that scenario, how there could be any silver lining, but there was. The judge had said, "I made it clear at the outset that I had already completed my decision and written the judgment. The interest of justice does not indicate that I should reopen this case."

While Judge Killeen had been scrupulously careful not to indicate prematurely what his written judgment might contain, I concluded that there was good news to share with Jean. If the judge was not going to be influenced by the report of the Ontario Ministry of the Environment, which substantiated the evidence we had placed before him, and if we were to be denied the opportunity to get MacKenzie back on the stand, there could be only one logical explanation: the verdict had to be in our favour.

There was to be one more week of suspense before Judge Killeen finally issued his forty-page judgment. Killeen first picked his way through the legal niceties of the National Energy Board Act and the Railway Act. It will be recalled that two years earlier, when the judge asked whom he should believe, Geoff Bladon had responded to the effect that the judge would find the answer if he merely read his notes. It now became apparent that he had read his notes and had formed definite conclusions. The notes, and the numerous illustrations filed as exhibits, had combined to give the judge a clear impression of what had happened to our farms. He succinctly summarized Dr. Bob Quigley's findings and noted that "the regeneration of topsoil takes place at the historical snail's pace of about one inch every 1,000 years. In other words, the topsoil has been permanently disarranged and damaged." He then perceptively linked the evidence of our other consultants until he came to Norman Pearson, who "is a town and country planning expert. . . . His report (filed before me as exhibit 90) is, considered in retrospect, of a prescient character in that it zeroed in on all of the major issues put before me and proposed solutions or recommendations which if followed, would have eliminated, in my view, most of those issues now before me."

IPL's witnesses had also left deep impressions with the judge, though not along the lines John Brownlie might have liked. Recalled Judge Killeen, "Exhibits 19 and 20 (taken on April 15 and 22 respectively) show the Acton forces at work on tile correction and highlight the scope of this work and its undoubted adverse effect on soil's integrity." The confused testimony of Richardson and Todgham was not even rated as worthy of mention.

And then he came to IPL's big gun.

> I must confess that I found Dr. MacKenzie's approach to the problems at the Lewington and O'Neil farms, and his own findings thereon, somewhat anomalous and, more especially, unpersuasive. . . . I found the MacKenzie restoration proposal to be a far too simplistic approach to the kind of damage which has been wreaked upon the claimants' lands. . . . It is very clear to me that the restoration program design laid out in the report—and reflected in his recommendations before me—was very much of an experimental and tentative character. In cross-examination, he admitted the meaningful differences in soil and installation conditions which obtained in respect to the Manitoba and Saskatchewan test situation, making it an uncertain business to extrapolate from these results to the present case situation and, beyond that, acknowledged that his so-called "restoration program" was aimed at restoring productivity simpliciter, without real consideration of the interplay of complex factors arising from the incontrovertible evidence of permanent damage to the soil structures. In fact, during cross-examination, he further acknowledged that his manure and fertilizer program was a sort of suggested program on a wait and see basis, rather than a pre-emptive solution leading to certain results. I must say, in this context, that I found it hard to understand his antipathy to a topsoil replacement program. . . . I conclude, on the evidence, he was driven away from this approach by considerations of cost rather than efficacy.

Judge Killeen continued to exhibit a clear understanding of the significance of our presentations before the NEB.

> In the light of the serious and thoughtful complaints from Lewington and O'Neil and others like them about the harmful effects of pipeline construc-

tion from at least 1974, when the "Convenience and Necessity" hearings were held before the Board, I find it somewhat astonishing, to say the least, that Interprovincial took no steps to retain a consultant of Dr. MacKenzie's calibre until it was virtually too late to do anything to alleviate the concerns raised. . . . The date of Dr. MacKenzie's report to Interprovincial — May, 1976 — is a sad but clear reflection of Interprovincial's determination to take an approach of least resistance, involving lowest cost — and showing some considerable insensitivity to affected farmers — in the planning and progress of its work on this most recent pipeline installation.

Judge Killeen then explored the complexities and implications inherent in the legal precedents cited. And finally, compensation and damages. Once again, it became apparent that the judge had been listening intently to all the evidence relating to crop and livestock losses. These were duly itemized. But the big item was acceptance of topsoil replacement at $8,600 per acre. And better yet, Judge Killeen awarded costs for the hearings that stretched back to those before his colleague Judge McCart.

We had won! More importantly, it was a victory for all agriculture and the environment. Judge Killeen had assiduously touched every salient point. Hopefully, Geoff's prediction that Killeen would not err in law would be borne out. However, we were resigned to the prospect that Interprovincial would appeal. We faced yet another hiatus, yet another long and anxious wait.

But that did not stop us savouring the Killeen judgment and the ripples that flowed from it. One of Stu's neighbours, Ian Goudy, had been encountering similar problems when Union Gas laid its third pipeline through his farm. Goudy advised the Union Gas construction foreman that he should be aware of the Killeen judgment. The foreman walked over to his pickup truck and returned with a copy of the Killeen judgment and the comment "I carry it with me all the time."

The media had a field day with the judgment. That and other developments will be explored in the next chapter, on the media.

Farm and Country, probably Ontario's best-read farm publication, contributed to stimulating students to do their own research and projects. This was the sweetest touch of all. Perceptive young people had not seen it all as just a narrow conflict between a pipeline company and a couple of stubborn farm families. It gave them cause to look objectively at the whole fabric of society and the roles that they might play.

A new generation and our own could take solid comfort in Killeen's conclusion: "During the closing arguments, counsel for Interprovincial accused Lewington and O'Neil of trying to make a 'cause célèbre' out of this case, implying that their common allegations were either quixotic, or grossly inflated, or both. In what I have already said, and what I will say hereafter, I wish to make it clear that I have found the major thrust of the claimants' positions to have been made out overwhelmingly on the evidence."

CHAPTER 19

The Media

Has any reader ever found perfect accuracy in the newspaper account of any event of which he himself had inside knowledge?

—EDWARD VERRAL LUCAS

An entire chapter is devoted to the media because it was an integral part of the saga of how democracy came to the oil patch. Just like many of the other parts that interface to make the whole, a look at the media spans many of the foibles and failings of human nature. *Media* has been used in the broadest sense. Media, of course, include newspapers, periodicals, trade publications, radio, and TV. I have also included references to some company publications and reports published by the Canadian and the Ontario governments. It is this latter dimension that embraces some disturbing aspects of the integrity of the news that is promulgated. "News" stories in the more traditional media can frequently be traced to less than objective sources. No one would have appreciated such concerns better than George Orwell, author of *1984,* who clearly anticipated how news could be molded and manipulated.

I hasten to add that there is also a positive side. Gary May, later *London Free Press* bureau chief in Ottawa, was working in the Sarnia bureau when he covered the 1975 hearings described in Chapter 2. It is not easy for a reporter, working to a tight deadline, to sift from the forest of words what is really significant. I promptly wrote to him, "I would like you to know how much the farmers appreciated your lucid and concise reports. . . . Congratulations for a job well done under difficult circumstances." And to Clark Davey, managing editor of the *Globe and Mail:* "I much appreciate the thoroughness of the *Globe and Mail* investigating the problems relating to pipelines and agriculture." Clair Balfour's column in the Southam chain, which then included the *Financial Times,* precipitated my response that "my friends in sundry places from Montreal to Calgary have been sending me clippings which testify to your industry. It is most encouraging to see the tremendous interest this time around [1974]." Nor were the official court reporters overlooked. I wrote to owner Bob Young that "your colleague Doug Baker showed exemplary good humour and a very sound constitution in recording the marathon NEB hearing in Sarnia yesterday [September 4, 1975]."

To the credit of the *Globe and Mail,* Rudy Platiel reported on IPL's initiatives and farmers' reactions not only in western Ontario but also as the line snaked eastward to Montreal; such continuity is rare in the media. Platiel has a good nose for news and zeroed in on such significant revelations as "Oil could be flowing in pipeline before spill plans filed, NEB told."

So much for the bouquets. Now for some brickbats. The *London Free Press* owners have a virtual monopoly with the only daily newspaper in the city, the only TV station, and two of the most well-established radio stations. A laudatory front-page illustrated feature even used IPL's own brochure title, "On to Montreal." With its established base in London, the county seat and location of the courts of Judges McCart and Killeen, the *London Free Press* had a unique opportunity to provide accurate and comprehensive coverage. Stu and I feared what was to come when we sat in the court of Judge Killeen and overheard the *Free Press* reporter ask Irwin Lunn, who was sitting behind us, "Let me know if anything juicy happens." The search for something "juicy" overshadowed any awareness or understanding of what was happening. There was no reference to the unique features of the trial, the challenges to archaic legislation, or the interlocking roles of the expert witnesses. There were errors of fact. Jim O'Toole didn't rate a mention, but Peter O'Toole (better known for his movies) was quoted.

Channel 10, the TV station associated with the *London Free Press,* effectively covered major developments with reporter John MacDonald providing the continuity. News director Jack Burghard, subsequently a Liberal M.P. in London West and now deputy mayor of London, eloquently editorialized that the trial before Judge Killeen underscored the need for individuals to stand up to bureaucracy when they felt strongly enough about an issue. A curious lapse at Channel 10 was when Ross Daily explored the issues in his program "This Business of Farming." He interviewed people who had no connection with the trial while ignoring everybody who had been involved! When apprised by farmer Ian Goudy of this unprofessional lapse, Daily invited Stu O'Neil and myself to rectify the situation. We made reference to the judgment of Killeen during Daily's half-hour television program. Daily subsequently wrote with great enthusiasm of the extraordinary demand for copies, which the station had mailed to viewers at $10 each.

The Canadian Broadcasting Corporation's TV ombudsman, Robert Cooper, examined expropriation in 1974. Cooper, a lawyer who had turned to journalism, made it easy for viewers across Canada to relate to complex issues. The program's quarterback, Virginia Nelson, exemplified the thoroughness of the research that made the program so effective. She wrote, "We received a very good review in the Ottawa Citizen and in addition the Board of Transport, the Law Reform Commission and the Canadian Environmental Law Association have requested copies of the program. . . . Let's hope it will help in some way to encourage changes in legislation."

We are fortunate in Canada to have a national and an international radio service. Over the years, the CBC Radio farm specialists George Atkins, Glen Powell, Ron Neily, George Price, and Jim Caldwell (later, Progressive Conservative M.P. from the Windsor area) all explored the issues involving energy and agriculture. Other CBC Radio programs such as "Cross Canada Check-up" and "As It Happens" effectively examined everything from expropriation to the public hearing system as it relates to utilities and farmers.

I very rarely write a letter to the editor, but when the *Toronto Star* published a glowing feature entitled "An Historic Change in Our Life with Oil," based exclusively on an interview with David Waldon, IPL president, I wrote to say, "In view of the extensive documentation which was available to The Toronto Star it is singularly unfortunate that in 1976 you should publish a feature which ignores the sources which a more prudent journalist would have consulted."

The feature, written by business editor Jack McArthur, had been published on January 29, and by March 4 I had written a third registered/acknowledgement and receipt letter as the *Star* continued to refuse to publish my rebuttal and claimed that the original letter had been lost. Three months after publication of the Waldon interview, the *Star* was still digging in its heels. It reluctantly agreed to publish my letter, which had been censored to exclude any reference to Waldon. Direct quotes had been changed. The *Star* refused to provide any explanation of the elapsed time.

I declined to allow publication of such an emasculated letter and took the *Star* before the Ontario Press Council. Finally, on February 4, 1977, I appeared before the council in Toronto and found my adversary was Bordon Spears. Spears was variously editor of the *Financial Post, Maclean's* magazine, managing editor of the *Toronto Star,* member of the Kent Commission on the Media, university lecturer, and then the *Toronto Star*'s ombudsman.

I pointed out to the council that in our complex society, it is becoming ever more difficult for an individual to be a good citizen. The sustained procrastination of the *Toronto Star* and the paucity of complaints that reach the council served to underscore such a viewpoint.

Finally, on March 14, 1977, the front page of the *Toronto Star* featured an item bearing the headline "Star 'negligent' in handling of letter, Press Council says." Every member newspaper of the Ontario Press Council carried the decision in full under various headlines. "Complaint against Toronto Star upheld," said the *Kitchener-Waterloo Record,* while the *Hamilton Spectator* noted, "Council upholds farmer's charge." While victory was sweet, it was like everything else involved in making democracy work. It was a victory achieved at considerable cost in time and effort.

There were many instances of inaccuracies in newspaper reports and editorial comment that were followed up, but not pursued, all the way to the Press Council. John Walker Elliott took up the cudgels with the *Toronto Star.* An editorial had been sparked by Gene Whelan's suggestion that the federal government should pay for legal action by southern Ontario farmers against the building of the Sarnia-Montreal pipeline. The *Star,* in its February 21, 1974, editorial, had stated that "property rights in the settled parts of Canada are clearly established and generally well enough protected in expropriation proceedings. . . . We can be reasonably confident that the farmers whose land is crossed by the new pipeline will be fairly compensated." Said Elliott: "You may be confident, but the farmers are not! They have too many sad experiences."

Then, in May 1976, the Canadian Press reported at length on the speech given by Donald Ross, project manager for the new IPL pipeline, at the Canadian Pipeline Association meeting. A little digging confirmed that there was no such organization—there is a Pipe Line Contractors Association of Canada. Ross, allegedly, dwelt at length on the aesthetically pleasing aftermath of oil spills; there was no reference to igniting oil spills or the evidence before the NEB that there was no oil-spill policy in place.

Stu O'Neil was outraged by a column in the *Globe and Mail* by Kenneth McDonald, described as a Toronto writer. Stu's rebuttal included the following: "1. Mr. McDonald states 'everyone benefits.' Fact: IPL legal counsel stated on December 23, 1976, that legislation permits his client to turn Class I farmland into a wasteland. 2. Mr. McDonald asked, 'Are they unaware of the land reclamation practices followed by pipeline companies?' Fact: Mr. Waldon admitted that the applicant had no contingency plan for mitigation of damage to farmland."

In February 1975, I came to the defence of the *Globe and Mail* when an editorial had been criticized by Marshall Crowe, then chairman of the NEB. Crowe charged a lack of understanding and pointed to the prompt remedial action that he claimed followed oil spills. My published rebuttal, together with a picture of the smouldering ruins of John Walker Elliott's white ash grove was carried with the title "Scorched Earth Policy"; there was no reaction from Crowe.

When I appeared before the NEB in Ottawa on May 17, 1974, I referred to a CP (Canadian Press) story from Ottawa that included many of the more spurious aspects of the media. For example:

•"Federal experts indicated Wednesday that there is little foundation to charges that a Sarnia-to-Montreal oil pipeline would damage Southern Ontario farmland." Neither the "experts" nor their expertise were identified.

•"One National Energy Board engineer who has been associated with pipeline work on the Prairies and throughout Ontario said he had, 'Never seen harmful effects from pipelining' on cultivated land. On the contrary, crops appeared to grow better over a filled in pipeline ditch." No documentation was offered in support of this claim. Perhaps it traced to the sort of "research" referred to earlier, funded by a pipeline company and carried out exclusively in unusually deep topsoil in which aeration could have been a factor in any crop improvement.

•"Engineer A. V. Deugue of the NEB said, 'Pipeline construction produced no farming difficulties.' " In view of the documentation available in the NEB files and library, such a statement was irresponsible; it could, however, have influenced readers not in possession of the facts.

•And with reference to the land area affected by the then-proposed Sarnia-Montreal pipeline, the story carried this statement: "Somebody's obviously grinding a hatchet for some other reason," said a federal pipeline specialist. Once again, neither the specialist nor his speciality were identified. The impugning of the motives of opponents to the way the pipeline was to be installed, in the complete absence of any supporting evidence, is the sort of journalism that often brings the media into disrepute.

Bechtel is the common denominator in the following diverse projects: a billion-dollar hydroelectric project in Newfoundland, an iron-slurry pipeline in Tasmania, a pipeline linking European nations, a mass-transit system in Washington, D.C., and IPL's pipeline to Montreal. The Bechtel Corporation was founded at the end of the nineteenth century by Warren Bechtel. He was, appropriately, a builder of railroads. With its world headquarters in San Francisco, Bechtel has grown to become the largest engineering, consulting, and construction company in the world. Less is known about Bechtel than about companies of comparable size because it is privately owned. Such company alumni as George Shultz, regarded as number-two man in President Reagan's cabinet, are better known.

With the big bucks generated by its projects, Bechtel Canada can invest lavishly in media advertising such as its "Plain Talk" series. One of those columns featured Earle Stobart, manager, Environmental Department, Bechtel Canada Limited, who said:

> Mankind relies on the environment for climate regulation, fresh air, fresh water, food — for life itself. . . . There is a too widely held opinion that resource development per se constitutes wilful destruction of the environment. . . . On the Sarnia-Montreal pipeline extension project, the [Bechtel environmental] department was involved before, during, and after construction. Our environmentalists assessed sensitive areas in advance, prepared reports and procedures for the National Energy Board, and monitored relevant construction daily. Although it is not possible to eliminate all environmental impacts from major projects, it is possible to minimize these effects by long-range planning. And it is much more beneficial (usually cheaper) to design environmental protection into the project beforehand, rather than attempt to add it on after the fact.

Amen. Such statements would surely be very reassuring to any reader not aware of the actual destructive pipeline practices. Comprehensive research and monitoring by Agriculture Canada proved that significant crop losses were still apparent on the right-of-way ten years later.

Bechtel could also afford to send Stobart on the speaking circuit. For instance, on February 1, 1977, he told the Cambridge, Ontario, Rotary Club: "By making everyone, from the project manager down to the bulldozer operator, aware of the need to protect the environment and thus preserve the quality of life, we can eat our cake and have it too."

A year later, Stobart was still eulogizing the protection of the environment in the Montreal-Sarnia pipeline project. He told the Kiwanis Club of London that "after all work was done and all environmental protection accomplished, the pipeline route was completely surveyed and returned to original condition." Stobart clearly demonstrated that he would be very comfortable with Alice in Wonderland and that his thinking was much along the lines anticipated by George Orwell. "Some property owners en route forced expropriation," wrote Stobart. He chose to ignore the reality that it had been demonstrated to the satisfaction of the NEB and the courts that expropriation was a direct result of the failure of IPL to negotiate acquisition of additional working rights.

On November 23, 1976, the omnipresent Stobart teamed up with Alex Ramsay, also of Bechtel, now head of the IPL right-of-way department, to address the Canadian Land Reclamation Association on "Restoration of Agricultural Productivity Along a Major Pipeline Right-of-Way."

How many people were influenced by this barrage of published words, speeches before service organizations, and papers before professional organizations? On the other hand, how many people heard Dr. Angus MacKenzie floundering in court on these very topics, and how many people read Judge Killeen's evaluation that he found the work of MacKenzie, and in effect Bechtel, "unpersuasive"?

IPL, in the 1981 edition of *The Piper* (an IPL magazine distributed to nine thousand involved landowners) states, "When Interprovincial Pipe Line Limited began construction of its Montreal line in 1976, largely through federal government insistence, its agricultural restoration program gained full stature." While it may have achieved its full stature, it was a shrivelled and shrunken stature; once again, the integrity of the claim must be judged in the light of evidence given by IPL-Bechtel representatives before Judge Killeen.

A four-colour full-page advertisement of the Gulf Oil Corporation asked, "Where's the best fishing in the Gulf of Mexico? Just look for an offshore oil platform." Such a soporific advertisement has to be seen in the light of the wild well in Mexico's Bay of Campeche, which spewed well over 3 million barrels of crude oil before it was controlled. Or the *Exxon Valdez* Alaskan crude-oil disaster, which disgorged 11 million gallons into pure northern waters. Or the *Amoco Cadiz,* which spilled seven times that volume off the coast of Brittany.

One can also legitimately question the editorial philosophy of such trade publications as *Oilweek,* which initially chose to dismiss my environmental concerns as "amusing." Subsequently, *Oilweek* has published reference to the fact that the NEB has been dissatisfied with IPL's environmental studies and sent them back to the drawing board. *Oilweek* has also published a special supplement generated by PACE, Canada's Petroleum Association for Conservation of the Environment. *Oil-*

week now appears to have discovered the environment, but long after needless damage had been perpetrated.

I have used a liberal definition of *media* because there is a grey link between government publications and the more conventional media. In March 1980, I received from the Land Resource Research Centre of Agriculture Canada various scientific publications, including *Effects of Pipeline Construction on Soils and Crops,* by A. J. Stewart, and A. F. MacKenzie, "Department of Renewable Resources Macdonald College of McGill University." No reference is made to MacKenzie's role on behalf of IPL-Bechtel. And then on October 6, 1981, I found an Agriculture Canada publication in our mailbox—unaddressed and unwrapped. It was also published by the Land Resource Research Institute and entitled *Impact of Installation of an Oil Pipeline on the Productivity of Ontario Cropland.* Credit was given to such people as MacKenzie, Neilsen, and Ramsay, with no indication that MacKenzie and Ramsay had been employed by IPL-Bechtel or that Neilsen was MacKenzie's student. Once again, the work of people like Quigley and Pearson did not rate a mention, although their work has been instrumental in changing the ways pipelines are installed.

The bothersome part of such government publications is that they are taken at face value and the advice publicized in the farming press. Farmers are nonchalantly advised to find out about company policy and to negotiate before they sign. This only serves to distort the reality, which includes extreme difficulty in gleaning company policy and use of the club of expropriation in lieu of negotiation.

This look at the media has been sombre and singularly lacking in humour. John Schmidt is a great bear of a man and a character in his own right. He wrote the column "Agriculture Alberta" in the *Calgary Herald.* He has assiduously recorded the conflicts of pipelines and agriculture in *the* newspaper in the oil patch. It is Schmidt's unpublished idiosyncrasies that add a dash of humour.

"You've been caught speeding!" Jean told me. I didn't think that this was so, but looked closely at the envelope from the Ayr Police Department, Ayr, Ontario. I noted that the postmark was Ganges, British Columbia, and told Jean, "I expect that it is from John Schmidt, who probably came home to see his dad."

I never knew John to use a conventional notebook or his own stationery or that of the *Calgary Herald.* His letters may come from any part of the world and on an intriguing variety of corporate letterheads. A letter from Tel Aviv was on the letterhead of a Vancouver investment firm and in a CN envelope.

Prior to the 1979 IPL annual meeting, Schmidt inherited twenty-five of the company's shares and promptly castigated IPL president Bob Heule for wasting shareholders' money on conflicts and lawsuits with farmers. Replied Heule: "With respect to the Lewington decision, the Company feels that it was wrongly decided and has launched an appeal. . . . Our policy has been—and continues to be—to disturb the land as little as possible during construction and to assist the owner in bringing affected land back to full production quickly." Such a statement has to stand beside the boast of making a wasteland, which was repeated in the courts of Judge McCart and Judge Killeen by IPL's legal spokesman. In typical IPL fashion, Heule did not retract his inaccurate statement to shareholders when his company's appeals turned to ashes in the Supreme Court of Ontario.

Another note from John Schmidt confirmed that he had provided some links when he covered a fertilizer price-fixing conspiracy trial. Jake Howard was representing Imperial Oil and inquired after the health of Larigmoor Pattillo, a registered Holstein calf named in honour of his visit to us with Arthur Pattillo. The lawyer representing Sherritt Gordon chuckled that he had clipped a report of the Killeen judgment and was going to tape it to Brownlie's locker at the Cambridge Squash Club in Toronto.

Farm & Country was among the many farm publications that reported the Killeen judgment, and events leading up to it, in great detail. Editor John Phillips won the 1982 top award from the Canadian Farm Writers Federation with his "Court Ruling Backs Farm Compensation."

And that feature inspired Nancy Tindall to research and write the winning project to celebrate the thirtieth anniversary of our local Medway High School. She was among the students who took a keen interest in making democracy work. She is also among that new generation featured in the next chapter.

CHAPTER 20

A New Generation

There are times when we need education in the obvious more than investigation of the obscure.

—OLIVER WENDELL HOLMES

I t was obvious to our lawyers, our consultants, our friends, a handful of politicians, and ourselves that there were aspects of society that screamed for change.

How could it be appropriate, on this crowded planet, to have legislation that condoned turning productive soil into a wasteland? How could a society that prided itself on being a democracy retain a legal system that gave the takers of land access to what they wanted while the owners need not even be notified of a hearing affecting them? How was it possible for the harsh, archaic, and repressive Railway Act to survive intact? Totalitarian rulers put down all opposition, and that is precisely what the Railway Act continued to legalize. All this—obvious to a relative few but obscure to the vast majority.

As we struggled to change a manifestly unfair system that constrained justice, a new and inquiring group entered the scene—the students. Some interested and involved students were mature, at the Ph.D. and postdoctoral levels. The others were students in public and high schools, in community colleges, and in universities. It was the involvement of these students of different age groups, educational levels, and areas of expertise that contributed to making the struggle so rewarding.

Wrote Norman Pearson on receipt of *Pipeline Construction Impact on a Cattle Farm, Bryanston, Ontario:* "Larigmoor Farm must be the best researched farm in the world. Many thanks to Quigley et al. who have produced a really fine piece of research reporting which I am glad to have, and have enjoyed reading."

Larigmoor Farm provided Dr. Roy Turkington with the "laboratory" needed for some aspects of his postdoctoral studies and the location needed by a few of his colleagues. In addition, Turkington got much more than he had anticipated, as he reveals in writing about his "gut reactions" from the vantage point of 1985. "A solitary farmer taking on the might of the oil industry was crazy! An individual with obvious altruistic goals didn't stand a chance! (I say altruistic because I don't think that any court settlement could adequately compensate for the financial losses, the stress and the tension.) I was pleasantly surprised to see firsthand that democracy can be made to work; but democracy doesn't always reward efforts." These latter concerns relate to academic integrity and the conflicts revealed in the funding of research. It is fair to say that Turkington is an even better educator as a result of his involvement in making democracy work.

A strong contingent of students from the department of plant sciences at The University of Western Ontario came daily to Judge Killeen's court, sparked by the interest of Dr. Paul Cavers. Today, one of his former students, Dr. Susan Weaver, is a research scientist at Agriculture Canada at Harrow, and the impact of her weed research is being felt across the province of Ontario. Muriel Heagy (now Mrs. Peter Andreae and the mother of three children) generated a lot of relevant information in her own right and worked closely with Bob Quigley, Roy Turkington, and Al Tomlin. Muriel made a presentation on land reclamation at the annual meeting of the Canadian Botanical Association. She recalls that "the pipeline case influenced my choice of the natural revegetation of gravel pit slopes for my M.Sc. thesis."

The Bryanston cattle farm referred to above was of course Larigmoor, which is located at Bryanston but has an Ilderton, Ontario, address. The ninety-one-page report was published in May 1979 and represented the first such interdisciplinary project to my knowledge. Spearheading the project were Bob Quigley and one of his technical associates, geographer Anne Bohdanowicz at The University of Western Ontario. The chapters on plant sciences and plant ecology were written by Muriel Heagy and Roy Turkington. Al Tomlin contributed a further dimension, which will be explored in some detail in the chapter "Soil Isn't Just Dirt." Requests for copies of the report came from such diverse quarters as Alberta Power, Ontario Hydro, and the Upper Thames River Conservation Authority.

The year 1979 also witnessed the granting of the degree Master of

Engineering Science to Stephen Eccles, whose thesis was entitled "Agricultural Impact of Pipeline Installation, Birr, Ontario." Stephen was another of Bob Quigley's students, and his 204-page thesis contributed to the filling of a substantial research gap. Stephen's research was done on the farm of Stu O'Neil, which is located at Birr and has a Denfield address.

Another master's student at UWO with whom we worked closely was Michael Wyness whose interests spanned journalism and political science. He was a frequent visitor to Larigmoor Farm and carted away documents by the armful to continue his own research.

David Evaniew came to us via farmer Andrew Kittmer, of Lakeside, Ontario, who had led a group of interested members of the National Farmers' Union to observe the court of Judge J. F. McCart. Evaniew, who hailed from Calgary, Alberta, was then in his fourth-year honours program in environmental studies at the University of Waterloo. After his second year at university, he had taken a year off to tour Scandinavia, Europe, and North Africa, and perhaps that view of the world encouraged him to participate in change. In 1977, he was involved in drafting a policy for Waterloo County's input for the Official Plan, so that there was adequate representation of the interests of agriculture. The Evaniew aftermath once again demonstrated the web of gossamer threads. While doing research in her work as policy planner with the city of Peterborough, our daughter Ann wrote in 1985, "I thought you would be interested in the enclosed draft Official Plan for the Region of Waterloo. I have never seen such a hydro, gas, oil and communications line policy before."

Jean and I made the time to work with any students, at any level, who displayed an interest. Our only provisos were that they do their own research and that we receive a copy of their project report. One of the better ones was completed by Noreen Finlay and Diane Klopp, who were then students at the London campus of Fanshawe Community College. They concluded that "there is a great feeling of helplessness among the farmers. Everyone is sympathetic, but nothing changes. Yet, the farmers did stand up for their beliefs, and that in itself is a step forward."

Nancy Tindall grew up on a dairy farm at Lucan, Ontario, and was a student at our nearby Medway High School when the writings of John Phillips in *Farm & Country* sparked her interest. Jean and I probably spent more time with Nancy than with any other student because she exhibited such infectious enthusiasm. But when, after considerable effort on her part, the project was completed, it was too biased in our favour. We were very proud of Nancy when she tore it up, expanded her own research, and did the project again. Fortunately, she was rewarded with the top mark in the competition that celebrated the thirtieth anniversary of Medway High School.

Today, Nancy and her husband, Ron Cunningham, have two young children and operate their Merry Meadow Farms at Mar in Ontario's Bruce Peninsula. Recently Nancy wrote,

> I do recall how I felt throughout the whole endeavour. I felt mostly anger towards government and its legislation. As farmers, we struggle with the elements, with sickness in our herds, with machinery breakdowns, and numerous other factors. Yet, we survive. The expropriation of farmland, the destruction of farmland by people who obviously don't have any sense of right or wrong, we don't need. We shouldn't have to deal with it. It is thrilling and fulfilling to realise that at last the struggle has been fruitful. It is a truly huge success to know that years of court proceedings have brought about definite changes in the actual procedures for the installation of pipelines through farmland.

Morley Salmon, like many of the other students, now has a family and is succeeding in business. Morley was different from most of the other students in that his concerns stemmed from personal experience on his father's London Township farm. The Salmons had suffered at the hands of Union Gas and its multiple pipelines. Readers may recall that Morley was introduced in Chapter 2 when he rendered yeoman service in a marathon appearance before the NEB. Morley Salmon's major project in earning a degree from UWO in geography dealt with the effects of Union Gas pipelines through the townships of West Nissouri and London. In his thesis, Morley explored the following hypotheses:

• That the installation of the Union Gas pipelines changed soil structure.
• That the installation disrupted drainage.
• That the aftermath included increased farming and maintenance costs.
• That the absence of environmental-impact studies and implementation of good pipelining practices have adversely contributed to the effect of pipelines on agriculture.

Morley carried out in-depth interviews with affected farmers, took numerous pictures to illustrate his thesis, made good use of available references (including NEB transcripts and the preliminary reports of Dr. Bob Quigley), and concluded with special thanks to "Mr. and Mrs. Lewington who helped enormously in gathering research material, helping me get organized, and checking my work."

And then in 1976, Morley appeared on behalf of his father Ernie before the Ontario Energy Board. Since Union Gas had a provincial charter, it came before a provincial energy board. The board's Reasons For Decision record the involvement of Morley and other farmers who have been mentioned earlier—including Ron White, Ian Goudy, and Ken Patterson.

When Morley Salmon graduated from UWO, he asked for a reference to assist him in his search for a job. I was confident in writing a reference for Morley because I had been involved with him over a period of years and had been impressed by his industry and thoroughness. But would a reference from me help? In our earlier search for expert witnesses, we had been turned down by "professionals" whose survival at universities depended on their ability to attract funding from industry. Such members of the academic fraternity thought that their survival might be jeopardized by any involvement with us.

One of Morley's more promising applications had gone to Dome Petroleum. Morley was selected out of some 180 other applicants for an interview. The first provocative statement during that interview was "I see that you are involved with that bugger Peter Lewington." How should a young university graduate applying for his first job respond to such provocation? Morley's response was an unequivocal "Yes, I am very proud of that association." Morley got the job! I can only surmise that the Dome Petroleum official wanted to know whether Morley was a fair-weather friend; if he would stick to his convictions, despite putting himself at risk, he was just the sort of recruit that Dome Petroleum wanted.

And some of the involved students were family. Barry O'Neil, the eldest son of Stu and Jocelyn, following graduation from the University of Guelph worked in extension with young farmers. He is now field manager for Hamilton Sod. He can relate more effectively to farmers and their problems having been a shrewd observer of the events in Judge Killeen's court that he witnessed as a teenager. "I was thrilled out of my boots when Mr. Brownlie and Co. discussed how they were going to cross-examine my father the next day, while I was still sitting in the room. It was like getting a preview of a math exam. I was fascinated by the strategy of the court battle . . . the thinking, the bluffing, and the lying."

Our own children, Ann, Jennifer, and Roger, endured a lot of the pipeline controversy during their years in public and high school and university, and latterly in their careers. Ann, in retrospect, thinks that her career as a planner was influenced by our initiatives in preparing documentation, retaining consultants, and making presentations before the courts. Writes Ann: "I am not sure that democracy works, but that it can be made to work. Because I had the opportunity when I was growing up to see how the individual fared against the system, I feel that I have a greater empathy for people who have to deal with the system. In recent years I have been able to negotiate results that have mostly satisfied the various parties. I think that my experiences at home made me a better planner."

In its September 1984 edition, *Flare Magazine,* in a feature entitled "Quest for the Best," profiled twenty-five people described as "role models for Canadian women." In reference to Jennifer, it included this comment: "Credits grass roots writing style to rural Ontario upbringing and informed family debates." As her parents had been a thorn in the side of government for so long, we feared there might be an adverse reaction to Jen in her varied writing assignments, often involving government, but happily this did not occur. The many pipeline-related experiences contributed to Roger's maturity and added to his success in a career spanning conservation and erosion control.

And finally, the views of Norman Pearson, who wrote to say:

> The reactions of *this* student may be helpful. Today the advice came that I was awarded the Degree of Doctor of Philosophy (Land Economy and Ecological Planning) for a two-volume, 500-page dissertation on the "Impact of Pipelines On Agriculture in South-West Ontario" (1979). Since the impetus to do it and the main case study included in it both came from your courageous fight and the experience of Larigmoor Farm, I hasten to send you a copy with my very warmest thanks and appreciation. In 1956, in my first week as the newly-appointed Director of Planning for the Hamilton-Wentworth Planning Area Board, the board members, who were very fine citizens, took me to numerous farms and escarpment crossings by pipelines and utilities, and asked what planning skills could do to mitigate or prevent the damage. And there began a lifelong interest and concern for this problem. My planning board sent me to almost every hearing in the region and all abutting regions to file briefs and to protest; and it was like sending letters to a black hole, or making speeches in oblivion. The material accumulated, but the opportunity to do definitive, predictive research only arose when you asked me to be your consultant. Your disaster proved the whole point of my dissertation, and I am so very proud to be associated with your endeavours which have produced a new era in pipelining. As a graduate student of mature years, it made me extremely sad to see the environmental movement becoming increasingly irrelevant. It was a refreshing change to find a citizen who believed in the kind of fight that John Hampden (or

thousands of others who fought for freedom) epitomized; people who believe that a citizen in a free democracy is the best force for a better environment. I also found respect for our judges who could use all this scientific evidence and who could understand predictive planning in a landmark case.

Norman characteristically signed a recent letter "A lifelong student." Hopefully there will be many readers who also aspire to be lifelong students — to question the way society operates and to explore what they might contribute to make it work better.

During the 1970s, I began to fear that we had created a boomerang effect that would later come back to haunt us. It will be recalled that during the early years of our thirty-year struggle, environmental-impact studies were unknown, and there was no scientific resource to which we could turn relating to mitigation of damage to farmland during pipeline construction. Having achieved some victories in the courts and having funded the first objective research, we created a backlash. Papers were published and pronouncements were made, either by people who were, and in some cases continued to be, pipeline company consultants or by their students, who were awarded master's and Ph.D. degrees and in their turn became pipeline company employees. References were made above to the pipeline installation in the deep and rich chernozem topsoil. This specious and self-serving "research" was exposed in court only by the alertness of our expert witnesses Jim O'Toole and Bob Quigley. It was then that I had the first misgivings. Would students of the future be able to distinguish the documented research of a Dr. Quigley from that generated by consultants hired by pipeline companies or by their students who owed their experience to pipeline funding?

By the spring of 1988, our worst fears were confirmed. Jean and I worked with a young farmer, Darryl Bycraft, who was about to graduate from the diploma course at the University of Guelph and was preparing his final class assignment. It was a fact sheet on the impact of pipelines and the restoration of agricultural land. His original draft included some half-dozen sections on such themes as restoring productivity and organic content. Darryl was unable to provide any documentation for these assertions, only simplistic and plausible claims made by pipeline personnel. By referring to the nine volumes of the transcript of Judge Killeen's court, we were able to give him an entirely different perspective.

But what of all the other students, now and in the future? A disturbing situation can only deteriorate. The research initiated by ourselves and our consultants was a historic aberration. I know from my investigations as a farm writer that there is an apparently unavoidable bias in virtually all research. In an era of escalating costs, candidates for master's and Ph.D. degrees depend financially, in part, upon commercial funding. This is not necessarily bad. However, it is potentially a bear trap for students of the future who may be unaware of the commercial connections. There is a potential bias in the very choice of research topics. Who, for instance, is going to fund research into the impact of pipeline construction on earthworms and other beneficial denizens of our good soils?

I have dwelt at some length on the dilemmas faced by students who sincerely researched the issues that are the basis of this book. My concern was sparked by several recent library computer searches that revealed either a paucity of information or a bias in the completeness of the material available. The Epilogue refers to one hopeful contribution to a solution.

CHAPTER 21

The
Supreme
Courts

The easement agreements did not permit the appellant
[IPL] to come on the lands and leave them as wastelands.
The appellant would be expected to leave the lands in sub-
stantially the same condition as they were before
entry. . . . The appeal is dismissed.
                              —JUDGE JEAN MARC LABROSSE

We found, as others had found before us, that the mills of justice grind exceeding slow. But at last, yet another hiatus ended with the IPL decision to appeal the conclusions of Judge Killeen to the Supreme Court of Ontario. It had been a cliff-hanger, with Brownlie delaying notification of appeal until the very last day.

According to the notice of appeal issued by Blake, Cassels and Graydon on January 19, 1979, Killeen had really screwed things up. His award was against the evidence and contrary to law; he had erred in permitting more than three expert witnesses; he was wrong in failing to restrict his award to the 30-foot strip of temporary working rights; he had not accepted the evidence of Dr. MacKenzie; and he had been too liberal in attaching a rate of 6 percent, rather than 5 percent as provided by the Interest Act of Canada, on his award (which continued to be inaccessible to us, pending any appeal). As interest rates were then climbing to some 19 percent, Brownlie looked unduly parsimonious.

Who should represent us before the Supreme Court of Ontario? Jean and I pondered this with Stu and Jocelyn O'Neil and had to conclude that we had no information or experience upon which to base a decision. We concluded that the decision would be best left to Geoff Bladon. If he chose to argue the appeal, he would continue to have our confidence. However, if he preferred to retain counsel who specialised before the Supreme Courts of Ontario and Canada, we would accept all the legal and financial consequences of such a choice.

On a long shot, Geoff telephoned a former classmate to see if John Josiah Robinette might be available. "Within ten minutes I had his telephone acceptance," reported a jubilant Geoff Bladon. J. J. Robinette is the son and the father of successful lawyers. He was a brilliant student and a gold medallist at the University of Toronto in political science and then a gold medallist in law at Osgoode Hall Law School. Despite his youth, on graduation he taught law and was fondly and favourably remembered in later years by his students, who themselves capped illustrious careers with distinction on the bench of various supreme courts in Canada. Robinette's subsequent career made him a household word. He shone in everything from lurid criminal cases to the complexities of combines litigation and the intricacies of repatriation of the Canadian Constitution. His clients ranged from those charged with bank robbery or murder to corporations such as Union Gas, to the government of Canada and people like the articulate Jane Jacobs, who opposed construction of the Spadina Expressway through the heart of Toronto.

Robinette clearly had a versatile practice and a diverse clientele. While I had not kept a box score, he seemed to have won more than his share of cases. With acceptance of Geoff's brief in the fall of 1979, the forthcoming appeal promised to become a battle of the titans, as Blake, Cassels and Graydon and McCarthy and McCarthy (the latter is now McCarthy, Tétrault, with 450 lawyers) vied as the largest legal firms in Canada, with teams of some 160 lawyers each. Not that Robinette appeared to be a team player; he was reputed to be an individual who preferred to do his own research. The September 1979 issue of *Canadian Lawyer,* in a feature entitled "At the Head of His Class," noted that "his peers say J. J. Robinette is the best courtroom lawyer in the country. His record says believe it."

I promptly wrote to Mr. Robinette to express our pleasure that he had accepted Geoff's request to defend our interests and advised him:

We have endured five pipelines through land we farm. The most disastrous was the third installed by IPL; one can only regard the havoc they created as wanton and wilfull as they were in possession of the research funded by my wife and myself which could have mitigated a great deal of damage. We had 14 inches of topsoil and the unique asset of an aquifer in the area of the easement and working rights. By disregarding all prudent precautions IPL turned the beneficial asset of the aquifer into a liability. They disrupted the natural drainage and jeopardized our source of water. We are now purchasing feed to sustain a smaller herd than we maintained before the third entry of IPL . . . at which time we had been able to also sell Certified seed and surplus forage.

The first item in the Osgoode Hall notices in the *Globe and Mail* of January 14, 1981, read, "Court of Appeal peremptory list for today at 10:30 a.m. Courtroom I; Interprovincial Pipe Line Limited v P. Lewington." It was thus seven years since IPL entered our farm with a warrant, five years since Judge Killeen's court, and the fourth anniversary of the day we had been promised judgment. This January 14 promised to be more productive.

We arrived at Osgoode Hall, the bastion of the Law Society of Upper Canada since 1797, and were impressed by the colonnades and acres of blue carpeting. We passed galleries of large oil paintings of former justices. We gathered in the impressive Courtroom I, with its royal coat of arms and the legend *Dieu et mon droit* ("God and my Right"). The high-ceilinged courtroom was immaculately cleaned and varnished. Beautifully crafted oak pews rose in a semi-circle from below the raised dais. It was a light, bright room with colourful red leather desktops and blue padded seats.

And there we met the legendary Robinette of whom so much had been heard and more expected. He was then into his seventies and celebrating his fiftieth anniversary since being called to the bar. Years ago, Oscar Wilde had observed that we all get the face we deserve by the time we are fifty. Robinette had a full and interesting face that looked like it could easily crinkle with good humour. It was the face of a man who had enjoyed his life and work to the full, but in moderation. He exuded an air of restrained confidence and competence, and we immediately felt we were in good hands. He was assisted by Geoff Bladon, who had previously made three trips to Toronto to brief Robinette. Geoff modestly referred to his own considerable role as that of "observer."

At 10:37 A.M., the president of the court, Mr. Justice John Arnup, enters with his fellow justices Blair and Weatherston. The triumvirate of judges then write furiously while a brooding silence settles over the court. Eventually Arnup indicates he is ready for action, and the three judges receive copies of a brief from John Brownlie.

Brownlie is clearly uncomfortable as he begins his preamble with the admission that "it is a tricky problem to know whether this is the right court." The biter bit! For nearly thirty years, IPL had been telling us that we were in the wrong court. Now the company and its legal representatives experienced the problems firsthand. They had no precedents to guide them. Farmers were not supposed to win in the courts, and pipeline companies had never before been obliged to appeal.

John Brownlie seems to touch all the points of the compass. A Saskatchewan finding indicated that the appeal should go to the Court of the King's Bench. The Ontario Court of Appeal is the correct court, and "Your Lordships have got to hear this appeal." And eventually the confused admission that "I don't know where I should go with this appeal."

It appears to be the sort of legal conundrum the judges enjoy. Mr. Justice Arnup sends the clerk scurrying, apparently to find references in vintage law books, but the clerk returns empty-handed and sits down without even a glance to or from the bench. The brilliant red telephone on the clerk's desk remains unused. Could it be that some call may be necessary to resolve the morass of conflicting references? It is anticlimactic to find that it is merely a whisper phone that the clerk can use without distracting the court.

While we chafe at the unexpected and costly delay, Arnup enjoys the debate, which has apparently been precipitated by his own alertness the day before. Eventually, the president of the court invites Robinette's views. He has a clear voice that carries throughout the courtroom and has the essential inflection to maintain interest and attention. Robinette has no doubt that this is the wrong court. Brownlie should have lodged his appeal in the Divisional Court of the Supreme Court of Ontario. Lunn is now represented by London lawyer Reg Lamon, who doesn't appear to have a handle on what is happening and merely says, "I have nothing to add."

Hours later, after an adjournment, Arnup announces the decision. This is indeed the wrong court, and the appeal must be heard in the Divisional Court.

Geoff Bladon laments that everybody loses. Robinette, in his very courteous way, apologises for having to concede that it is the wrong court. "But we have to protect the integrity of the Court." And then we get a glimpse of why Robinette is held in such regard by his peers. He delivers an afterthought with a shy smile. "I was glad to get out of there. Arnup is a black-letter judge who interprets the law very narrowly."

The Osgoode Hall proceedings duly noted that "the appeals are adjourned to the Divisional Court pursuant to Rule 225 (2)." And so began another uneasy hiatus from the courts.

The Supreme Court of Ontario, it appeared, is composed of a covey of judges who variously appear in the different branches of the court. The Ontario Court of Appeal is one branch, and the other goes through the High Court of Justice and then slips into a Trial Division, where cases are heard before a single judge, and the Divisional Court, which has a panel of three judges.

Promptly on time on September 22, 1981, Justices Galligan, Catzman, and Labrosse entered, and all sat down, only to write furiously. This seemed to be an endemic quality in justices of the Supreme Court of Ontario. This time around, Brownlie had the assistance of his colleague Miss L. D. Robinson.

Brownlie provided a succinct synopsis of the saga, stretching back to the 1950s. He made sustained efforts to prove that Killeen had erred. Justices Galligan and Labrosse soon demonstrated that they were very familiar with the nine volumes of the transcript of Killeen's trial. Commented Galligan: "Judge Killeen made very strong conclusions on very strong evidence that your people went and made a mess." Reacted Brownlie: "I don't want to go into that." To this, Galligan responded: "You may have to; you are challenging a very experienced judge."

Brownlie concluded one extensive dissertation with the thought "If I am right . . . " Labrosse countered with "I am not prepared to assume that you are right; I have serious questions. This case is about negligence; you screwed it up." But Brownlie also made some telling points and Jean passed me a note that it was like a pendulum.

During the morning recess, IPL's right-of-way chief Bob Dunsmore volunteered that the controversy had gone on too long and that the changes in federal legislation had come twenty years too late; he made no bones that he now felt that these were beneficial changes. Unfortunately such concern would better have been directed to his hard-nosed superiors.

On resumption, Brownlie had a field day with the number of witnesses Killeen allowed on our behalf and in contravention of the Railway Act: "I am at a disadvantage because I only called one agronomist and he did not find favour with the learned arbitrator," regretfully concluded Brownlie. Brownlie persisted, only to run into a blockbuster from Galligan, who said, "You are asking us to buy that MacKenzie was right, when the trial judge specifically rejected his evidence as unpersuasive."

During the afternoon, Linda Robinson appeared to have made a telling point as Labrosse gestured for assistance from a clerk, but the clerk was not sent to the library for research, only to recharge Mr. Justice Labrosse's pen, which had run dry.

Linda Robinson explored at length the IPL theme that any remedial action should be within the constraints of what is practical and possible. To this, Labrosse reacted in earthy language, which one had not expected in the august surroundings of the Supreme Court. "If you break my leg off, you have to compensate me because you can't give me back my leg. There is no market value for my leg. You cut the Lewington farm in half. If the proper procedures had been followed, there would have been no problem. You were negligent."

The next day, Linda Robinson continued and deplored the "economic waste" inherent in Killeen's judgment. This struck us as a curious contradiction in light of the repeated boasts that it was quite legitimate to make a wasteland of good farms.

Brownlie and Robinson had clearly read their case law. In support of their position they referred even to the Supreme Court of Oklahoma and a decision on the strip-mining of coal. But Linda Robinson asserted that "nothing has been found to endorse the decision of Judge Killeen." That was no surprise, as the whole concept of the case was without precedent.

As the morning dragged on, the clerk buried himself surreptitiously in a paperback on baseball as there were no other demands on his time.

A singularly unfair aspect of the case surfaced as Linda Robinson continued to try to erode Killeen's award. The court, it appeared, could reduce the award but not increase it.

I don't know what law students did for the rest of that day, but I question whether they could have learned more than by sitting in the court, held spellbound by Robinette. The three justices had previously asked both Brownlie and Robinson to speak up. They had no such complaint with Robinette, for whom every word counted. Robinette, a true orator, didn't rely on volume but an interesting use of cadence. Sometimes his voice would drop, and the court would still hear as a hush descended.

Justice Galligan didn't buy all Robinette's arguments: "A serious problem in this case is that the award would place the respondents in a far better position than they were before." But Robinette swiftly demolished such an idea, elaborated on the correctness of Killeen's judgment, and substantiated his arguments with a reference to the Court of Appeal in England. During the afternoon of the second day, Robinette did what we had hoped he would do. He explored the ramifications of negligence in construction on an easement, which inevitably precipitates a total farm problem. He handed the judges my black-and-white enlargements that had been accepted by Killeen as exhibits. Exclaimed Galligan: "It looks like trench warfare in World War One!" Geoff Bladon regarded that as the turning point.

Another key point made effectively by Robinette was the disruption of farming operations and the need for continuity in successful farm management. These were the sort of key points that farmers had hoped to see recognised in law for many years. Respect for Robinette grew by the hour. He had fantastic recall and raised and demolished every point made by Brownlie and Robinson. One was left with a feeling that it would be churlish to do anything but agree with him. He similarly picked his way through the transcript of Killeen's trial and demonstrated an impressive grasp of even the most complex agricultural issues. My notes made while he was speaking show another important characteristic: "I am amazed at the ease with which R can find the document and the exact passage he wants, while continuing with his clear and precise delivery all made in carefully structured sentences."

Throughout the four days before the Divisional Court, Robinette was only once caught flat-footed. And it was then that we benefitted from Geoff Bladon's foresight in retaining counsel well known to Supreme Court judges. With Robinette in difficulty interpreting Dr. Roy Turkington's evidence, the president of the court called for an early luncheon adjournment. While John Robinette might be Canada's top lawyer, he claimed no special farming expertise. I diffidently explained to him how he might recoup. A lesser person might well have brusquely dismissed advice from a layperson, but as Geoff had earlier told us, Robinette was more likely to listen than to tell you what he was going to do.

John Robinette used the luncheon recess to explore the points I had raised with him. During the afternoon, he spoke eloquently for some two hours and on concluding, turned to me and asked with an infectious grin, "How did I do?" It was this sort of rapport that had carried us through many difficult times. In contrast, the representatives of Bechtel and IPL sat in distant parts of the courtroom and had no communication during the proceedings with either of their lawyers.

John Robinette had devoted a great deal of his time to establishing the validity of Judge Killeen's apparent contravention of the Railway Act. On behalf of his client, Lunn, Reg Lamon had no such concerns because his client had not called any witnesses! Having enjoyed the free ride to the Supreme Court, Lunn was quite happy to see us founder in our attempt to change an archaic system.

In an impassioned oral judgment Mr. Justice Labrosse, speaking on behalf of the panel of judges, stated that "no substantial wrong or miscarriage of justice has been occasioned by the number of expert or opinion witnesses who testified before the arbitrator."

The judgment of Killeen was upheld; IPL's appeal was dismissed with costs awarded to us.

But even that did not end the battle. Brownlie was nothing if not tenacious. He brought an action before the Ontario Court of Appeal for leave to appeal to the Ontario Court of Appeal. This time around, the hiatus was mercifully brief. On November 16, 1981, we were scheduled to go back into Courtroom I and appear before yet another panel of judges. The omens were not good. There was a morning fog, which made it difficult to check our Simmental beef cattle, and we would never dream of leaving without doing that. Jocelyn O'Neil came with us, and we struggled through the persistent fog to Toronto, only to find that Justice Arthur Jessup had convened his court, assisted by Justices Houlden and Morden.

Jessup appeared to be in a black mood, and we wondered if some of that attitude stemmed from our late arrival. However, Jessup's irritation was not biased. He cut John Brownlie off in midsentence, and the three justices abruptly retired to chambers.

I took advantage of the recess to visit the washroom; Jean volunteered that this was not prudent, and I responded that it was essential. It was also unfortunate. In my momentary absence, the three justices had returned and delivered their decision. After thirty-two years, I had missed the finale! We were not prepared for such speed.

Once again, the court upheld the judgment in our favour. IPL was once again saddled with court costs and was denied any appeal to the Ontario Court of Appeal, a decision that also denied appeal to the Supreme Court of Canada. In a jubilant mood, we congratulated John Robinette, who responded with a warm smile that "I work for everybody . . . but this one was fun."

We thanked Geoff Bladon again for his years of dedicated and often inspired legal counsel. It was a memorable day!

The mood was apparently different at IPL's head office. On November 26, 1981, John Brownlie telephoned Geoff Bladon to advise that he had strict instructions from his client that the cheques when issued to us would come from his trust account and not directly from Interprovincial. That way, we could neither frame nor photocopy the IPL cheques!

The decision of the court was greeted enthusiastically by the press. The banner front page of *Farm & Country* trumpeted, "Farmers Win Land Victory. Expropriators Must Now Replace Precious Topsoil." A feature recalled some of the highlights, and an editorial noted, "We can take pride in a resounding victory achieved by two stalwart Middlesex farmers. After a long and gruelling fight with a pipeline company they have won a stunning triumph. A triumph not only for themselves but for all Ontario farmers facing land expropriation."

Huron County farmer Gordon Hill, who had tried to help while president of the Ontario Federation of Agriculture, was quoted in the same edition: " 'The decision is a landmark for Ontario farmers. . . . Peter (Lewington) has won the war in the farm battle against utilities and their arrogant expropriation practices. Farm people now know they don't have to be raped when dealing with utilities.' "

By the following spring, Canada Law Book Limited had published the court's decision in *Land Compensation Reports*. It was indeed, as Gordon Hill had said, a landmark decision. The next two chapters will explore the reactions of the National Energy Board and a wide variety of companies involved in the construction and operation of pipelines.

CHAPTER 22

The
NEB
Revisited

Our greatest business in life is not to see what is dimly at a
distance, but to do what lies clearly at hand.
— THOMAS CARLYLE

The National Energy Board now has a staff of well over four hundred and a budget in excess of $25 million. NEB responsibilities include the regulation of about 35,000 kilometers of oil and natural gas pipelines. The NEB controls the export of oil, which peaked at over 80 million cubic metres; natural gas, which exceeded 28 billion cubic metres; and electricity of up to 35,000 gigawatt hours annually.

In 1984 the minister of supply and services Canada published the silver anniversary publication, entitled *National Energy Board — 25 Years in the Public Interest.*

In his Introduction, the then chairman Geoffrey Edge wrote, "What was new was the fact that for the first time an independent tribunal had been created to provide advice to the federal government on certain major energy matters based on the evidence put before its members at public hearings. In casting back over the past 25 years, it is easy to overlook one remarkable feature of the organization — the smooth and harmonious functioning of the Board itself. . . . Over the years the members have come from widely different backgrounds." Well, Edge was entitled to his views and had the funding to present them in a glossy four-colour publication. My own views and conclusions, based on painful exposure to the NEB, are rather different.

Several of the early chapters of this book are critical of the board. Such criticism is documented and valid. I differ from Edge's conclusions on just about everything. My concern is that the board has not always acted independently, as it is empowered to do by legislation. It repeatedly failed to act in matters of agriculture and the environment, having heard evidence put before it in public hearings. The members, far from coming from widely different backgrounds, come predominantly from the oil and gas industry and politics. The regulators became the mirror image of those regulated.

It is significant that the NEB's glowing quarter-century self-portrait makes no reference to agriculture or the environment. Despite the evidence and concerns placed before it, it was 1972 before the board hired anybody with any expertise in the environment.

A harsh reality is that the NEB continued to be reactionary. Change is forced upon it by exterior and interior forces. Jack Stabback, an old oil and gas man, was perhaps the most reactionary board member it was my misfortune to appear before; he was promoted to be the fourth chairman of the NEB. Among the board staff, the one I found least receptive to agriculture and the environment was Robert Stead; having served eleven years as secretary of the NEB, he spent four years as a board member.

Having reiterated my concerns over the board, I hasten to exclude the staff from such censure. When I returned to visit the NEB in 1985, I received a warm welcome from Yorke Slader, who has since been succeeded by Louise Meagher as secretary. He responded to my questions frankly and to the best of his ability. When he didn't have the answers, he found them. He arranged for me to meet with board staff whose responsibilities affect agriculture and the environment the most. They in turn had prepared a very useful compendium of information in response to my written inquiries. The subsequent interviews were objective and productive. Once again, I had free access to the board's extensive library.

Ulana Perovic, assistant coordinator of information services, had plenty of good news for me. The NEB embarked on a series of Information Bulletins in September 1983:

•Number 1, entitled *Route Approval Procedures,* refers to several changes of benefit to landowners. For instance:

> First the company is required to serve a notice on all owners of land proposed to be acquired and to publish a notice in at least one issue of a publication which is circulated in the area. . . . If the board receives any statement opposing the route, it holds a local public hearing to hear representations from all interested persons. The local public hearing affords landowners and affected parties an opportunity to take part in the determination

of the final route. The board has the authority to allow any reasonable costs incurred by a person in making representations at such a hearing, and such costs are then payable to that person by the company. . . . If the parties cannot agree on the compensation payable for the acquisition of lands, or for damages resulting from the company's operations, the company or the landowner can apply to the Minister of Energy, Mines and Resources to request negotiation or arbitration. . . . Every landowner has the option of receiving compensation, either in a lump sum or in annual or periodic payments which are subject to review every five years.

This latter innovation will be welcomed by landowners who prefer what amounts to a rental agreement. When IPL installed its third line, landowners who requested such an agreement were refused, but Ontario Hydro was able to extract such an agreement from IPL when the pipeline was installed through the corridor acquired earlier by Ontario Hydro from farmers.

•Number 2, *The Public Hearing Process,* is a good-news–bad-news situation. It notes that, "Board counsel does not play an adversarial role and does not oppose or support either the Applicant or any intervenor." This is a welcome change from the time when it was asserted by board counsel that I should be held in strong confines and was singled out to be the last to make an intervention. The bad news refers to the appeal procedure. "A decision or order of the Board may be appealed to the Federal Court of Appeal on a point of law or jurisdiction. . . . Judgments of the Federal Court may with leave be appealed to the Supreme Court of Canada." Extensive correspondence with Ian Blue, when he was a board counsel, confirmed that this is a very murky and difficult appeal procedure, and Blue knew of no instance when it had been carried out. In effect, there is no responsive appeal procedure; even the most unreasonable and arbitrary decision of the board still consigns the affected landowner to grapple with the costs and complexities of Canadian courts.

•Number 3, *Non-Hearing Procedures,* deals with such things as minor changes to a power line. Of interest to agriculture is the item "Leave to cross a pipeline." Under Section 77 of the act, no road, ditch drain, or utility may cross a pipeline, and no excavation or construction may be carried out on the right-of-way, without leave of the Board. Such leave is normally granted without a hearing.

•Number 4, *How to Intervene,* contains information essential to anyone contemplating such a step. It notes that "as a general principle, the Board seeks to hear the views of all parties." There continues to be no assurance that the board will subsequently act logically, rationally, and forthrightly, having heard such views. In this regard, the board will be judged by its record.

•Number 5 is entitled *The Board's Publications.* The NEB is a major publisher and routinely supplies numerous libraries across Canada, the United States, Australia, England, Switzerland, West Germany, and New Zealand.

•Number 6 deals with regulatory information about tolls and tariffs.

•Number 7 describes the resources and services of the NEB library. A library is nothing without a good librarian, such as Nancy Park. When I researched *Canada's Holsteins,* I received tremendous help from the librarian of Agriculture Canada, a schoolmate of our children and a fellow graduate of Medway High School. Nancy Park is another Medway graduate, and for good measure her father had been a buyer of our certified bird's-foot trefoil seed.

•Information Bulletin Number 8 deals with electric power, another responsibility of the NEB.

•Number 9, which was published in June 1985, is entitled *Protection of the Environment — Pipelines.* The Introduction asserts:

> The protection of the environment is a major concern of the National Energy Board in the construction and operation of oil and gas pipelines. . . . The construction of pipelines is normally carried out with due regard for the environment, but if poorly planned and inadequately monitored, can cause a variety of adverse impacts. For example, in the case of agricultural lands, loss of topsoil, soil compaction and drainage alteration are of particular concern. . . . Important environmental issues associated with pipeline projects in southern Canada include the protection of agricultural lands, particularly the sensitive clay soils found in southern Ontario and southern Quebec. . . . Wherever possible, routes are chosen to avoid particularly sensitive areas such as fields with tile drainage or with soil types susceptible to damage. Construction is usually scheduled during the dry summer months or the winter when soil damage is less likely to occur. By storing topsoil separately from sub-soil during construction, soil fertility can be maintained. . . . The Board uses two means of ensuring that companies comply with applicable environmental requirements and effectively deal with any unforeseen problems that may arise as work progresses. First, the pipeline company must have full-time inspectors on site to oversee all of the activities of contractors and to ensure, among other things, that the requirements with respect to environmental matters are being properly fulfilled. Second, Board inspectors periodically visit the project to monitor the condition of the right-of-way and any other relevant matters, and to help resolve any unanticipated difficulties. . . . The Trans Quebec & Maritimes Pipe

Line was built in Quebec through valuable agricultural land and Board inspectors monitored pipeline construction to ensure that the company implemented measures such as topsoil stripping and separation, subsurface drainage repair and post-construction tillage. . . . Landowners who feel that the activities of a pipeline company are adversely affecting their properties can bring their concerns to the Board's attention. The Board will then investigate the complaint. If the complaint is valid, the Board will inform the pipeline company of the problem, request that it contact the landowners concerned, and report to the Board on the outcome of the discussion, including any action proposed to resolve the problem. . . . The company must establish procedures that are to be implemented in the event of an emergency. The Board requires detailed reports of all incidents involving personal injury or fatality, or a leak, break, fire, explosion, or failure on or malfunction of pipelines under its jurisdiction. . . . In a continuing effort to maintain high standards of environmental protection, the Board encourages participation in discussions with the general public, other provincial and federal government departments and agencies, and oil and gas transmission companies.

Phew! Has the world witnessed a more sweeping change of attitude since Saul took the road to Damascus? The magnitude of change can only be appreciated when one reflects on the earlier attitudes, which included total ignorance of farm drainage, condoning massive burning of oil spills, failure to monitor pipeline construction, and continuing willful ignorance of agriculture. The NEB now has fifteen professionals on staff with special expertise in many aspects of the environment. When Yorke Slader circulated all companies under the board's jurisdiction on requisite environmental information in the fall of 1984, he confirmed that the NEB had indeed accepted as part of its mandate protection of the environment.

The rigid and entrenched positions of the NEB had been rendered untenable in the light of Judge Killeen's findings and the subsequent success of John Robinette in ensuring that the decisions became entrenched in Canadian law. The NEB had learned that it could no longer throw farmers to the mercy of the Railway Act; times and legislation had changed. The Expropriation Act was amended. The changes referred to in the above information bulletins were made possible by the sweeping changes in the National Energy Board Act in 1983. No longer could the board condone the destruction of farmland following the publicity of the Senate Special Committee on the Northern Pipeline and the conclusions of Judge Thomas Berger. These are very welcome changes, and the NEB is to be congratulated, regardless of the motivation for change. But that does not mean that all is well or that vigilance can be relaxed.

In December 1982, Jean Chretien, then minister of Energy, Mines and Resources, announced the appointment of a task force to report on pipeline construction costs. The organizations contacted during the task-force investigation included numerous federal and provincial regulatory agencies, pipeline contractors, unions, pipeline suppliers, pipeline companies, and the producers and industrial users of energy. The report, when issued in June 1983, noted that "a related cause for delay in construction start-up can be the failure of project sponsors to allow sufficient time for the necessary regulatory review and approval process, or the failure to submit a well-planned and documented application." However, the task force totally ignored landowners, the environment, and the reality that a couple of farmers could delay even Canada's biggest pipeline projects in the absence of concern for the environment.

An even more ambitious study was that conducted by the NEB into pipeline construction costs 1975–1985. The charts showed such items as steel and labour going up like a Saturn rocket. However, the voluminous report made only a fleeting reference to the cost of land.

It is logical to extrapolate from such reports that the land cost in pipeline construction is a very minor component. It is a further reasonable assumption that a pipeline company can still install its pipelines economically across farmland, providing that it has good pipeline practices and procedures. Probably the biggest landowner-related cost of IPL in installing its third pipeline on the O'Neil and Lewington farms would have been the legal fees paid to Blake, Cassels and Graydon. IPL's drainage contractor, Ken Acton, was paid over $20,000 for work at Larigmoor Farm; practically all of that work would have been unnecessary had the company listened to Drs. Quigley and Pearson or implemented our advice on how to install a pipeline through an aquifer.

Some recent NEB decisions substantiate that the board really does mean business in environmental affairs. Dissatisfied with IPL's environmental impact studies for its Norman Wells pipeline, the company was sent back to generate further studies.

A milestone for the NEB and pipeline construction was the rerouting of the Q and M pipeline to minimize the impact on Quebec agriculture. Traditionally, pipeline construction and urban concentration have been on the best (and limited) farmland. Through the cooperation of the NEB and the pipeline company, the earlier preferred route along the fertile south shore of the St. Lawrence River was abandoned. This deference to good farmland was followed by the change in the North Bay shortcut of TransCanada Pipe Lines, which was previously planned to go through artificially drained farmland between North Bay and Ottawa.

Jim Hodges, assistant director for the environment and right-of-way branch of the NEB, says, "The board is very receptive to the private landowner now."

The merits of planning to mitigate damage to and even avoidance of aquifers are now considered among the board's newer priorities. The changes in the attitudes of pipeline companies are exemplified by Trans-Canada, which now submits more environmental-impact studies than even the expanded NEB environmental staff can cope with.

In total, these beneficial changes are particularly welcome to farmers in both Canada and the United States because such major companies as TransCanada and IPL, through their various associated companies, are very active on both sides of the forty-ninth parallel. There are, of course, reciprocal interests. The Federal Energy Regulatory Commission (FERC) is the U.S. counterpart of the NEB; the NEB environmental branch staff were kept posted by FERC on the St. Clair Pipelines Limited crossing of the St. Clair River because this is yet another pipeline installed partly in both countries.

Because most of the changes made by the NEB relate to common-sense environmental-impact planning, the avoidance of problems, and mitigation of damage to farmland and river crossings, they will likely contribute to lower, not higher, pipeline costs in the future.

While the progress that I was happy to learn about while visiting the NEB is a quantum leap, it continues with unabated momentum. To this point, I have recognized the courteous help of NEB staff and have reserved my censure for the appointed board members. The happy finale of visiting the NEB is that I can now express my appreciation to Roland Priddle, the current NEB chairman. He was a relatively junior civil servant when I first appeared before the NEB. He was the most receptive to my concerns even then, and I believe that had he been promoted much earlier, many of the problems and conflicts between agriculture and pipelines would never have been allowed to fester.

The most objective way to indicate the extent of these welcome changes is to reproduce Roland Priddle's own overview of what the NEB has done since the 1975 pipeline construction through Larigmoor Farm.

Initially, the Board's environmental requirements for projects were determined on a case-by-case basis, but soon it became apparent that a more effective process was needed. In 1976, therefore, the Board introduced general guidelines respecting environmental information to be submitted with applications to construct pipelines in ecological regions of Canada. After a trial period, and after allowing for comment from the public and industry, the guidelines were reviewed and, in 1978, incorporated into the Board's

Rules of Practice and Procedure, thus formally becoming the Board's environmental information requirements for applications to construct pipeline facilities.

In response to increased pipeline construction during the late '70's, the Board began to conduct regular environmental inspections of pipeline construction and operating facilities, not only as a means of ensuring that the Board's environmental conditions to certificates were being properly implemented, but also as a way for Board staff to observe first-hand the effectiveness and practicability of various environmental protection measures. Thus began an important learning process which has culminated in a number of important regulatory initiatives at the Board in the '80's.

Perhaps the most important of those has been the adoption by the Board of an issue-oriented approach to environmental protection. From the initial stages of project development, companies are encouraged to identify in their applications those environmental concerns which may not be addressed adequately using standard practices. In such instances, special protection or impact mitigation procedures would have to be devised by the company and approved by the Board prior to the start of construction.

In addition, the former regulations respecting gas pipelines and oil pipelines have been replaced by the new Onshore Pipeline Regulations which have adopted an issue-oriented approach. The Regulations require companies to conduct environmental inspections and maintain throughout the construction period a list of environmental issues which is modified continually as new issues arise and others are resolved by effective mitigative or restorative measures. Ti ? issues list then forms a basis for all post-construction monitoring by the company, with the ultimate goal being that all issues are resolved. The environmental issues list is also used by the Board to focus its environmental audits during and after construction. Looking to the future and the likely development of hydrocarbon resources in Canadian offshore areas, the Board will soon promulgate its Offshore Pipeline Regulations. Those Regulations will also have a strong environmental component which will incorporate the environmental issues list concept.

Over the years, other major changes have taken place at the Board that directly affect the selection of pipeline routes. The first improvements were achieved as a result of Senate-initiated amendments to the National Energy Board Act, which provided an opportunity for landowners to inquire more fully into the appropriateness of the detailed route selected by a company. Other improvements related to landowners' rights in seeking compensation with respect to both the acquisition of easements and in the event of damages resulting from the construction or operation of pipelines.

In March 1983, legislation was introduced that described new requirements controlling routing and land acquisition. Its effect was the creation of a two-stage route approval procedure involving a certificate stage for the general route, and a new detailed-route stage. The purpose of the latter is to provide landowners an opportunity to express their concerns to the Board without having to participate at the general facilities hearing. To encourage public participation, an improved process of public notification was developed, detailed-route hearings are held in the affected communities and intervenors are compensated for any reasonable costs they incur in order to appear.

The exercise by landowners of their rights in the event of disputes over compensation for the acquisition of easements, or over damages resulting from construction or operation of the facilities have also been improved as a result of the new legislation. Where necessary, unresolved matters of compensation between a landowner and a company can be taken to the Minister of Energy, Mines and Resources for negotiation or arbitration. These new procedures seem to be generally acceptable to the Canadian public. In the six years since the legislation was introduced, there has been only one case where contentious matters between a pipeline company and a landowner could not be resolved other than by arbitration.

A September 1989 initiative of the Board relates to early public notice for proposed facilities. A draft Memorandum of Guidance on Early Public Notification of Proposed Applications which will provide for public input as early as possible during the planning and development stage of a project has been sent to interested parties for comment. The new procedure would require a company to implement a public information program to explain a proposed project and its potential environmental and social effects, as well as allowing an opportunity for public comment.

Today, the Board regulates a total of about 35,000 km of pipeline in Canada, and although it has responded in the past to a diversity of environmental challenges, perhaps the greatest challenges lie ahead. As hydrocarbon reserves in frontier areas are developed, it will be the Board's responsibility to ensure that the associated pipelines are built and operated in a way that affords maximum protection to the environment. The construction of a Mackenzie Valley gas pipeline may be the first of those projects. In its regulatory and advisory capacities, the Board considers that part of its mandate is to ensure that Canada's energy policies are consistent with the principle of sustainable development so that future generations of Canadians will enjoy the benefits of both abundant energy resources and a healthy environment. I can assure you that the Board will continue and improve its efforts to ensure careful protection of the environment and safeguarding of landowners' rights in the construction and operation of pipelines in Canada.

The NEB now has a comprehensive summary of good practices for acceptable environmental protection. Reference to just a few of the key points will confirm that both attitudes and procedures have changed dramatically for the better:

•Archeological surveys. Special care is warranted in carrying out archeological surveys at streams and river crossings or other areas along the right of way. (Judge Killeen would have appreciated this!)

•Trenching. Topsoil should be stripped and stockpiled separately from the subsoil in order to avoid mixing. Where terrain instability may be encountered during trenching, proper dewatering, bracing, or other suitable means should be provided to ensure the stability of the trench and side slopes. (This would take care of the problems encountered when an aquifer is breached.) The time interval between trenching and back-filling should be kept to a minimum. (Readers may recall that during the winter of 1975–1976, as much as seventeen miles in a stretch of open, vulnerable trench were exposed to the elements.)

•Backfilling of the trench should be carried out carefully with the placement of subsoil first, then followed by topsoil. Backfill "roaching" or "mounding" over the trench is essential to accommodate later subsidence.

•Restoration on agricultural lands should include complete repair of all drainage tiles, erosion control, removal of rock and stones, careful replacement of topsoil, decompaction of soils, and plans for continued monitoring of crop growth and productivity.

And so by 1989, the NEB had implemented my ten points (and much more!), which had been dismissed in 1967 by *Oilweek* as the aberrations of a disgruntled farmer. The icing on the cake had come in March 1983 when land-acquisition procedures under the NEB Act were amended. The amendments traced to the mortal wounding of the Railway Act in the court of Judge Killeen and subsequently in the appeals to the Supreme Court of Ontario.

Roland Priddle has the last word: "Under the current NEB legislation, once the plans and profiles and books of reference had been approved (which could involve a public hearing) and only if the company were unable to conclude an agreement with the owner, the company could apply in writing to the NEB for what is now referred to as a right-of-entry."

CHAPTER 23

Ideas
Incorporated

We act wisely when all other possibilities are exhausted.
—ANONYMOUS ENGLISH PHILOSOPHER

L ast spring, we removed a fence we had erected nearly thirty years ago. When the old fence bottom was plowed, the soil had a beautiful, mellow, and friable structure. It was in even better condition than other parts of Larigmoor Farm that had never been touched by pipeline equipment. It provided an indication that modern farm equipment, even when used with extreme care, can contribute to soil compaction. No farmer worth his salt will drive a tractor over clay or clay-loam soils when there is the slightest danger of soil compaction due to excessive moisture. The broad significance of soil compaction is now being appreciated by scientists, regulatory authorities, and regulated companies.

The NEB now has the expertise to evaluate the costs and benefits of new construction. It has the specialists in fish and wildlife biology who can assist in mitigating the impact of construction, especially in those more northerly latitudes where damage tends to be permanent. A measure of the change at the NEB is that delegations come from overseas to learn how damage can be mitigated, and NEB personnel are invited to participate in symposia abroad.

There have been comparable sweeping changes in attitudes in the provinces. For instance, the Ontario Energy Board published environmental guidelines for the construction and operation of hydrocarbon pipelines in Ontario. No longer will a pipeline company get away with a "windshield appraisal" by driving down the highway or a routing that consists of drawing a line from A to B. On the subject of agricultural lands, the guidelines state, "The use of food land for pipelines and related facilities should be minimized. . . . Accordingly, the use of the lowest capability agricultural land is preferred for optimum route selection. . . . Prime agricultural lands, generally considered as Classes 1–3 in the CLI (Canadian Land Inventory) capability classification and speciality crop lands should be avoided."

Earlier, reference was made to the initiative in the regional municipality of Waterloo, Ontario, in drafting a policy for hydro, gas, oil, and communication lines. One proviso is that "lines are to be located in such a manner to minimize their impact on people, the adjacent uses of land, the ecology and the environment."

The Senate of Canada, as detailed earlier, contributed to the reform of some of the more archaic aspects of the laws relating to expropriation. A further initiative of the Senate was the report on soil conservation by its Standing Committee on Agriculture, Fisheries, and Forestry. That report, entitled *Soil at Risk,* observed that "the installation of oil and gas pipelines and surface mining activities are the two major causes of soil mixing and disturbance on agricultural land in Canada. Of all the surface mining activities the extraction of coal, sand and gravel most affect agricultural soils."

The area of land disturbed for the extraction of sand, gravel, and stone in Canada is estimated at 78,000 hectares (1 ha = 2.47 acres). The strip-mining of coal in Alberta, Saskatchewan, and New Brunswick involves another 12,000 hectares. The Senate report states,

> Renewed interest in coal as a fuel for the generation of electricity and for industrial processes probably means that further large areas of prairie soil will be disturbed. Some 80% of Alberta's shallow coal deposits are in agricultural regions. Alberta now has strict regulations involving the reclamation of land used for strip mining. It takes an average of five years for reclamation to be completed and a further five years before the soil returns to a productive state capable of supporting agriculture.

We saw earlier that *Oilweek* could explore two decades into the future with the president of Imperial Oil without making any reference to the environment. Today, no energy company annual report is considered complete without some environmental commitment. Through a combination of public-policy and free-enterprise wheeler-dealing, Petro-Canada has become number one at Canada's gas pumps. Its annual report acknowledges "a special responsibility to find a balance between the need to provide further sources of hydrocarbons for Canada, and the requirement that the country's environment be respected." The annual report of Suncor, Inc., notes that in 1985–1986 there were further investments in protection of environmental quality in order to comply with Alberta government regulations. Ontario Hydro recently displaced Hydro Quebec as the largest Crown-owned corporation in Canada. Ontario Hydro has had a very checkered career in farmers' perceptions as a result of its installation of transmission lines through farmlands. A further concern over Ontario Hydro is the generation of electricity at thermal plants, with the inevitable contribution to acid rain. It is encouraging to find that Ontario Hydro "recognizes that economic development must be consistent with protection of the natural and social environment. Ontario Hydro realises that because it is part of the problem, it must be part of the solution."

There are encouraging indications that confrontation is giving way to cooperation.

Facility Siting and Routing '84 Energy and Environment, the proceedings of a symposium held at Banff, Alberta, was published in two volumes by the Environmental Protection Service of Environment Canada. The sponsors included two consulting and planning firms, Acres and MacLaren. The government of Canada was involved through Environment Canada and the Department of Fisheries and Oceans. And the sponsors from the energy industry were Nova Scotia Power, Petro-Canada, and Union Gas. The list of participants reveals even more how times have changed, for included are the Honourable Thomas Berger; Ms. Connie Hunt, of the Canadian Institute of Resources Law at the University of Calgary; and Ken Berry, environment inspector, Westcoast Transmission. The corporate representatives also came from Union Gas, Alberta Power, Chevron Canada, Nova Corporation, TransCanada Pipelines, Dome Canada, PanCanadian Petroleum, TransAlta Utilities, and Esso Resources. It is of interest to note that the representatives of the Canadian corporate sector had titles like Manager Environmental Affairs or Environmental Biologist. Jim Hodges attended as chief of the Environment Division of the NEB. Regulatory authorities were there from most Canadian provinces, many U.S. states, and as far afield as Norway. The participants came from many different disciplines, including biology, geography, planning, and environmental law. A comparable interdisciplinary involvement was seen in the participation of various other provincial, state, and federal departments. Given that Banff is a nice place to be in the spring, it must still be recognised that such a cosmopolitan gathering interested in energy and the environment would have been unthinkable even a very few years ago.

But have the energy companies really changed? To find out, I sent a form letter to the chairman, president, or chief executive officer of just about every pipeline company in Canada.

The first response came from Darcy McKeough, a former high-profile Ontario cabinet minister who was then chairman and president of Union Gas of Chatham, Ontario, who wrote, "Dear Peter, If I hadn't realised that your letter was a form letter I would have been very upset. Frankly we at Union Gas are doing a damn good job after a few mistakes in the past. We can always do better and are working at that very hard. . . . This pipe line laying corporation at least is way ahead of you!" In yet another of those gossamer threads, the then environmental planner at Union Gas turned out to be the son of the scoutmaster I had been fortunate in finding when I formed a Sea Scout group. I was pleased to hear from Ian Moncrieff that Union Gas had environmental policies and environmental protection specifications and corporate policies relating to the environment and agricultural research. Union Gas put some teeth into its regulations and empowered his associates to dismiss contractors' workmen who are incompetent or careless. There were comprehensive guidelines for the topsoil inspector, and diaries and reports must be maintained. The trenching specifications included the following:

> Where tile drain is encountered, the contractors shall dig the ditch so that the pipeline be laid over or under such tile with a minimum clearance of 15 cm. At the time such tile is damaged, the contractor shall carefully and immediately mark the location of such damaged tile at the trench and both sides of the easement and install a plugging device approved by the company and supplied by the contractor on the downstream opening of the damaged tile so that foreign material will not be allowed to enter the tile. At no time will bags be permitted for this plugging purpose. These plugs will remain in place until the contractors' tile repair crew begin to repair the damaged tile.

It is ironic that Moncrieff has now left Union Gas and his Consolidated Environmental Group Ltd. has been allocated $130,000 by a group of farmers who were given $208,400 by the Ontario Energy Board to finance opposition to the Union Gas fourth pipeline through Middlesex County farms.

The response from TransCanada Pipelines was also prompt and encouraging. The company's Environmental Affairs Department was then headed by the very experienced W. Ross Milne who had the backing of three environmental analysts and a support staff. Their mandate is detailed in the company's *Environmental Protection Practices Handbook,* which is periodically revised. It begins with a statement which is a commitment to agriculture and the environment: "It is the policy of TransCanada Pipelines Limited to design, construct and operate its facilities in a manner which reduces short and long-term negative impacts on the environment. In practice this involves compliance with the regulations and guidelines of the National Energy Board, and applicable federal and provincial legislation, and with all Company commitments to governments, interest groups and landowners."

The philosophy of TransCanada — and it does have a philosophy — is of interest to anyone even indirectly involved with energy and the environment. First, there is an environmental department, which is allocated the resources to impact beneficially on the construction and operation of pipelines. A second important point is that environmental protection is not the exclusive prerogative of that department. "The success of the environmental programs depends on the interaction and cooperation among construction and field operations personnel, engineers, technicians, right-of-way agents and environmental specialists. The multi-disciplinary and inter-departmental approach through to environmental protection is therefore employed."

Interest in the environment is not restricted to intramural resource personnel. "Liaison with technical experts in the public and private sectors, such as regional and district biologists, foresters, water quality experts, soil scientists, geologists, and archaeologists is routine in order to obtain new information and state of the art advice on various matters relating to the company's facilities."

An important part of the TransCanada philosophy is that concern for agriculture and the environment is not an afterthought; it is integral to good planning and pipeline practices.

For instance, "TransCanada rights-of-way have traversed a wide variety of agricultural land uses which vary in intensity and productivity, such as pasture, orchards, field and speciality crops. In each of these cases, experience has shown that the effects of pipeline construction can be limited to the short-term, provided adequate, mitigative and restorative measures are applied."

These are some of the fundamentals of the policy to mitigate damage, and they include construction when soils are normally dry or sufficiently frozen. Another relates to topsoil. "The mixing of topsoil and subsoil may result in the reduction of crop productivity and is therefore a major concern in agricultural lands. Care will be taken to ensure that the correct amount of topsoil is removed, stored separately from the spoil pile and subsequently replaced with a minimum of handling."

TransCanada policies confirm an awareness of the testimony before Judge Killeen. For instance, relative to Dr. Roy Turkington's input, it observes, "The introduction of dormant weed seeds from below normal cultivation depth is possible during topsoil stripping and trenching and this may result in the subsequent spreading of weeds along the right-of-way. Care will be taken to ensure that weeds are controlled on the right-of-way and that spreading of weed seeds along or off the right-of-way is minimized by washing down equipment, establishing a crop cover, harrowing et cetera."

TransCanada does not duck the crucial issue of cessation of construction in the event of soil or weather conditions that would lead to irreparable damage. In this regard it is light years away from IPL, which recognized availability of enough riprap to hold up heavy equipment as the only constraint.

To substantiate further that TransCanada does have a philosophy, one need only turn to the sections on wetlands and forests; it is most encouraging to find reference to concern for any "aesthetic depreciation of the landscape."

Husky Oil Limited, which is 67 percent owned by Nova, an Alberta Corporation, has both an Environmental Affairs and a Native Affairs Program. Nova itself has an Environmental Affairs Department with a mandate "to give priority to matters of air and water quality, soil conservation and agricultural productivity, wildlife and noise control." The Nova environmental department is staffed by professionals with a variety of backgrounds, including soil science; this makes good a deficiency that was evident in much of the pipeline construction in Canada in earlier years. The advantage of such an in-house environmental department is evident in the filing of applications with regulatory authorities. The natural evolutions that follow include monitoring and inspection during construction and environmental research and development.

Some of the Nova pipeline construction is through land that has a topsoil stratum of 150 mm or less (in Imperial units, perhaps three inches). In 1980, Nova developed a machine specifically designed for stripping of frozen topsoil. The merits of this initiative have been documented in subsequent successful pipeline construction.

The now defunct Versatile Corporation was among the companies hard hit by the National Energy Program through its interest in Bralorne Resources and the reduced demand for its Versatile farm equipment, as a result of declining farm income and the drought that ravaged the 1985 wheat crop in the southern Prairies. However, G. Martin Greer, Versatile's vice-president and general counsel, wrote to say, "We share your concern with respect to the use of agricultural land and a considerable amount of the company's research and development activities relate to conserving agricultural land and increasing its productivity."

My enquiries extended to the changing corporate structure in Canada, but with meagre results. A. E. Downing, chairman and CEO of Hiram Walker Resources Limited, declined to take a position, despite the fact that Walker held a 34 percent interest in IPL. PanCanadian Petroleum is today Canada's number-one oil and gas producer, but is 87 percent owned by Canadian Pacific Enterprises Limited (CPE), in turn owned by CP. CPE president, S. E. Eagles, responded that "any pipeline installation would be carried out in full recognition of and compliance with, such requirements as may be determined by the regulatory authorities. . . . The regulatory approval for any pipeline installed would take into account the topsoil and drainage protection provisions which are considered to be necessary."

As we are currently witnessing an accelerating concentration in a few corporate hands, it behooves top management to take a closer involvement in the land-use activities of subsidiary companies or those in which there are major investments.

Westar Petroleum Limited is a member of the B.C. Resources Group, operates some seven hundred oil and gas wells, and has a pipeline complex, primarily in Saskatchewan. Westar president David Banks responded frankly that his company did not have a written environmental policy, had not done any agriculture-related research, and did not have an environmental department. However, he stressed that

> Westar Petroleum adheres to policies established by the provincial and local governments in the provinces in which we work. On both drilling and pipeline operations, the topsoil is removed during the period of oil field activity and replaced so that normal agriculture may continue when either the well is drilled or the pipeline is in service. Pipeline operations are discontinued during periods when the rights-of-way become impassable. Aquifers, when encountered, are sealed from the trenches with non-porous material or quickly backfilled with the indigenous material.

Hallelujah! How refreshing it is to find an oil and gas executive with an awareness of how an aquifer can be traversed with minimal disruption.

TransAlta Utilities Corporation is another energy company that has an awareness of aquifers and policies for cessation of construction in the event of adverse weather. The company's Environmental Planning Section is headed by a Ph.D. biologist. The TransAlta initiatives in minimizing environmental impact include tests, demonstrations, and research. The Plains Coal Reclamation Research Program is a joint research project in concert with the government of Alberta. The company-financed programs relate to local farm management and a series of demonstrations assessing the benefits of mulching, manuring, topsoiling, fertilizing, and planting legumes. Some of the TransAlta activities include open-cast, or strip, coal mining, and a series of plots is designed to show the possibilities in land reclamation. The McAllister Whitewood trials involve a ten-year demonstration in crop rotations and fertilizing techniques.

As a matter of principle, TransAlta stockpiled topsoil and organic material long before this was mandatory; the replacement procedures are designed to minimize damage to drainage patterns or soil productivity.

The response of Bob Heule, then IPL president, included the welcome admission that "much has been learned from past pipeline construction projects respecting mitigation of impacts on the environment, particularly on agricultural land." It came as a surprise to learn that the funding of the pipeline impact research at Macdonald College of McGill University had been jointly funded by IPL and Agriculture Canada in 1977–1979. Heule provided no specifics on environmental policies or procedures and forwarded the correspondence for action by Dr. A. F. MacKenzie at Macdonald College, but there the trail died, and no information was made available to me.

However, Heule had included an article published in the August 1982 *Right of Way* magazine. It was written by Alex Ramsay, a student of MacKenzie who was then working for IPL and subsequently became the company's right-of-way chief. The title of that article was "To What Extent Is Topsoil Conservation Necessary in Pipelining?" IPL stood out in my inquiries as the only pipeline company questioning such practices. This situation was exacerbated by Ramsay's selection of published references that included items Judge Killeen had questioned, while the omissions embraced all of the research that positively influenced the judge.

Notwithstanding such discouraging setbacks, I continued to monitor IPL. I am happy to say that as with the NEB, a new era appears to have dawned. In 1989, IPL, perhaps the oldest and the largest pipeline company in North America, adopted an environmental policy. This is such a welcome milestone that it is reproduced in its entirety.

Interprovincial Pipe Line Company
Lakehead Pipeline Company Inc.
ENVIRONMENTAL POLICY

1. The protection of the environment is an integral element in conduct of company business.

2. The company will ensure that adverse environmental effects are

minimized through careful planning, implementation of effective protection measures, and monitoring company activities.

3. Company rules and procedures for environmental protection will comply with government regulations and standards, and be consistent with industry codes and guidelines.

4. The company will minimize consequences of emergency events by ensuring prompt and effective response.

5. The company will provide appropriate training to ensure employees understand their responsibility to protect the environment.

6. Employees and contractors must follow company environmental rules and procedures and must carry out work in an environmentally responsible manner at all times.

7. The company will provide the public and government with relevant information regarding planned activities and will actively respond to their concerns.

8. Environmental damage resulting from company actions or actions of its contractors will be repaired in a timely and efficient manner.

9. Environmental research will be encouraged, supported and undertaken when necessary to improve company environmental protection and reclamation procedures.

I am also indebted to John Hayes, IPL environmental coordinator, for some company documents that confirm that the intent of the environmental policy is being implemented now that IPL has an environmental team effort with the capability to monitor pipeline construction. For instance: "Conservation of topsoil from degradation due to pipeline construction was a major objective." "Topsoil/subsoil mixing can adversely affect agricultural capability. Dilution of organic matter and changes in texture affect the moisture and nutrient-holding capacities of soil, as well as the structural and drainage characteristics." "Travel of heavy equipment can cause compaction of soils resulting in poor internal drainage and restricted plant rooting." "Potential for wind erosion was reduced during construction by minimizing the width of the cleared right-of-way and by minimizing the amount of grading employed in right-of-way preparation." "Improperly conducted pipeline construction can interfere with normal uses of lands crossed and adjacent to the right-of-way." "Since pipeline construction activities in special land use areas such as cities, towns, rural residential subdivisions, and golf courses can cause an inconvenience to the populations affected, special measures were required to minimize impacts during construction."

As a result of staff and consultant initiatives, IPL now has an "Environmental Issues" list as part of the planning process. The company also now recognizes that "all potential unresolved environmental issues cannot be determined from conditions at completion of construction. Therefore post-construction monitoring programs will be implemented with the objective of identifying any unresolved issues. IPL is committed to ensuring that all lands disturbed during construction are stabilized and returned to productive use."

So much for the individual companies. What is the industry doing collectively for its environmental image? The Canadian Petroleum Association (CPA) is the umbrella organization that embraces most of Canada's oil and natural gas industries and the pipelines that take their products to market. Ian Scott, senior coordinator, Pipeline Division of CPA, exhibits an infectious pride in what the association is doing.

The CPA Pipeline Environmental Committee is responsible for researching-generating any specific environmental information affecting pipeline construction. It liaises with federal and provincial governments, identifies environmental problems, recommends solutions, and establishes annual objectives.

CPA is big in publishing, and its bibliography alone is a large volume. *Guidelines For The Reclamation Of Linear Disturbances* is a clear, colourfully illustrated, and comprehensive mine of information. It cites much of the information that has become available, chiefly since the late 1970s, from such diverse sources as the Alberta Land Conservation and Reclamation Council, and the U.S. Environmental Protection Agency.

The CPA environmental initiatives are both responsive to public concerns and responsible in their factual documentation. For instance, there is an annual published summary of *Pipeline Performance,* warts and all. CPA has developed *Environmental Operating Guidelines.* Bill Hopper, chairman of both Petro-Canada and CPA, says that "our 'Environmental Code of Practice' breaks important new ground. It makes an important contribution to establishing a single, high environmental standard for industry to adhere to. It creates a bridge of understanding about our environmental commitment between the industry and governments, environmentalists, its customers and other industries."

CPA is also active in education. Its 1990 training sessions included courses on Environmental Land Management, Environmental Planning for Linear Development, and Pipeline Environmental Inspection.

One of the most ambitious CPA initiatives was its third pipeline conference, which was held in 1989 with the theme "Pipelines in Transition."

In 1989, CPA joined forces with the Independent Petroleum Association of Canada for a task force on "Oil Spill Preparedness on the Upstream Petroleum Industry." The chairman, J. J. O'Connor, who is also president of Mobil Oil Canada, observed, "While we have concluded that generally we do, and have done, a good job of protecting the environment and have adequate preventive policies and measures in place, we can do better. There is no room for complacency in dealing with this most important issue. Our recommendations reflect that. Once implemented, they will do much to assure Canadians of our willingness and ability to deal with this aspect of our business." The report puts its money where its mouth is and advocates the investment of some $15 million over the next five years "to prevent and control onshore and offshore oil spills more effectively."

Oil and the environment interface on the East and the West Coasts of Canada and in the North in such areas as the Beaufort Sea. The issues involving spills from marine tankers are being explored in a study sponsored by the Petroleum Association for the Conservation of the Canadian Environment (PACE).

None of the corporate or industry environmental entities quoted (with the exception of IPL) participated in any of the NEB hearings in which I participated in the 1960s and 1970s. In the 1990s it is good to be able to report that so many sound environmental practices have been adopted and that the momentum for beneficial change continues.

CHAPTER 24

Soil Isn't Just Dirt

A clod of earth, seemingly simple and lifeless, is now known to be highly complex in structure, its particles most elaborate in their composition, with numerous invisible crevices inhabited by prodigious numbers of living organisms inconceivably small, leading lives of which we can form only the haziest conception, yet somehow linked up with our lives in that they produce the food of plants which constitute our food, and remove from the soil substances that would be harmful to us.

—SIR JOHN RUSSELL

The interesting people we met and the areas of knowledge that they opened for us to enjoy are among the continuing by-products, the bonuses, of bringing democracy to the oil patch. As long as I can remember, I have had a respect for the soil and an awareness of stewardship of the soil, but I had no inkling of the wonderful world that lay beneath my feet.

In 1978, Jean and I enjoyed the opportunity to explore the agriculture of Brazil and Peru. In Brazil, we were impressed by the vigor with which erosion problems were being enthusiastically tackled. In Peru, we witnessed the tragedy of a country that neglected agriculture. Everywhere we went we gathered soil samples for Dr. Al Tomlin, who had arranged with Canadian quarantine authorities for us to return with them in sealed metal containers. We gathered soil samples on the contoured hills of Parana, high in the Andes, in the upper reaches of the Amazon Basin, from the terraces of Machu Picchu, and from a compost heap on a dairy farm near Pôrto Allegre in the Brazilian state of Rio Grande do Sul.

Those soil samples confirmed that soil isn't just dirt. We had returned with a wide variety of microscopic species. All the samples were autoclaved once positive identification was made to preclude the risk of introducing to Canada some soil-borne disease. One specimen, a soil mite and a denizen of that compost heap, *Neogamasellevans sp. near brevitremata Karg,* turned out to be a species new to science and is now preserved in perpetuity in plastic at the Canadian National Collection in Ottawa.

It was Bob Quigley who had first sparked our interest in a totally new dimension for us. He had involved his colleague at UWO, Dr. Jim Zajic, who holds a master's degree in soil microbiology from Wisconsin and a Ph.D. from the University of California. In the court of Judge Killeen, Geoff Bladon had completed the lengthy introduction of Zajic when John Brownlie jumped to his feet. "Your Honour, to interrupt my friend, I think we have arrived at the grand moment. The Railway Act says: 'The arbitrator shall examine on oath or solemn affirmation such witnesses as may appear before him, but no more than three expert or opinion witnesses shall be called on behalf of any party.' " It was then that Killeen spoke of his higher duty to arrive at the truth, so Zajic's testimony became part of the transcript. Because it linked with several other developments outside the court, I postponed detailed reference until this chapter.

Most people, if they give it any thought, probably think that soil is inhabited only by such visible creatures as earthworms and grubs. Zajic's speciality is the inhabitants that can't be seen with the naked eye. Said Zajic: "Microbes are a unicellular form of life; you need a microscope or an electron microscope to see them. They have all the properties of life. They are able to reproduce. They have all the requirements of life. They need organic matter. They need energy. They need cations and anions which are essential for life processes. They represent a simple but a very complex entity unto themselves."

Court Exhibit 37 was a sample of good soil, rich in organic matter. Jim Zijac fingered a tiny pinch of that soil and told the court:

> A gram of this soil could contain up to one hundred fifty thousand different species of microbes. What do I mean by a species? If you take man, *homo sapiens,* that represents a species. When I say one hundred fifty thousand species, I am describing a very complex number of microorganisms, each representing a different form of life, each having specific nutrient require- ments and specific environmental needs, and carrying on an interdependent type of relationship as far as all these microbes are concerned. That same gram could have billions of microbes.

Geoff Bladon, chameleonlike, had been obliged to immerse himself once again in an entirely different discipline of science. As he led Zajic on a conducted tour of the soil, our lexicon of terms increased dramatically.

The microbial species, it appeared, were divided between the *autotrophes* (generally the plants), which live on mineral matter and fix energy, usually solar, and the *heterotrophes* (generally the animals), which live on organic matter. Earlier, our knowledge of Latin had increased; now our neglected Greek education received an assist from Dr. Zajic. *Heterotrophic,* derived from the Greek words *hetero* and *trophes,* meaning "other" and "nourishment," respectively. And so began yet another archaeological expedition that linked the inhabitants of soil to pipeline practices.

Failure to conserve the topsoil, which is the only soil stratum uniformly rich in organic matter, results in a surface material that is low in organic matter. Hence it is subject to erosion and "puddling," or soil compaction, leading to a lack of oxygen, an aerobic condition.

Explained Zajic:

> Since the oxygen supply is limited, or there is no oxygen present, the microbes have to get oxygen from someplace else. They scavenge the oxygen from nitrate, and in so doing reduce that nitrate to gaseous nitrogen. It is a step-wise process, and nitrogen will be lost to the atmosphere; that's denitrification. Nitrate is needed for plant growth or for soil fertility. If you have a well-aerated soil, you can have nitrification. If there is oxygen, ammonium is oxidized to nitrate. So the microbes will either denitrify or nitrify, depending strictly on the amount of oxygen that is present. It acts like a switch. Another compound that is needed by plants is sulphate; in an anaerobic soil the sulphate is reduced to sulphides and thus converted into a form that is unavailable for plant growth.

And then Jim Zajic got into another area that confirmed relevance to the subject at hand and the need for his special expertise to complement that of Bob Quigley, Roy Turkington, and Jim O'Toole.

We had concentrated on bird's-foot trefoil production for several very good reasons. Once bird's-foot trefoil becomes established, it lasts virtually forever. The seedpods, as they mature, form in the shape of a bird's foot and ultimately literally explode and begin trefoil regeneration. Trefoil is a legume high in protein, but unlike alfalfa, it does not have the hazard of bloat, which can kill an animal following ghastly agony. Trefoil enjoys another attribute of economic benefit in an era of high energy costs. While the costs of nitrogenous fertilizers so essential to economic growth had climbed astronomically, the trefoil plant could happily go on generating its own nitrogen.

Jim Zajic explained that the legume species, in addition to such forages as trefoil and alfalfa, included the white beans and the soybeans grown by Stu O'Neil. These legumes need the help of microbes if miniature nitrogen factories are to develop. Explained Zajic:

> The rhizobium bacteria infect the roots of legume plants and form a nodule. We say they are symbiotic because it takes the plant and the microbe working together. Neither the plant alone nor the microbe alone can fix nitrogen. If you want to take advantage of nature in adding atmospheric nitrogen to a soil in a form that is readily usable by plants, the nitrogen-fixing microorganisms and the nitrogen-fixing populations are very important. They add nitrogen to the soil in a form that can be utilized by a plant and at no cost to the farmer. If a farmer attempted to put the same level of nitrogen on in terms of ammonia or nitrate or urea, the chances are he would burn any subsequent crop. Nitrogen fixation is very beneficial and profitable to a farm operation.

And the key to all this beneficial activity beneath our feet was the organic content of the soil. Earlier testimony had established that it would take ten tons of manure per year for seventy-five years to achieve a 1 percent increase in the organic content of the soil. In this regard, Zajic said, "It's a very delicate system that has built up over hundreds and thousands of years. You disturb that, and it could even be geological periods of time to get back to the same basic soil structure."

The interrelationship of microbial populations and soil pH were examined and then another jawbreaker had to be spelled for the benefit of the court reporter. *Mycorrhizae,* a branch of the mycorrhizae microbes, grow right next to the roots of plants. They specialise in the transfer of cations and anions from either a mineral form or a soluble form and assist in getting them to the root system of the plant. "If the organic matter decreases, you are not going to get the mycorrhizae populations," said Zajic.

Al Tomlin subsequently contributed the chapter on soil animals in *Pipeline Construction Impact on a Cattle Farm,* referred to earlier. Dr. Tomlin and his colleagues in the soil zoology group at the London Research Centre of Agriculture Canada became involved on Bob Quigley's invitation.

Sink a shovel just about anywhere in the undisturbed soil of Larigmoor Farm, and you'll come up with some earthworms. In the disturbed and compacted construction area, even if you could get a shovel into the ground, you would not find the soil inhabited by earthworms. Dr.

Tomlin's sampling was much more sophisticated, and his laboratory procedures included the use of the Tullgren funnel method for extraction of soil arthropods. Concluded Tomlin:

> The pipeline construction had a marked affect on earthworm populations by reducing the numbers of the two dominant earthworm species. The results of the arthropod survey are more difficult to interpret. The most apparent difference was the large population of astigmated mites which had built up in the right-of-way. The species involved was probably feeding on surface litter that probably accumulated because of reduced earthworm populations. The generally larger gamasine mite population found in the right-of-way was probably preying on the large population of astigmated mites. The podurid springtails had significantly larger populations on the easement on five of six sampling dates. Presumably they were taking advantage of some food source or were under reduced pressure from predation, compared with the control area. In general, the construction has had direct effects on soil animal populations. Inversion of subsoil with topsoil has removed the upper humus layer as a habitat for earthworm species. Compaction of the soil and the pipe overburden has excluded deep burrowing worms such as *Lumbricus terrestris*. Despite the gross insult, the soil, or more correctly the soil fauna, has suffered from the construction process. It is a hopeful sign that there are several species of animals which are able to exploit the situation by colonizing the pipeline soil overburden and establish life processes which will lead to a broader species base and eventually to a better quality soil. Just how long this might take, however, is at present unknown.

In June 1985, The University of Western Ontario was host to the Canadian Congress of Biology. A major symposium, which attracted a lot of interest, was entitled "It's Not Just Dirt — The Relationship among Soil Biota, Structure and Fertility." It was chaired by Dr. Tomlin. He pointed out that "the soil beneath your feet can teem with life; but the number of species is in inverse proportion to the disturbance of the soil. The greater the disturbance, the fewer the species." The participants came from Canada, the United States, and the United Kingdom, and together demonstrated just how much there is to learn about that largely unappreciated "dirt" that is so often taken for granted.

Dr. Stephen Nortcliff, of England's University of Reading, enjoys that rare gift of making his subject come alive for an audience: "Soil is not static, it is not inert. Soil is a living, biological entity," declared Nortcliff. "The soil will not always be there, no matter what man does to it. For most practical purposes, soil is a nonrenewable resource. Good soil management should seek to prevent degradation; prevention is always better than cure."

In his delightful book entitled *Down to Earth,* Nortcliff explored his favourite subject in greater detail.

> Soil contains a multitude of living organisms, some visible, others microscopic and invisible to the naked eye. These organisms form a complex food web within the soils; one group consumes plant litter, another group consumes the by-products of the first group, while a third group preys on the first two. A small spoonful of dry garden soil may contain about twice as many soil bacteria as there are people in the world! There can be well over five tons of bacteria per hectare of soil. Soil fungi may be equally numerous. Both these micro-organisms help to break down the fresh organic litter at the surface into humus. Figures for the larger soil organisms can be equally remarkable: for example, in a typical lowland pasture the weight of cows on the soil surface will be considerably less than the combined weight of the earthworms below the soil surface. . . . Soil is a vital component of the natural environment. The manner in which it has developed, and is still developing, must be understood if we aim to minimize its destruction and maintain it for future generations.

This chapter has been all about land, which must be very much alive if it is to feed and clothe the growing world population. For many readers it may come as a surprise that the soil beneath their feet can be so fascinating and fruitful. An anomaly is that for every person captivated by living soils, there are thousands who have been entranced by the dead soils of North America. As *Conserving Canada's Resources* observed, "Tourists find the eroded 'hoodoos' of Banff picturesque; they marvel over the wild beauty of the badlands of South Dakota, the many-coloured pillars of Bryce Canyon in Utah, and the shimmering Jacob's coat of the Arizona desert; but they seldom give a thought to the fact that these are dead lands. They died because they were unprotected from sun and wind and denuded of water . . . and such may become millions of acres of Canada unless heed is given quickly to conservation."

A final footnote is for any remaining readers who question the significance of soils in their own lives. Aureomycin is probably the antibiotic that has exerted the greatest influence on world food supplies. Aureomycin was refined by Lederle Laboratories, Pearl River, New York, from the fungus *Streptomyces aureofaciens,* which was discovered in the soil in a field of timothy.

CHAPTER 25

A Winning Blueprint

He who fears being conquered is sure of defeat.
—NAPOLEON BONAPARTE

S electing the most appropriate quotation for this concluding chapter proved to be difficult. Should I use the prayer of St. Francis of Assisi, who asked for the courage to achieve change and the wisdom to know what could not be changed? Or should it be the words of that aggressive builder of the Canadian Pacific Railway, Sir William Cornelius Van Horne. He believed that "nothing is too small to know, and nothing too big to attempt"; that combined insight with a determination to complete the job at hand.

While Napoleon is a flawed character in history, he was dead-on when he said, "He who fears being conquered is sure of defeat." If not fear, the apparent inevitability of defeat deters many people from becoming actively involved, even though they may be very concerned about an issue. One of the most depressing aspects of our involvement in trying to make democracy work was to encounter so many people who knew that we were doomed to lose. As one of my neighbours declared at the outset in abject defeat, "What can you do . . . they've got the government at their back!" There was no comprehension that he was the government or that his forebears could conceivably have given their lives in defence of some principle of freedom.

The first essential of a winning blueprint is not confidence in success but a commitment to try to achieve change. Indulging in the expectation of success would have been insupportable in the light of the legislation and the apparently endless unfavourable precedents for farmers and the environment. The chances of ruinous failure were present until the Supreme Court of Ontario ruled out any further appeal.

Many times, farmers came to us and asked whether they should fight. Routinely I responded that I could not advise them. There could be no assurance of ultimate success, but there were real and increasing financial, physical, and mental pressures in bucking an entrenched and unfair system. Each individual has to decide, given his or her temperament and resources, whether surrendering would be more debilitating than struggling. A merciful aspect is that the problems and the challenges come in small increments; seldom does one face a single momentous and cataclysmic decision. With each new hurdle, large or small, there often comes a little bit of hope.

One must be cognizant of the effect any protracted effort has on one's own family. Barry O'Neil reminisces:

> Since the age of 12 I had a rather negative attitude towards pipelines; that attitude stemmed from a farm operation called stone picking! From that point, my attitude improved very little. The court cases with IPL did two things for our family; they pulled and they strained. At times it really pulled our family together. We spent days taking pictures and yields and writing letters. I was fairly involved in some of these activities and learned a great deal. However, with a court case comes pressure, and pressure can certainly strain a family. Mum and Dad kept most of the pressure to themselves, but I still felt it. The great thing is that now no one should have to do this ever again.

No reader can be in any doubt about how much I owe to my own family and my closest neighbours. One Christmas Eve, John Walker Elliott came to bring his greetings. Jean, looking out into the twilight, asked John to invite his friend, who appeared to be sitting quietly in the pickup cab, to come on in. The "friend" turned out to be a beribboned lamb, John's Christmas gift to us!

And our friends who became consultants, our consultants who became our friends! When I insist that we are in their debt, they counter that they are in ours. If I may use one of those ten-dollar words that sprinkle the various court proceedings, it is a symbiotic relationship. Barry O'Neil expresses it more simply when he says, "I met a whole new group of interesting and knowledgeable people with whom I felt comfortable." This is the human factor, something unique to each individual and each family!

And the time! Quite apart from anything detailed thus far, there was input to such organizations as the Ontario Pipeline Coordinating Committee of the Ontario Energy Board. If anyone like the chairman of that committee, D. R. Cochran, showed any interest, I always responded positively. Such essential liaison is both time-consuming and expensive in the aggregate, but often it was bread upon the waters. The initiatives spread out like ripples on a pond until they gained enough momentum to effect legislative change.

I supported any organization that might conceivably contribute to bringing democracy to the oil patch. I joined the Ontario Federation of Agriculture and the National Farmers Union. I became a charter member of the Canadian Land Reclamation Association and contributed financially to the Canadian Environmental Law Association. However, since virtually all organizations have to cater to the many and often divergent priorities of their members, sometimes one has to go for the jugular and go for it alone.

Sometimes the confrontations were of the bare-knuckles and toe-to-toe variety. Such heat can generate light and a mutual respect for the protagonists. I have been very encouraged by three opportunities to address various symposia of right-of-way organizations in North America.

I personally find it much more difficult to cope with stonewalling techniques. Despite the passing of ten years, smoke is still coming from one of my letters to Jack Stabback, but the total NEB response was "Dear Sir: I have been directed by the Board to acknowledge receipt of your letter of October 16, 1975 addressed to Mr. J. G. Stabback, Associate Vice-Chairman of the Board. Yours truly, Robert A. Stead, Secretary."

The *Financial Post* of July 1975 included this comment. "People who really want to guide or influence government policy are wasting their time dealing with members of parliament, senators, and usually even ministers." This is the height of cynicism but unfortunately it has a measure of truth; all too often we lost a point because we didn't enjoy access to the inside track. But, to hew to such a cynical line is to negate our democratic system. Throughout this narrative I have repeatedly cited the efforts and involvement of numerous backbenchers in both the Liberal and the Progressive Conservative parties. I have also paid tribute to Bill Stewart when he was Ontario Minister of Agriculture and Food, Gene Whelan when he was federal Minister of Agriculture and John Wise the more recent minister who also played a crucial role while in opposition. But, we were never partisan. Letters and briefs were sent to all political parties. As the New Democratic Party (NDP) espoused social justice it was curious that it never followed through effectively at either the federal or provincial level. When I wrote to Tommy Douglas, leader of the NDP in Ottawa I was advised that he was out of the city. Judging by my mail he never returned. Stephen Lewis, later Canada's Ambassador to the United Nations, was leader of the NDP in opposition in the Ontario Legislative Assembly. He replied in a different vein than Robert Stead to my letter to Stabback by saying, "It is a very strong letter and I agree with it in its entirety." But nothing else happened. The moral is, touch all of the political bases but avoid playing partisan politics.

Another, often neglected, aspect of a winning blueprint is simply expressing thanks for assistance and involvement. It is very time-consuming, but in this age of electronic communications, people do appreciate the courtesy of a letter, no matter how brief.

It is said that he who hesitates is lost. I suggest that he who loses his cool is even more lost! Despite the many provocations, we never strayed beyond the strict confines of the law, and despite the stresses and strains, never overstated our case. We were never called upon to make a retraction. It is not only important to be right; it is important to be able to prove that you are right. And that calls for a discipline that doesn't come naturally to me. It involves including the date, time, identity, and affiliation of a telephone caller and the matters discussed. Such details can be recorded with any assurance of accuracy only if the notations are made at the time. It is vital to keep an accurate diary of any and all events and to make the entries promptly on the day of any event.

Time and again, the additional cost of using registered and acknowledgement-and-receipt mail paid off. For instance, IPL's Gordon Sheasby had charged that I had refused to negotiate. He was then confounded by the admission of Bob Dunsmore, under oath, that he had received a registered letter that read in part, "I am prepared to negotiate with responsible IPL officials at any mutually agreed time and date."

When I made my diary entries, I had no thought that the diaries would one day be seized as court records and that three IPL lawyers would sit up much of the night exploring them as they framed questions for the next day. As the entries were purely factual and scrupulously accurate, I had nothing to fear from such an inquisition. Because the Supreme Court of Ontario lost all of these diaries and many of our other exhibits, it was fortunate for us that appeal to the Supreme Court of Canada was denied. We would have been like Marshall Wyatt Earp, without his six-guns.

We have seen how judges at the County Court level and at the Supreme Court level appreciate good pictures and coloured slides. They can assist judges in their search for the truth. It is said that the camera doesn't lie, but of course photographs can. How is the court to know whether a picture was taken on the date claimed? When I pictured some of the worst devastation created by IPL, I often included a copy of that day's newspaper, floating in the foreground. This proved to the satisfaction of the court that the picture could not have been taken earlier; the picture could have been taken only after that specific IPL construction initiative.

But having gone to all that trouble, one still needs the element of luck. On November 28, 1976, I wrote to my photographic processor, David Hunsberger, in St. Jacobs, Ontario: "Dear Dave, Please do this as soon as possible. It is a 36 exposure roll of Kodak Tri-X which is part of our photographic documentation needed for our court case next week against Interprovincial." Unfortunately, the post office delivered only a tattered envelope with my request; the film had been lost forever.

In many instances, an individual in fighting an entrenched system has to operate at a disadvantage and continually has to come from behind. That makes it implicit that no stone, however unpromising, can be left unturned. The Bibliography at the back of this book is but a sample of the documentation assiduously garnered over some forty years.

There is, of course, a world of difference between being in possession of relevant facts and presenting them in a convincing manner to a court or tribunal. The Ontario Federation of Agriculture has this advice on a speech formula: (1) Stand up; speak up; shut up. (2) Have something to say; say it; sit down. (3) Be sincere; be brief; be seated. Much more comprehensive advice can be found in the *Guide Book on How to Prepare Cases for Administrative Tribunals*. This was first published by The Consumers' Association of Canada in 1977. The introduction explains that "this guide book is like a map; it does not tell you where to go, merely how to get there. It cannot serve as a substitute for solid experience, extensive preparation, or creative imagination."

There are specific publications that relate to specific areas of society. For instance, Saskatchewan Agriculture has published a little booklet entitled *Negotiating Surface Rights*. And then, also within the energy industry but with implications far beyond such confines, is the NEB's own information bulletin, *How to Intervene*.

For most of our involvement, it was a do-it-yourself project. But latterly there have been two major changes. At both the provincial and the federal levels there are now precedents that it is in the public interest to assist citizens financially in making their presentations. This has occurred with farm groups combatting Ontario Hydro, and there is the

NEB example of financial assistance by companies at the local hearing level. Another basic change is that more lawyers have become interested in issues involving the environment and individual rights. A generation ago it was virtually impossible to find a lawyer with expertise in such areas, and it was even less likely to find one who had any expectation of success before the courts. It is now more likely for a court or tribunal to listen to the testimony of an expert witness. We were fortunate in putting together a team of expert witnesses whose special areas of expertise interlocked like pieces of a jigsaw puzzle. It is most encouraging that the takers of land are now adopting such an approach. When Ontario Hydro advertised for another plant ecologist, the advertisement included the following paragraph: "This opportunity will interest a physiological plant ecologist able to conduct research with a multidisciplinary team of biologists."

I have already observed that mercifully we cannot see all of the problems that lie ahead. The other side of this coin is that there are unexpected benefits. When I made a plea before the Ontario Law Reform Commission for the appointment of judges on merit rather than on the basis of political patronage, I could not have anticipated the long-range results. A continuing pleasure has been the friendship of Gaylord Watkins, who was so effective with the Law Reform Commission of Canada. It was also encouraging to provide written testimony for the Canadian Bar Association Special Committee on the Appointment of Judges in Canada. When the chief justice of Canada, the Right Honourable Brian Dixon, addressed the Canadian Bar Association in 1984, he said, "The public is entitled, in my opinion, to be reassured that our judges are appointed on the basis of merit and legal excellence alone."

The related committees of the Canadian Bar Association led to the publication in the fall of 1985 of *The Appointment of Judges in Canada* and *The Independence of the Judiciary in Canada*. The findings are largely encouraging to anyone wishing to see uniformly high standards of excellence and independence in the appointment of our judges. It still remains to be seen whether the good intentions of the Canadian Bar Association will be followed by a rejection of patronage and an endorsement of merit by the provincial and federal governments of Canada.

As matters now stand, an individual contemplating initiatives that could lead to litigation should consider the wide range in competence of judges before whom they may appear. We were singularly fortunate in coming before a thoughtful judge who expressed a commitment to arrive at the truth, and most importantly, one who did not negate that by making mistakes in law.

My work as a farmer and farm writer often led to useful contacts and information. It meant the opportunity to attend the Drastically Disturbed Lands Seminar in Ohio, to witness land being reclaimed from the sea in Holland, and to observe how the Israelis use impoverished soil and minimal water supplies to grow bountiful crops. One cannot be exposed to such things without being motivated to believe that the energy equation in Canada has to include concern for the land and the environment. As a nation, we have not appreciated nature's bounty.

Some energy companies have clearly demonstrated that they can prosper without injuriously affecting a landowner or the land. They have grasped the essential truth — and the economic benefits — of good planning and practices that mitigate damage. It is doubly rewarding for them to find that doing what is morally and aesthetically desirable is also the most profitable course of action. And that has to be a very important benefit of bringing democracy to the oil patch.

These beneficial changes might never have occurred, and certainly not when they did, without the fortuitous gossamer threads that linked the efforts of so many people. Some of them were good, some were bad, and some were totally indifferent to balancing the energy–environment equation.

It is important to note that our expert consultants never publicly advocated any particular point of view regarding pipeline construction. Their comments were confined to the facts available to them and were made in a courtroom. We knew that we enjoyed their confidence, and we knew that they were convinced that our cause was just, but very properly, they realized that their essential contribution was to remain unassailable expert witnesses.

In the Preface and in numerous chapters, I have acknowledged debts to many fine and talented people. The last words appropriately should mention Jean, Stu, and Jocelyn, who with me agonized over so many problems — and never gave up.

EPILOGUE

The bottom line of the battle that began in 1949 is that we won. We won despite a flawed system, overwhelming odds, and archaic legislation. Winston Churchill once said that "democracy is the worst form of government . . . except for all the others." The victory reaffirmed that while democracy does not necessarily work, it can be made to work. I hope that this message will be heard wherever concerned individuals and organizations face an entrenched bureaucratic system.

After all the trauma and tension that the underdog encounters in any legal system, it was gratifying that the courts clearly discerned not only the truth but the whole truth. The courts also discerned what was objective bona fide research and what was suspect and self-serving.

The broader implications can now be seen in the legislative changes, sweeping reforms of such federal legislation as the National Energy Board Act and the Expropriation Act. Particularly gratifying is the reality that no one will ever again have to endure the inequities of the Railway Act and its indifference to agricultural technology.

The law is not unchanging, nor is it written on stone tablets; it evolves with precedents that create new and hopefully fairer laws. The various court proceedings and the judgments are now there to guide those who come after us. There is a wealth of documentation that previously did not exist.

Timing in life is everything; fortuitously, the critical decisions were made during worldwide environmental concerns. Would any lawyer think it prudent today to boast of the power to make a wasteland of prime farmland? Would the current chief executive officer of an energy corporation tell a legal inquiry that physically holding up heavy construction equipment with riprap was the criterion for pipeline construction involving bad weather and Class I farmland?

Perhaps the most significant accomplishment has been the interdisciplinary effort. It was the complementary expertise that provided the key to breaking the logjam that had endured for a century. Too often the explosion of knowledge has led to insular thinking. Our consultants, researchers, and friends demonstrated together that with dedication, all of the diverse pieces could be fitted together to make a more environmentally sensitive future.

A regret in such a lengthy saga is that some of the large cast of characters have gone to their reward. Along the way there were pivotal changes I vividly recall; the late former chief justice for Ontario, James McRuer, epitomized just such a significant watershed. He would have relished the outcome.

Will it all prove to have been worthwhile? Dr. Al Tomlin is one who gives a resounding affirmative response: "I hope that if anyone tries to cut environmental corners in the future, they will be blown right out of the water."

But will they? Some of the research that was demolished in the court of Judge Killeen appears, after a lapse of many years, in a published feature article in the magazine *Right of Way*. Hugh Fletcher, a Middlesex County farmer whose father, Dunc, purchased Holsteins from us years ago to become premier exhibitor at the county Black and White Show, is questioning the currently planned installation of a 42-inch diameter gas line. He complains that he can't find a useful paper trail. He is not alone. Librarian Gabriel Pal at the McLaughlin Library of the University of Guelph kindly undertook an extensive computer search for me. He too came up with listings that are only a minuscule part of the total literature of which I am aware. An even more ambitious computer research by Dr. Tomlin in the United States revealed similar problems.

Many years ago when the then president of IPL was questioned under oath, he said that his company had no record of a requested document. He added, "I expect that Mr. Lewington has a copy." I did!

I am delighted that the D. B. Weldon Library at The University of Western Ontario has accepted what had become our pipeline archives. Cupboards, drawers, credenzas, and much of our basement have yielded their paper hoard. This information will now be available to researchers everywhere, in perpetuity. My wife, Jean, who has endured so much pipeline paranoia, was glad to see it go! So was I. After forty years, it is finally out of my system, and that's a relief.

The response of Dr. George Pedersen, UWO president, was as follows:

> I am writing to accept your donation of a collection of books and documents which record your successful court battle to restrict the rights of access of utility companies to farmland for construction projects and to ensure, when such access is granted, that the negative impact upon the land is appropriately minimized. Yours was an epic and precedent-setting struggle for the protection of farmland and the rights of farmers. We are proud of the part members of Western's faculty played in it. It was also a proud moment for us when we honoured you in 1987, with a Doctor of Laws degree, *honoris causa,* for your singularly important contribution to agriculture and the protection of the rural environment.
>
> As you already know, this unique archive will be housed in the Regional Collection located in The D. B. Weldon Library. Undoubtedly, it will be an invaluable resource for those students and faculty at Western who have a research interest in environmental issues pertaining to farmland whether they be in the Faculties of Business, Engineering, Law, Science or Social Science. Similarly, it will attract interest from many outside our University.
>
> I also want to take this opportunity to say how grateful we are for your thoughtfulness in donating this material to Western. Your interest in having this material preservered here for purposes of consultation and research is deeply appreciated.

The University of Western Ontario is an apt choice. Dr. Bob Quigley and his students involved in intricacies of soils, Dr. Paul Cavers and his students in plant sciences, and Dr. Al Tomlin and his colleagues in Agriculture Canada are all based in London, Ontario. UWO is also noted for its Faculty of Law, and this provides a link with Geoff Bladon who, following a term as chief judge in the Territorial Court of Yukon in Whitehorse, is now teaching law at the University of New Brunswick in Fredericton. It is of further relevance to note the changes at the UWO School of Business Administration. Dr. Donald Simpson, director, Centre for International Business Studies, added a course in 1990 on Managing Sustainable Development. This initiative promptly kindled interest at several other universities cognizant that business corporations now have to adjust to a new environmentally conscious era.

A 1978 publication of the University of Illinois noted that "the landowner has an opportunity to assert his rights and protect his interests when the utility company first offers to negotiate a contract for the purchase of the right-of-way." Canadian landowners theoretically also had such rights. What they lacked was the opportunity to exercise those rights. Hearings were not advertised and even when they were, they were frequently an arbitrary insult to justice. At times, it was like the famed Hampton Court maze, minus an exit.

Now landowners have not only far greater rights, but access to the knowledge to ensure that rights can become reality. Canadians now have greater legislated rights to the access of information.

Larigmoor Farm is in the Medway Valley watershed. This small river is a mere twenty miles from its source to its confluence with the river Thames beside The University of Western Ontario. There are already nine pipelines in the valley, ten if you count the environmentally destructive sewer that is bigger than some of the pipelines. There are pipeline easements across both the research farm of environmental sciences of The University of Western Ontario and the London Research Station of Agriculture Canada.

Some of the best farmland in all Canada lies in the Medway Valley. There is also an Indian archaeological site, a beaver dam, terminal moraines, and Larigmoor Farm, which was once a glacial lake left by the late Wisconsin Glacier, which gave us the parent material which weathered to become our deep topsoil—and the aquifer that IPL never did comprehend.

The Medway watershed attracted settlement because of many attributes. In the future, it could attract the interest of professionals in every discipline from law to planning, from sociology to agriculture and environmental protection. It is still our home and farm, but it has become a living laboratory. The initiatives and the research that were generated in response to the environmental insults perpetrated have a direct relevance for the millions of people who live in the Great Lakes region of Canada and the United States, and far beyond.

Throughout this book, Agriculture Canada is portrayed with black or white hats, like the cowboys in a B movie. The Land Resource Research Centre of Agriculture Canada in Ottawa monitored the long-term effects of the IPL pipeline to Montreal and concluded that "effects of soil mixing on chemical properties was still apparent, despite good crop management. With the exception of alfalfa, field crop yields in the Right of Way were reduced by an average of 28% ten years after installation." That need not, and must not, be allowed to happen again.

No longer will a farmer whose land has been expropriated for a pipeline be obliged to suffer in silence while a judge—quite legitimately—rules that "drainage is no concern of this court!" How could such tyranny survive for so long in an agricultural county in which governmental departments exhorted farmers to invest in drainage systems? How was it possible for an archaic legal system to survive when it negated any drainage rights?

The biggest bottom line is that Judge Killeen's arbitration decision can now be seen as a watershed of beneficial change and environmental concern.

In 1979, Norman Pearson, in his doctoral dissertation, concluded that "what appears to be needed in the research and development area is a Canadian Pipeline Research Institute where all the disciplines involved in these interface and conflict situations can work together in an exploratory situation."

Perhaps the Canadian Petroleum Association can expand its promising initiatives to achieve this sensible and practical goal.

Directory of Organizations Involved with Energy, the Environment, and Land Use

Aggregate Producers Association of Ontario, 3701 Chesswood Drive, Suite 209, Downsview, Ontario M3J 2P6

Agricultural Institute of Canada, 151 Slater Street, Suite 907, Ottawa, Ontario KIP 5H4

Agriculture Canada, 930 Carling Avenue, Ottawa, Ontario KIA PC5

Alberta Chamber of Resources, 1403 Baker Centre, 10025 106th Street, Edmonton, Alberta T5J 1G4

American Agricultural Law Association, 1025 Thomas Jefferson Street NW, Suite 700, Washington, DC 20007

American Farmland Trust, 1920 N Street NW, Suite 400, Washington, DC 20036

American Society of Farm Managers and Rural Appraisers, 950 S. Cherry Street, Suite 106, Denver, CO 80222

Appraisal Institute of Canada, 309-93 Lombard Avenue, Winnipeg, Manitoba R3B 3B1

Arctic Petroleum Operators Association, #310, 505 8th Avenue SW, Calgary, Alberta T2P 1G2

Association of Ontario Land Economists, 210 Sheppard Avenue East, Willowdale, Ontario M2N 3A9

Association of Peel People Evaluating Agricultural Land (APPEAL), P.O. Box 532, Streetsville, Mississauga, Ontario L5M 2C1

British Columbia Utilities Commission, Board of Trade Tower, 2100-1177 W. Hastings Street, Vancouver, British Columbia V6E 2L7

Canadian Agricultural Economics and Farm Management Society, 151 Slater Street, Suite 907, Ottawa, Ontario KIP 5H4

Canadian Association for Rural Studies, c/o E. A. Cebotarev, Secretary, College of Social Science, Dept. of Sociology and Anthropology, University of Guelph, Guelph, Ontario NIG 2W1

Canadian Association of Geographers, Burnside Hall, McGill University, 805 Ouest, Rue Sherbrooke, Montreal, P.Q. H3A 2K6

Canadian Association of Municipal Administrators, 112 Kent Street, Suite 1318, Ottawa, Ontario KIP 5P2

Canadian Association of Petroleum Landmen, 800 6th Avenue SW, Suite 960, Calgary, Alberta T2P 3G3

Canadian Association of Well Drilling Contractors, 603 7th Avenue SW, Suite 414, Calgary, Alberta T2P 2T5

Canadian Bankers' Association, 2 First Canadian Place, P.O. Box 348, Toronto, Ontario M5X 1E1

Canadian Bar Association, 130 Albert Street, Suite 1700, Ottawa, Ontario K1P 5G4

Canadian Consulting Agrologists' Association, #22, 44 Wellington Street East, Toronto, Ontario M5E 1C8

Canadian Electrical Association, One Westmount Square, Suite 580, Montreal, Quebec H3Z 2P9

Canadian Environmental Law Association, 243 Queen Street West, 4th Floor, Toronto, Ontario M5V 1Z4

Canadian Environmental Law Research Foundation, 243 Queen Street West, Suite 400, Toronto, Ontario M5V 1Z4

Canadian Federation of Agriculture, 111 Sparks Street, Ottawa, Ontario KIP 5B5

Canadian Gas Association, 55 Scarsdale Road, Don Mills, Ontario M3B 2R3

Canadian Geotechnical Society, 602-170 Attwell Drive, Rexdale, Ontario M9W 5Z5

Canadian Institute of Planners, 30-46 Elgin Street, Ottawa, Ontario KIP 5K6

Canadian Land Reclamation Association, Box 682, Guelph, Ontario NIH 6L3

Canadian Nature Federation, 75 Albert Street, Ottawa, Ontario KIP 6G1

Canadian Petroleum Association, 3800 150 Sixth Avenue SW, Calgary, Alberta T2P 3Y7

Canadian Real Estate Association, 99 Duncan Mill Road, Don Mills, Ontario M3B 1Z2

Canadian Seed Growers' Association, Box 8455, Ottawa, Ontario K1G 3T1

Christian Farmers' Association of Ontario, Box 220, Drayton, Ontario NOG 1P0

Consumers' Association of Canada, 251 Lawrence Avenue West, Ottawa, Ontario K2S 5J3

Energy, Mines and Resources Canada, 580 Booth Street, Ottawa, Ontario KIA OE4

Energy Resources Conservation Board of Alberta, 640 Fifth Avenue SW, Calgary, Alberta T2P 3G4

Environment Canada, Ottawa, Ontario K1A 0H3

Farm and Land Institute of the National Association of Realtors, 430 N. Michigan Avenue, Chicago, IL 60611

Farm Credit Corporation, 434 Queen Street, Ottawa, Ontario KIP 6J9

Federal Energy Regulatory Commission, 825 N. Capitol Street NE, Washington, DC 20426

Federation of Ontario Naturalists, 355 Lesmill Road, Don Mills, Ontario M3B 2W8

Fisheries and Oceans Canada, 200 Kent Street, Ottawa, Ontario KIA 0E6

Foodland Alert, Box 220, Drayton, Ontario NOG 1P0

Greenpeace Foundation, 2623 W. Fourth Avenue, Vancouver, British Columbia V6K 1P8

Independent Petroleum Association of Canada, 707 7th Avenue SW, Suite 700, Calgary, Alberta T2P 0Z2

Industrial Gas Users Association, 170 Laurier Avenue West, 11th Floor, Ottawa, Ontario KIP 5V5

Institute for Environmental Policy and Stewardship, University of Guelph, Guelph, Ontario NIG 2W1

Institute of Pedology, Guelph Agriculture Centre, P.O. Box 1030, Guelph, Ontario NIH 6NI

Interhome Energy, Inc., 3200 Home Oil Tower, 324 Eighth Avenue SW, Calgary, Alberta T2P 2Z5

International Joint Commission, 100 Metcalfe Street, Ottawa, Ontario KIA OH8

International Right of Way Association, 9920 La Cienega Boulevard, Suite 515, Inglewood, CA 90301

Izaak Walton League of America, 1701 N. Fort Myer Drive, Suite 1100, Arlington, VA 22209

Justice Canada, Justice Building, Kent & Wellington Streets, Ottawa, Ontario KIA OH8

Land Improvement Contractors of America, 1300 Maybrook Drive, Maywood, IL 60153

Land Resource Research Institute, Agriculture Canada, Ottawa, Ontario KIA OC6

Lands Directorate Environment Canada, 20th Floor, Place Vincent Massey, 351 St. Joseph Boulevard, Hull, Quebec KIA OE7

Law Reform Commission of Canada, 130 Albert Street, Ottawa, Ontario KIA 0C6

Manitoba Department of Energy & Mines, Petroleum Branch, 555-330 Graham Avenue, Winnipeg, Manitoba R3C 4E3

National Energy Board, 473 Albert Street, Ottawa, Ontario KIA OE5

National Farmers Union, 250C Second Avenue South, Saskatoon, Saskatchewan S7K 2M1

New Brunswick Public Utilities Board, Provincial Building, 110 Charlotte Street, Saint John, New Brunswick E2L 2J4

Newfoundland Commission of Public Utilities, Prince Charles Building, P.O. Box 9188, St. John's, Newfoundland A1A 2X9

Niagara Escarpment Commission, 232 Guelph Street, Georgetown, Ontario L7G 4B1

Northwest Territories Public Utilities Board, P.O. Box 697, Yellowknife, North West Territories X1A 2N5

Nova Scotia Resources Development Board, P.O. Box 519, Halifax, Nova Scotia B3J 2R7

Ontario Coalition to Preserve Foodlands, Box 220, Drayton, Ontario NOG 1P0

Ontario Energy Board, 9th Floor, 14 Carlton Street, Toronto, Ontario M5B 1J2

Ontario Farm Drainage Association, Box 99, Ailsa Craig, Ontario N0M 1A0

Ontario Federation of Agriculture, 491 Eglinton Avenue West, Suite 500, Toronto, Ontario M5N 3A2

Ontario Federation of Anglers and Hunters, Box 28, Peterborough, Ontario K9J 6Y5

Ontario Ministry of Agriculture & Food, 801 Bay Street, Toronto, Ontario M7A 1B2

Ontario Municipal Board, 180 Dundas Street West, Toronto, Ontario N5G 1E5

Ontario Petroleum Association, 2300 Yonge Street, Toronto, Ontario M4P 2C6

Ontario Rural Geographers Group, Geography Department, University of Windsor, 401 Sunset Avenue, Windsor, Ontario N9B 3P4

Ontario Society of Farm Managers and Rural Appraisers, 40 Pondview Crescent, Guelph, Ontario N1E 3K1

Parks Canada, Ottawa, Ontario KIA 0H3

Pipe Line Contractors Association of Canada, Room 400, 698 Seymour Street, Vancouver, British Columbia V6B 3K7

Public Utilities Board for the Province of Alberta, 11th Floor, Manulife House, 10055 106th Street, Edmonton, Alberta T5J 2Y2

Public Utilities Board for the Province of Manitoba, Room 1146, 405 Broadway Avenue, Winnipeg, Manitoba R3C 3L6

Public Utilities Commission Federation, Court Building, Suite 501, 134 Kent Street, P.O. Box 577, Charlottetown, Prince Edward Island CIA 7L1

Public Utilities Review Commission of Saskatchewan, Sturdy-Stone Centre, 122 Third Avenue North, Saskatoon, Saskatchewan S7K 2H6

Régie de l'Électricité et du Gaz, 2100 rue Drummond, Montreal, P.Q. H3G 1X1

Royal Canadian Geographical Society, 488 Wilbrod Street, Ottawa, Ontario KIN 6M8

Sierra Club, 530 Bush Street, San Francisco, CA 94108

Sierra Club of Ontario, 191 College Street, Toronto, Ontario M5T 1P9

Sierra Club of Western Canada, 314-620 View Street, Victoria, British Columbia V8W 1J6

Soil and Water Conservation Society, 7515 N.E. Ankeny Road, Ankeny, IA 50021

Supreme Court of Canada, Supreme Court Building, Wellington Street, Ottawa, Ontario KIA OJ1

Transport Public Utilities Board, P.O. Box 2703, Whitehorse, Yukon Y1A 206

GLOSSARY

Acid rain: Precipitation acidified by atmospheric pollutants such as the oxides of sulphur and nitrogen.

Aquifer: A pervious geological formation containing water, which may be easily withdrawn for use.

Bacteria: Microscopic single-celled organisms that break down organic material.

Barrel: A traditional unit of measurement in the oil industry. The volume is thirty-five Imperial gallons or forty-two U.S. gallons, and the weight of a barrel varies according to the liquid's specific gravity.

Bulk dry density: The mass of oven-dry soil per unit bulk volume, including air space.

Canada land inventory (CLI): An inventory of Canadian soil resources that classifies land from that which has no constraints of soil, climate, or drainage on production through to land that has no agricultural potential.

Catch basin: Usually a precast concrete structure located adjacent to a drainage tile system and covered at ground level with a rodentproof grid; designed to accelerate entry of water to the tile system and avoid soil erosion.

Chernozem soils: A zonal group of soils having deep dark to nearly black surface horizons and usually rich in organic matter developed under temperate and cool subhumid climates.

Corn heat units (CHU): Based on daytime temperatures above 10 degrees C and nighttime temperatures above 4.4 degrees C. The sum of these heat units between normal planting date and the date when a killing frost can be expected one year in ten constitutes the available CHU in a specific area; Larigmoor Farm has 2800 CHU. In contrast, the Prairie regions, where corn is marginal, may have only 1900 CHU.

Cubic metre: A current oil measurement equal to 6.3 barrels.

Drainage: Some soils are self-draining; others require a complex of tile or tubing buried at perhaps one metre with an outlet to an open drainage ditch or watercourse.

Environmental impact: Any alteration to the environment caused by man and affecting human, animal, fish, and/or plant life.

Expert witness: A witness with special or exceptional knowledge.

Expropriation: The legal process by which there is a permanent or temporary transfer of ownership without the owner's consent.

Fine-textured soil: A soil composed predominately of silt and clay-sized particles.

251

Gigawatt hour: One million killowatt hours; a unit of bulk energy.

Habitat: The natural or normal environment of a plant or animal.

Humus: The dark organic component of soil created by the partial decomposition of vegetable or animal matter in the upper soil horizon. Adequate organic content is an essential for viable crop production; the humus content also influences the effectiveness of herbicides and insecticides and the ability of legumes to fix nitrogen.

Hydrocarbon: Any chemical compound composed only of hydrogen and carbon atoms; for instance, crude oil or natural gas.

Land: The total natural and cultural environment within which production takes place.

Land classification: The classification of land according to its productive capability; an integral part of the Canada Land Inventory.

Land leveling (irrigation): The reshaping of the ground surface contours to facilitate the uniform application of irrigation water or improve drainage.

Leaching: The process by which water percolating through soil removes soluble constituents.

Liquified natural gas (LNG): A contradiction in terms which refers to, for instance, propane gas, which is formed from natural gas through processes of condensation and absorption and stored under pressure to keep it in its liquid state.

Litter: The crop residue or trash left on the surface from agricultural activity; partially decomposed organic material. Also the natural plant and animal material (leaves and feral pellets) accumulating on the soil surface.

Loam: A desirable, permeable, friable, organic soil type composed of approximately equal parts of sand, silt, and clay. Soil types range from sand to loams to clay loams and clays with an ascending proportion of fine-textured soil particles. The smaller the particles, the greater the need for drainage and avoidance of compaction.

Mycorhiza: The morphological association, usually symbiotic, of fungi and roots of seed plants.

Negotiation: A mutual discussion with the object of reaching an agreement.

Percolation: The downward movement of water through soil.

pH: A numerical expression ranging from 0 to 14 of soil acidity. A pH of 7 is neutral; less than 7 is acidic; and more than 7 is alkaline. The soil pH affects what crops can be grown successfully.

Pig: Also known as a scraper. A device used to test and clean the interior of a pipeline. Pigs range from simple devices to separate different hydrocarbons, or they may involve sophisticated inspection and detection devices such as those for checking of welds.

Proved reserves of oil and gas: The volumes of oil and gas that can be demonstrated by geological and engineering data to be recoverable with reasonable certainty under existing economic and operating conditions.

Right-of-way: A strip of land that a transmission or pipeline company has acquired on a temporary or permanent basis through negotiation or expropriation upon which it can perform construction and maintenance.

Soil: Soil is a natural material developed from weathered minerals and decaying organic matter covering the earth in a thin layer. It is a natural medium on the surface of the earth in which plants may grow.

Spoil: The subsoils (as opposed to the topsoil) removed during pipeline trenching excavation.

Spread: A unit of pipeline construction involving every facet. The length of a spread may be influenced by the weather, the season, and the terrain.

Surface rights: A Canadian phenomenon under which the landowner's rights are restricted to the surface, while the mineral, oil, or gas rights may be owned by the provincial government and may be leased to a third party.

Tile: A misnomer that can apply to any structure of wood, plastic, stone, concrete, or baked clay, which is usually buried at depths up to one metre as part of a drainage system. Water gains access to the tile either through joints between tile or through perforations in the tile. The laterals may be four inches in diameter; the headers that gather the water from the laterals may be eight inches or more in diameter; and the tile system involves increasing-diameter tile until the outlet to an open ditch or stream is reached.

Transmission line: A line used for the transmission of electric power at high voltage; such lines are normally overhead but may be buried.

BIBLIOGRAPHY

Anstey, T. H. *One Hundred Harvests*. Agriculture Canada Research Branch Centennial, 1986.

Batten, Jack. *Robinette, the Dean of Canadian Lawyers*. Macmillan, 1984.

Bell Canada. Letter to the Author from E. G. Gill, Manager, Right of Way and Liaison Defining Corporate Drainage Policy, December 1985.

Berger, T. R. *Northern Frontier Northern Homeland*. The Report of the Mackenzie Valley Pipeline Enquiry, Minister of Supply and Services Canada, 1977.

Blair, J. M. *The Control of Oil*. Pantheon, 1976.

Bosworth, D. A., and Foster, A. B. *Approved Practices in Soil Conservation*. The Interstate, 1982.

Bothwell, R., and Kilbourn, W. *C. D. Howe*. McClelland & Stewart, 1979.

Bregha, François. *Bob Blair's Pipeline*. James Lorimer, 1979.

Canada. Agriculture. *Grasses of Ontario*. Supply and Services Canada, 1980.

_____. "Impacts of Installation of an Oil Pipeline on the Productivity of Ontario Cropland." Land Resource Institute Contribution no. 66, 1981.

Canada and World Food. The Royal Society of Canada and the Agricultural Institute of Canada, 1977.

Canada. Director of Investigation and Research Combines Investigation Act. *The State of Competition in the Canadian Petroleum Industry*, vols. 1–7. 1981.

Canada. Energy, Mines and Resources. *An Energy Policy for Canada*. 1973.

Canada. Environment. *Lands Directorate Publications*. March 1981.

_____. *Energy and Environment*. April 1984.

Canada. Gazette. *An Act to Establish the Northern Pipeline Agency*. April 12, 1978.

_____. *National Energy Board Rules of Practice and Procedure*. April 22, 1978 and December 8, 1978.

Canada. Information. National Energy Board Act, 1971; Amendments, 1974.

Canada. Law Reform Commission. *Expropriation*. Working Paper #9, 1975.

_____. *Report to Parliament on Expropriation*. January 1976.

_____. *Report on Expropriation* (Gaylord Watkins Special Consultant). 1976.

_____. *The Legal Status of the Federal Administration*. 1985.

Canada. The National Energy Board. *Order No. OH 1–67*. February 14, 1967.

_____. *Report to the Governor in Council*. March 1967.

_____. *Reasons for Decision*. May 3, 4, 5, 1967.

_____. *Report to the Governor in Council*. May 1973.

_____. *Order No. OH-1-74.* May 14–17. May 21–22. October 9, 10, 1974.

_____. *Order No. MH-1-75.* September 4, 5, 8, 1975.

_____. *Report to the Governor in Council.* October 1975.

_____. *Staff Study of the Cost to Pipeline Companies of NEB Regulation of Pipeline Construction.* June 1983.

_____. *Route Approval Procedures.* October 1983.

_____. *The Public Hearing Process.* October 1983.

_____. *The Board's Publications.* February 1984.

_____. *The N.E.B. Library.* May 1984.

_____. *Environmental Information.* October 11, 1984.

_____. *Rules of Practice and Procedure.* October 17, 1984.

_____. *Protection of the Environment.* June 1985.

_____. *Onshore Pipeline Regulations.* June 28, 1985.

_____. *Summary of Good Practices for Acceptable Environmental Protection.* 1989.

_____. *Rules of Practice and Procedure.* 1989.

_____. The National Energy Board and Protection of the Environment. Letter of Chairman Roland Priddle to the Author, November 24, 1989.

Canada. *National Energy Board. Twenty-five Years in the Public Interest.* Minister of Supply and Services Canada, 1984.

Canada. Queen's Printer. The Railway Act. R.S., c.234, s.1.

_____. The National Energy Board Act.

_____. The Expropriation Act.

Canadian Land Reclamation Association. *Inaugural Proceedings.* University of Guelph, December 1975.

Canadian Petroleum Association. *Environmental Operation Guidelines for the Alberta Petroleum Industry.* September 1988.

_____. *Oil Pipeline Performance Review.* 1989.

_____. Pipeline Conference: "Pipelines in Transition," vols. 1, 11. 1989.

_____. *Public Consultation Guidelines for the Canadian Petroleum Industry.* October 1989.

_____. *Environmental Code of Practice.* Undated.

_____. Pipeline Division series of booklets: *Pipelines in Canada,* 1987; *Environmental Issues/Land Reclamation, Waste Management, Sour Gas, Water, An Overview, Bibliography,* 1989.

Canadian Petroleum Association for Conservation of the Environment (PACE). *An Industry Overview for Government and the Public.* Undated.

CanPac '80. *The First Canadian National Power Alcohol Conference.* Biomass Energy Institute, Inc., 1980.

County Court of the County of Middlesex. *Cross-examination of David G. Waldon, President, Interprovincial Pipe Line Limited,* November 12, 1975.

_____. *Cross-examination of R. O. B. Richardson, President, Richardson Real Estate Limited,* November 12, 1975.

_____. *Decision of Judge J. F. McCart,* November 25, 1975.

_____. *Conditions Established by Judge J. F. McCart,* November 28, 1975.

_____. *Transcripts, vols. 1–9: Interprovincial Pipe Line Limited and Peter Lewington et al. re. The National Energy Board Act and the Railway Act,* December 1976.

_____. *Arbitration Decision of Judge Gordon Killeen,* December 28, 1978.

Donahue, R. L. et al. *Our Soils and Their Management.* The Interstate, 1983.

Finlay, Noreen, and Klopp, Diane. *Sarnia-Montreal Pipeline.* Fanshawe College, April 1976.

Fritsch, A. J. *Community at Risk: Environmental Dangers in Rural America.* Renew America, 1989.

Gray, Earle. *Impact of Oil.* Ryerson Press, 1969.

_____. *Super Pipe.* Griffen House, 1979.

International Institute for Land Reclamation and Improvement. *Drainage Principles and Applications.* 1974.

Interprovincial Pipe Line Limited. *Application to the National Energy Board to Construct a Pipe Line Extension from Sarnia, Ontario, to Montreal, Quebec,* Parts 1–4. March 1974.

_____. *Application to the N.E.B. Appendix IV re. Environmental Assessment.* Undated.

_____. The Piper. Interprovincial Pipe Line Limited/Lakehead Pipe Line Company, Inc. *An Ongoing Agricultural Restoration Program,* pp. 10, 11. 1981.

_____. *A Review of Pipeline Impacts on Agricultural Lands.* Environmental and Right-of-Way Branch. September 1984.

_____. *Post-Construction Environmental Report.* June 1987.

_____. *Environment Issues Report.* October 1988.

_____. *Monitoring and Restoration.* December 1988.

_____. *Environmental Policy.* January 1989.

Kilbourn, W. *Pipeline.* Clarke, Irwin, 1970.

Landsburg, S. "Effects of Pipeline Construction on Chernozemic and Solonetzic A&B Horizons in Central Alberta." *Canadian Journal of Soil Science* (May 1989).

Laxer, James. *The Politics of the Continental Resources Deal.* New Press, 1970.

Leggett, R. F. *Glacial Till: An Inter-Disciplinary Study.* The Royal Society of Canada in Cooperation with the National Research Council of Canada, 1976.

Lewington, Peter. "Expropriation and the Farmer." *Saturday Night Magazine,* pp. 14, 15, 40, May 9, 1959.

_____. *Address to the National Energy Board of Canada.* February 14, 1967.

_____. "Topsoil Preservation." *Point of View,* Canadian Broadcasting Corporation, July 20, 1970.

_____. *Address to the Ontario Law Reform Commission.* March 29, 1971.

_____. *Address to the American Right of Way Association.* September 18, 1972.

_____. "Ontario Drainage Justice." *Drainage Contractor* 4, no. 1 (1978): p. 120.

_____. *Address to the London, Ontario Science Teachers Professional Development Day.* March 3, 1978.

_____. "Tomorrow's Lessons from Yesterday and Today." Editorial, *Drainage Contractor* 5, no. 1 (1979).

_____. *Address to the Ontario Society of Farm Managers and Rural Appraisers.* September 24, 1979.

_____. *Address to the University of Guelph on Pipelines and Agriculture.* November 28, 1980.

_____. "Expropriation Precedents for Farmers." Editorial, *Agribook Magazine* 8, no. 3 (March 1982).

_____. *Address to the International Right of Way Association Educational Seminar.* September 18, 1985.

_____. *Address to the Ontario Farm Drainage Association.* January 22, 1986.

_____. "An Explosive Situation." *The Trenches* (the Ontario Farm Drainage Association Newsletter), March 1986: pp. 4–6.

_____. "The Green Appraiser." *The Canadian Appraiser* (the Official Quarterly of the Appraisal Institute of Canada), Spring 1990: pp. 17–19.

"LICA Survey Reflects a Redefined Industry." *LICA News* (the official publication of the Land Improvement Contractors of America), July 1989.

Lucas, A. R., and Bell, Trevor. *The National Energy Board Policy, Procedures and Practice.* The Law Reform Commission of Canada, 1977.

McCartney, Laton. *Friends in High Places. The Bechtel Story. The Most Secret Corporation and How It Engineered the World.* Simon and Schuster, 1988.

McRuer, J. C. *Royal Commission Inquiry into Civil Rights,* vols. 1–5. The Queen's Printer and Publisher, 1977.

Neilson, D. R. et al. *Soil Water.* The American Society of Agronomy, Soil Science Society of America, 1972.

"No Opposition to IPL Expansion Application." *Oilweek,* February 20, 1967, p. 23.

Nortcliff, Stephen. *Down to Earth.* Leicestershire Museums Publication no. 52, 1984.

Northern Pipeline Agency. *Alaska Highway Gas Pipeline Socio-Economic Terms and Conditions. Saskatchewan Segment.* May 1977.

_____. *Alberta Environmental Terms and Conditions. Alaska Highway Gas Pipeline.* September 1979.

_____. *The Alaska Highway Gas Pipeline Socio-Economic Terms and Conditions. Northern British Columbia Segment.* September 1979.

_____. *Northern British Columbia Environmental Terms and Conditions and Related Guidelines. Alaska Highway Gas Pipeline.* September 1979.

NOVA, an Alberta Corporation. *Environmental Policy and Principles.* January 15, 1983.

Olson, G. W. *Using Soils as an Ecological Resource.* Information Bulletin 6. Cornell University, undated.

Ontario. Energy Board. *Agricultural, Environmental and Resource Guidelines for the Contractor and Operator of Pipelines in the Province of Ontario.* December 1980.

Ontario Institute of Pedology. *A Guide to the Use of Land Information.* OIP Publication no. 79-2. Undated.

Ontario. Ministry of Agriculture and Food. *Drainage Guide for Ontario Publication 29.* AGDEX 752. Undated.

_____. *Agricultural Land Drainage in Ontario; the Final Report of the Select Committee on Land Drainage.* June 1974.

_____. *The Drainage Act.* 1975.

_____. *Annual Report of the Minister,* pp. 2–3. 1980.

Ontario. Ministry of the Environment. *An Environmental Study of the Interprovincial Pipe Line Ltd. Sarnia-Montreal Extension.* Environmental Approvals Branch, October 1978.

Ontario. The Ombudsman. *First Annual Report, 1975–1976.*

Ontario. *Royal Commission on Electric Power Planning,* vols. 1–9. Queen's Printer of Ontario, 1980.

Ontario. Special Committee on Farm Income. *The Challenge of Abundance.* 1969.

Ontario Soil and Crop Improvement Association. *Save Our Soil Conference.* December 8, 9, 10, 1980.

_____. *Agricultural Land Drainage-Ontario.* November 28, 1985.

Pattillo, Arthur. Letter to Jean Lewington, 1957.

Pearson, Norman. "Private Property Rights . . . for How Long?" *Appraisal Institute Magazine,* April 1976.

_____. *Food Land and Energy Planning,* vols. 1, 2. The Food Land Steering Committee, September 1976.

_____. "Educating Future Professional Land Economists." *Ontario Land Economist* 10, no. 2 (April 1979).

_____. "Impact of Pipeline on Farming in South-West Ontario." Ph.D. dissertation, International Institute for Advanced Studies. September 1979.

Pratt, Larry. *The Tar Sands.* Hurtig, 1976.

Prideaux, R. B. *Quality Control Survey of Plastic Farm Drainage Tile Manufacturing in Ontario.* July 10, 1985.

Productive Agriculture and a Quality Environment. National Academy of Sciences, 1974.

Quigley, R. M. "The Soil Column." *Geoscience Canada* 2, no. 2 (May 1975).

Quigley, R. M., and Bohdanowicz, A. *Pipeline Construction Impact on a Cattle Farm Ontario.* University of Western Ontario, 1979; reprinted 1989.

Ramsay, S. A. "To What Extent is Topsoil Conservation Necessary in Pipelining?" *Right of Way Magazine,* August 1982, pp. 25–29.

_____. *Interprovincial Pipe Line Limited Procedures to Be Followed by Drainage Contractors in Crossing IPL Pipelines.* Communication with the author, November 2, 1985.

Reclamation of Drastically Disturbed Lands. American Society of Agronomy,

Crop Science Society of America, Soil Science Society of America, 1978.

Resource-Constrained Economies: The North American Dilemma. Soil Science Society of America, 1980.

Right of Way Code of Ethics. International Right of Way Association, April 1985.

Ross, Lois L. *Prairie Lives: The Changing Face of Farming.* Between the Lines, 1984.

Salmon, Morley W. *The Effects of Ontario Natural Gas Pipelines on Four Farms.* University of Western Ontario, 1974.

Samson, Anthony. *The Seven Sisters: The Great Oil Companies and the World They Shaped.* Viking, 1975.

Schilfgaarde, Jan Van, et al. *Drainage for Agriculture.* American Society of Agronomy, 1974.

Sim, A. R. *Land and Community: Crisis in Canada's Countryside.* University of Guelph, 1988.

Smith, Philip. *The Trust Builders,* p. 6. Macmillan, 1989.

"Soil and Tillage Research." Institute for Soil Fertility 5, no. 2 (1987).

Soil Conservation Society of America. *Land Use: Tough Choices in Today's World.* Soil Conservation Society of America, 1977.

Soil Science Society of America, Special Publication Series, no. 5. *Field Soil and Water Regime.* 1973.

Stewart, A. J., and MacKenzie, A. F. *Effects of Pipeline Construction on Soils and Crops.* May 1979.

Stobaugh, Robert, and Yergin, Daniel. *Energy Future.* Random House, 1979.

Supreme Court of Ontario. Osgoode Hall Notices: Court of Appeal, Interprovincial Pipe Line Limited v. P. Lewington; January 14, 1981. Osgoode Hall Proceedings, adjourned to the Divisional Court; January 16, 1981. Osgoode Hall, Divisional Court, Interprovincial Pipe Line Limited v. Peter Lewington; September 28, 1981. Proceedings at Osgoode Hall, Court of Appeal, Interprovincial Pipe Line v. Peter Lewington; November 16, 1981.

Swayze, Carolyn. *A Life of Tom Berger.* Douglas and McIntyre, 1988.

Symington, D. F. "Land Use in Canada." *Canadian Geographical Journal,* February 1968.

Tarbel, I. M. *The History of the Standard Oil Company.* Norton, 1969.

Tick, Lorne. *Examinations of the Land and Related Public Policy Related to Temporary Working Rights and Easements Using the Example of an Interprovincial Pipeline.* York University, 1977.

Todd, Eric. *The Law of Expropriation and Compensation in Canada.* Carswell, 1976.

TransCanada Pipelines Limited. *Landowners' Guide.* Undated.

––––––. *Environmental Protection Practices Handbook.* June 1984, June 1986.

Union Gas. Communication of T. A. Vadlja, Senior Environmental Planner, with the author on matters of cleanup and tile repairs. January 25, 1990.

United Nations. Food and Agriculture Organization. *Agriculture: Towards 2000.* 1979.

United States. *Soil, The USDA Yearbook of Agriculture.* 1957.

_____. *A Place to Live, The USDA Yearbook of Agriculture.* 1963.

Warnock, J. W. *The Politics of Hunger.* Methuen, 1978.

Webber, L. R., and Hoffman, D. W. *Origin Classification and Use of Ontario Soils.* Publication 51, Ontario Ministry of Agriculture and Food, undated.

_____. *Ontario Soils.* University of Guelph, AGDEX 500, undated.

Winter, E. J. *Water, Soil and the Plant.* The Royal Horticultural Society. Macmillan, 1974.

Wishart, D. M., and Hayes, J. W. *Effectiveness of Soil Conservation Procedures Employed on a Recent Major Pipeline Construction in Western Canada.* Interprovincial Pipe Line Limited, 1988.

INDEX